CORNELL STUDIES IN CIVIL LIBERTY

GENERAL EDITOR: MILTON R. KONVITZ

The Guarantee Clause
of the U.S. Constitution

The Guarantee Clause
of the U.S. Constitution

by William M. Wiecek

Cornell University Press

ITHACA AND LONDON

First published 1972 by Cornell University Press.
Published in the United Kingdom by Cornell University Press Ltd.,
2–4 Brook Street, London W 1Y 1AA.

International Standard Book Number 0–8014–0671–4
Library of Congress Catalog Card Number 73-162542

PRINTED IN THE UNITED STATES OF AMERICA
BY VAIL-BALLOU PRESS, INC.

3 3001 00668 7619

To the memory of my father,

MICHAEL FRANK WIECEK

Acknowledgments

My foremost scholarly indebtedness in the writing of this study is to Stanley I. Kutler of the University of Wisconsin, who read and criticized an earlier version of the manuscript. Criticism of parts of that version by Paul Conkin and Richard Sewell, both of the University of Wisconsin, materially improved it. George Dennison of Colorado State University and William P. Murphy of the University of North Carolina Law School have read the entire manuscript; Marvin Gettleman of Brooklyn Polytechnic Institute has criticized portions of it. The staff of Cornell University Press offered useful substantive and stylistic suggestions.

Whatever virtues this study may have are due in large measure to these men. It would be most ungracious of the reader to attribute any of its flaws to them, especially since I did not always accept their suggestions. I alone am responsible for the book's faults.

My wife, Maryann Wiecek, took time out from her career and domestic activities to help in several ways.

The Faculty Research Council of the University of Missouri generously provided funds for typing drafts of this study, and I gratefully acknowledge this support.

WILLIAM M. WIECEK

Columbia, Missouri

Contents

Abbreviations

Annals	*Annals of Congress* [debates in Congress, 1789–1824]
Columbia Studies	Columbia University Studies in History, Economics, and Public Law
Elliot, *Debates*	Jonathan Elliot, comp., *Debates in the Several State Conventions on the Adoption of the Federal Constitution.* . . . (Philadelphia, 1901)
Farrand, *Records*	Max Farrand, comp., *The Records of the Federal Convention of 1787* (New Haven, 1937, rev. ed.). Citation is by volume and page, with parenthetical notation, where appropriate, of author and date.
Federalist	Jacob E. Cooke, ed., *The Federalist* (Middletown, Conn., 1961)
Globe	*Congressional Globe* [debates in Congress, 1833–1873]
Richardson, *Messages*	James D. Richardson, comp., *A Compilation of the Messages and Papers of the Presidents* (New York, 1897–1917)
Wm. & M. Q.	*William and Mary Quarterly* (3rd ser.)

Introduction

One of the more striking innovations introduced by the Philadelphia Convention in the 1787 Constitution was a clause in section 4 of Article IV that states: "The United States shall guarantee to every State in this Union a Republican Form of Government." This guarantee clause appears in an article of the Constitution that is a catchall of provisions dealing with intergovernmental relations. The remainder of section 4 requires the United States to protect each of the states against "Invasion" and "on Application of the Legislature, or of the Executive (when the Legislature cannot be convened) against domestic Violence."

The guarantee clause is unique in that it is the only restriction in the federal Constitution on the form or structure of the state governments. It empowers the federal government to oversee the organization and functioning of the states. It authorizes Congress and, perhaps to a lesser extent, the President and the Supreme Court to superintend the acts and the structure of the state governments and to inhibit any tendencies in a state that might deprive its people of republican government. Such a broad potential is rooted in the vague and unqualified wording of the clause. If fully realized, it would alter the delicate balance of power between the states and the nation in the American federal system. This sweeping yet recondite character of the clause has therefore discouraged its full implementation. The guarantee clause has emerged only fitfully and diffidently from desuetude because no one could foresee the consequences of its uninhibited application. For that reason, the clause is now just what Charles Sumner called it in 1867, "a sleeping giant." [1]

There are two ways in which this awesome potential of the clause can be better understood: we might resort to textual analysis or we might explore its history. Textual analysis of the clause does not tell us much about its meaning today. Felix Frankfurter once observed, apropos of reading statutes, that "some words are confined to their history; some are starting points for history. Words are intellectual or moral currency. They come from the legislative mint with some intrinsic meaning. Sometimes it remains unchanged. Like currency, words sometimes appreciate or depreciate in value." [2] Frankfurter's metaphor is strikingly appropriate to the guarantee clause. Its words are starting points for history; as time has passed, they have appreciated greatly in value. This is due partly to their ambiguity.

The clause is enigmatic, almost Delphic in its quality. Every important word or phrase in it is ambiguous and susceptible of widely varying definition. To illustrate: who shall enforce the guarantee and define the meaning of "Republican Form of Government"? One might assume, from the use of the words "The United States" and from the clause's location in Article IV, that responsibility for its

[1] *Congressional Globe*, 40 Cong., 1 sess., 614 (12 July 1867).
[2] Felix Frankfurter, "Some Reflections on the Reading of Statutes," *Colum. L. Rev.*, XLVII (1947), 525, 537.

enforcement was entrusted to all branches—legislative, executive, and judicial—of the federal government. For over a century following Chief Justice Roger B. Taney's opinion in *Luther* v. *Borden* (1849),[3] however, the federal courts usually declined to take a hand in construing or enforcing it. The Presidents likewise have paid little attention to the guarantee clause, following the lead of George Washington and John Adams in seeking their authority to suppress insurrections in the domestic violence clause instead.

The word "guarantee" is similarly amorphous. On its precise definition have turned the most important questions in the clause's history. How is the guarantee to be carried out? Does it imply only a suppression of unrepublican innovations by federal military force? Or does it convey a prophylactic, supervisory power to the federal government permitting it to prevent conditions from arising that could endanger the republicanism of the state governments? On what conditions does the guarantee become operative?

Last, what is "a Republican Form of Government"? By modern as well as past usage, it would seem to be the antithesis of monarchic and aristocratic government. Does it imply more? If it does—if it means that the states are to be held to current standards of "republicanism," with all that that nebulous word connotes—then the national government may define the content and standards of republican government and enforce its definition on the states.

Historical lexicographers give us only the vaguest help in translating the ambiguous commands of the clause into concrete prescriptions.[4] We must therefore turn to the clause's

[3] 7 How. 1 (U.S., 1849).
[4] See the entries "republic" and "republican" in: Samuel Johnson, *A Dictionary of the English Language* (4th ed., London, 1773);

history, comforted by Justice Oliver Wendell Holmes's reminder that the significance of words in a constitution "is vital, not formal; it is to be gathered not simply by taking the words and a dictionary, but by considering their origin and the line of their growth." The meaning of the clause can be found only in its past, illuminated by our sense of the needs of our society today. As Holmes put it elsewhere: "When we are dealing with words that also are a constituent act, like the Constitution of the United States, we must realize that they have called into life a being the development of which could not have been foreseen completely by the most gifted of its begetters. . . . The case before us must be considered in the light of our whole experience and not merely in that of what was said a hundred years ago." [5]

The clause was hammered out at Philadelphia in 1787 for two specific purposes: to permit the central government to suppress insurrections in the states and to forestall any relapse to monarchic or aristocratic forms of government. These dangers are obsolete today; the danger of rebellions against state authority dissipated by the end of Reconstruction and the threat of promonarchical backsliding vanished by 1800. But the clause did not thereby become a museum piece. It was soon put to other uses, taking on protean forms unforeseen by its framers. In drafting an assurance of repub-

---

Oxford English Dictionary; Webster's Second and *Third New International Dictionaries;* and Mitford M. Matthews, comp., *A Dictionary of Americanisms on Historical Principles* (Chicago, 1951); William A. Craigie and James R. Hulbert, comps., *A Dictionary of American English on Historical Principles* (Chicago, 1938–1944).

[5] *Gompers* v. *United States,* 233 U.S. 604, 610 (1914); *Missouri* v. *Holland,* 252 U.S. 416, 433 (1920).

lican government in the states, the framers were giving an open-ended command to posterity that each succeeding generation define anew the character of republican government.[6]

Early in the nineteenth century, the guarantee of republican government became associated with "higher-law" concepts as a restriction on legislative power. It constituted one of the few specific texts in the Constitution that might authorize transcendental restraints on the powers of the state governments. As such, abolitionists used it, unsuccessfully at first, as a weapon in their arsenal for the assault on slavery. At the same time, conservatives trying to stop state legislatures from implementing reform programs touted the clause as another bulwark in the defense of property against expropriative radicalism.

The guarantee clause was conceived in turmoil, and later disturbances promoted its most salient development. The most important in the ante-bellum years was Rhode Island's Dorr Rebellion of 1841–1842. Several important precedents were established by the Rebellion and by its judicial aftermath, the case of *Luther* v. *Borden* (1849). President John Tyler determined to support the extant or "legitimate" government of a state against those challenging its authority; Chief Justice Taney linked guarantee clause issues with nonjusticiable "political questions" beyond the competence of federal courts to resolve; and he held that responsibility

---

[6] For a valuable discussion of the concept of "open-ended intent" in constitutional interpretation, see Charles A. Miller, *The Supreme Court and the Uses of History* (Cambridge, Mass., 1969). See also Alexander M. Bickel, "The Original Understanding and the Segregation Decision," *Harv. L. Rev.*, LXIX (1955), 1–65. Compare with Frankfurter, J., concurring in *U.S.* v. *Lovett*, 328 U.S. 303 (1946).

for enforcing the guarantee of republican government lay principally with Congress.

During the Civil War and Reconstruction, the guarantee emerged briefly as constitutional authorization for a thoroughgoing program of Reconstruction. In early 1867, after passage of the first Military Reconstruction Act (2 March 1867), the clause reached the apogee of its historical development. It quickly fell into neglect, despite the persistent attempts of Senator Charles Sumner to exploit more extensive possibilities in it. In the 1870s Congress abandoned its interest in the guarantee of republican government, even though conditions in some southern states called for congressional or presidential application of the guarantee.

Since Reconstruction, the history of the guarantee clause has been a chronicle of missed opportunities and might-have-beens. After the turn of the century, Progressives and their opponents both resorted to the clause in efforts to promote or retard certain parts of the Progressive program, most notably the referendum, initiative, and recall. The United States Supreme Court reiterated its refusal to implement the guarantee clause in *Pacific States Telephone and Telegraph Co.* v. *Oregon* (1912), and interest in the clause subsided by the outbreak of the First World War.

The clause was again revived in the reapportionment controversies of the early 1960s. In seeking a constitutional mandate to the federal courts to correct the inequities of malapportionment, proponents of reapportionment construed the clause as a command to the federal courts to restore republican government to the states by striking at malapportionment, which they assumed to be antithetical to republican government. The United States Supreme Court, in *Baker* v. *Carr* (1962), rejected this contention, instead

6

suggesting that malapportionment violated the equal protection clause of the Fourteenth Amendment. In doing so, though, Justice William Brennan sharply narrowed the category of political questions that Chief Justice Taney had raised to prominence a century and a quarter before. Brennan thereby opened the doors of the federal courts to a broader range of guarantee clause questions than had been admissible under the political question doctrine. This development raises the possibility that federal courts will play a much greater role in implementing the guarantee clause and defining its contours than they have in the past. Perhaps today Sumner's 1867 prediction that "the sleeping giant is stirring" may be near fulfillment.

PART I

BEGINNINGS

I

Origins

The guarantee clause originated in the troubled 1780s, a by-product of what Bernard Bailyn has called the transforming radicalism of the American Revolution.[1] By 1786–1787 earlier inchoate fears concerning the independence and stability of the American governments had taken form. The related specters of tumult, anarchy, military dictatorship, and monarchical government haunted the imaginations of many influential Americans. These fears, even if exaggerated, had a basis in the very real instability of the frontier together with the expectably difficult postwar adjustment to national independence under a federal system of government. This reality and the fears it engendered stimulated nationalists at the Philadelphia Convention to insert the guarantee clause in the new Constitution. The clause derived from three interrelated phenomena of the late Confederation period: the altered ideology of republican government, Shays's Rebellion in Massachusetts in the winter of 1786–1787, and the rumors of monarchical government that circulated through the states during and after the Shays episode.

[1] Bernard Bailyn, *The Ideological Origins of the American Revolution* (Cambridge, Mass., 1967), 161.

If a consensus existed among Whigs after 1776 about any one thing besides the desirability of American independence, it was that their state and national governments were to be republican. This consensus dissolved, however, when Americans left the high-level abstraction of "republican government" and tried to specify its characteristics. The Philadelphia Convention, in drafting the guarantee clause and the state ratifying conventions in considering it, did little to reduce the ambiguity or fix the varied meanings of the concept.[2]

It might have been argued—and it was by a few Antifederalists in the ratification debates of 1788–1789—that the word "republican" in the guarantee clause was a sonorous but meaningless adjective.[3] Possibly, the word was not meant to have any strictly definable significance. Few of the delegates in Philadelphia tried to explain precisely the concept of republican government; the document they drafted abounds in vague words and phrases. The Convention was not a "seminar in analytic philosophy or linguistic analysis." [4] Because the Constitution is so much the product of compromise, we run a danger of reading history

[2] An outstanding effort at interpreting the meaning of republicanism in the late eighteenth century is Gordon Wood's *The Creation of the American Republic, 1776–1787* (Chapel Hill, 1969).

[3] See "The Albany Manifesto," signed by Robert Yates, John Lansing, and other New York Antifederalists, published in the New York *Journal*, 26 April 1788, reprinted in Cecilia M. Kenyon, ed., *The Antifederalists* (Indianapolis, 1966), 360; "A Columbian Patriot" (pseud. Mercy Warren), "Observations on the New Constitution, and on the Federal and State Conventions," reprinted as *Old South Leaflet No. 226*, Lawrence W. Towner, ed. (Boston, 1955).

[4] John P. Roche, "The Founding Fathers: A Reform Caucus in Action," *Am. Pol. Sci. Rev.*, LV (1961), 799–816, at 815.

backward when we construe it, seeing meanings in words and phrases that would surprise the men who used them. An attempt to find conceptual precision in a document whose most important immediate virtue had to be its acceptability may be misleading.

Thus the word "republican" may well not have had any single and universal denotation to the men who inserted it into the guarantee clause. It may, in fact, have had no meaning at all. John Adams complained late in life that "the word *republic* as it is used, may signify anything, everything, or nothing." He insisted that he "never understood" what the guarantee of republican government meant; "and I believe no man ever did or ever will." [5]

If the word did have a definable meaning it probably had several, and they may have been vague, ambiguous, multifarious, or conflicting. Adams believed that "there is not in lexicography a more fraudulent word." A republic might have been the antithesis of a monarchy or an aristocracy, yet Adams and others found no difficulty in imagining monarchic or aristocratic republics. Some of the framers and their contemporaries expected the concept of republican government to change over time, hopefully perfecting the experiment begun by the Revolution. The archnationalist Benjamin Rush expressed this idea with unmatched clarity:

There is nothing more common, than to confound the terms of *American revolution* with those of *the late American war.*

[5] Adams to J. H. Tiffany, 30 April 1819, in Charles Francis Adams, ed., *The Works of John Adams* (Boston, 1850–1856), X, 378; Adams to Mercy Warren, 20 July 1807, in "Correspondence between John Adams and Mercy Warren Relating to her 'History of The American Revolution,'" Mass. Hist. Soc., *Collections*, 5th ser. (Boston, 1878), IV, 353.

The American war is over, but this is far from being the case with the American Revolution. On the contrary, nothing but the first act of the great drama is closed. It remains yet to establish and perfect our new forms of government; and to prepare the principles, morals, and manners of our citizens, for these forms of government, after they are established and brought to perfection.

Reminiscing in 1816 on the early years of independence, Thomas Jefferson pointed up the semantic confusion: "In truth, the abuses of monarchy had so much filled all the space of political contemplation, that we imagined everything republican which was not monarchy. . . . Hence our first constitutions had really no leading principles in them." [6]

Jefferson's letter contains a hint that resolves some of the ambiguity in the term "republican" as it was used in the Confederation period. By 1787 most Americans considered a monarchy incompatible with the republican ideal. As James Madison put it: "Those who may lean towards a Monarchical Government . . . will of course abandon an unattainable object whenever a prospect opens of rendering the Republican form competent to its purposes." Closely related to this antimonarchical connotation of "republican"

[6] John Adams, "A Defence of the Constitutions of Government in the United States of America" (1787), in Adams, ed., *Works of John Adams*, IV, 370. For monarchic and aristocratic republics, see Adams' "Defence" and "Agrippa" (believed to be James Winthrop), in the Boston *Massachusetts Gazette*, 22 Jan. 1788, reprinted in Paul L. Ford, ed., *Essays on the Constitution of the United States* (Brooklyn, 1892), 104; Benjamin Rush, "A Letter to the American People on the Defects of the Confederation," reprinted in Hezekiah Niles, *Principles and Acts of the Revolution in America* (Baltimore, 1822), 402; Jefferson to Samuel Kercheval, 12 July 1816, in Paul L. Ford, ed., *The Writings of Thomas Jefferson* (New York, 1892–1899), X, 37.

was another: there was no place for an aristocracy in the American republic. The antiaristocratic impulse accounts for those provisions in the Articles of Confederation, the federal Constitution, and most state constitutions prohibiting the states and Congress from granting titles of nobility.[7] Like other elements that were subsumed in the guarantee of republican government, the antiaristocratic impulse became radically transmuted in time, so that what began as a mere prohibition of nobility, negative and almost truistic, ended as a sweeping positive affirmance of fundamental human rights. This is exemplified by the development of the republican government clause in 1787 in the Northwest Ordinance, a textual forerunner of the guarantee clause.

This republican government clause originated in Thomas Jefferson's 1776 drafts of a constitution for the state of Virginia. Recognizing that the ultramontane territory then claimed by Virginia would eventually become independent, Jefferson in his second-draft constitution provided for the territorial government and independence of "colonies" to

[7] James Madison to George Washington, 21 Feb. 1787, in Gaillard Hunt, ed., *The Writings of James Madison* (New York, 1900–1910), II, 315–316; see also "Camillus," in the Boston *Independent Chronicle* (1787?), reprinted in the Philadelphia *Daily Packet*, 13 June 1787; delegate Archibald MacLaine in the North Carolina ratifying convention, in Jonathan Elliot, comp., *Debates in the Several State Conventions on the Adoption of the Federal Constitution* (Philadelphia, 1901), IV, 10; and "Republic" in the *Oxford English Dictionary*, citing the 1771 British "Junius" letters. See modern discussions in Richard B. Morris, *The American Revolution Reconsidered* (New York, 1967), 39; George M. Dutcher, "The Rise of Republican Government in the United States," *Pol. Sci. Q.*, LV (1940), 199–206, Cecilia M. Kenyon, "Republicanism and Radicalism in the American Revolution," *Wm. & M. Q.*, XIX (1962), 153–182 at 165, and the same author's introduction to *The Antifederalists*, xxxiii.

be carved out of the area, which were to be "established on the same fundamental laws contained in this instrument & shall be free & independent of this colony and of all the world." This became a requirement of republican government in 1781 when Virginia ceded the territory to the Confederation Congress in a statute perhaps drawn by Jefferson. The cession's major proviso was "that the States so formed shall be distinct Republican States and be admitted Members of the Federal Union having the same Rights of Sovereignty Freedom and Independence as the other States." [8]

When Congress finally accepted the cession in 1783, it fused the 1781 formula with Jefferson's original version to require that the constitutions of the states created from the cession "shall not be incompatible with the republican principles, which are the basis of the constitutions of the respective states in the Union." Jefferson re-entered the picture with a proviso in his abortive ordinance of 1784 for the government of the Northwest Territories that "their respective governments shall be in republican forms, and shall admit no person to be a citizen who holds any hereditary title." Congress dropped this narrow concept of republicanism in favor of the broader formula, "that their respective governments shall be republican." [9]

---

[8] Julian P. Boyd, ed., *The Papers of Thomas Jefferson* (Princeton, 1950—), I, 352; IV, 386–388; p. 389 for Boyd's conjecture that Jefferson helped draft the ordinance.

[9] Worthington C. Ford *et. al.*, eds., *Journals of the Continental Congress* (Washington, 1904–1937), XXV, 678, 693–694; XXVI, 275–279. Jefferson, to Madison, 25 April 1784, explained that Congress dropped the prohibition of citizenship for persons with titles, not from any taste for aristocracy, but because it felt that the ordinance was the wrong place for the restriction. Boyd, ed., *Papers of Jefferson*, VII, 118.

When Jefferson's 1784 ordinance was abandoned for the 1787 Northwest Ordinance, drafted by Nathan Dane, the vague principle of republican government was transformed into a broad guarantee of civil liberty. In order to extend to the new states "the fundamental principles of civil and religious liberty, which form the basis whereon these republics [the extant states] their laws and constitutions, are erected; to fix and establish those principles as the basis of all laws, constitutions, and governments, which hereafter shall be formed in said territory," the Confederation Congress required, as "articles of compact" to "forever remain unalterable," the celebrated libertarian articles excluding slavery and assuring freedom of worship, habeas corpus, jury trial, due process, inviolability of contracts, public schools, just dealings with Indians, and federal supremacy. To clinch the point, Dane's ordinance required that "the constitution and government, so to be formed, shall be republican, and in conformity to the principles contained in these articles." [10]

The negative senses of "republican," that is, nonmonarchical and nonaristocratic, commanded the assent of most Americans in 1787. Beyond this it is unsafe to generalize about the precise meaning of the term. We can, however, try to give some form to the imprecise concepts of repub-

[10] The text of the ordinance is in Francis Newton Thorpe, ed., *The Federal and State Constitutions, Colonial Charters, and Other Organic Laws of the States, Territories, and Colonies now or heretofore Forming the United States of America* (Washington, 1909), II, 957–962. Dane's claim to authorship of the ordinance is asserted in his letter to Rufus King, 16 July 1787, in Charles R. King, ed., *The Life and Correspondence of Rufus King, Comprising His Letters, Private and Official, His Public Documents and his Speeches* (New York, 1894–1900), I, 289–290.

licanism that were, so to speak, in the air at Philadelphia in the summer of 1787. Although no one of these accounts for the definition of "republican form of government," we can describe characteristics of republican government that were widely held. Felix Frankfurter once suggested that the words of the Constitution "be read not as barren words in a dictionary, but as symbols of historic experience illumined by the presuppositions of those who used them." Finding these "presuppositions" can throw some light on the hopes and fears of the framers and can give us some idea of the evolution of the guarantee clause.[11]

Nearly all Americans were certain that they wanted no monarchy in either the state or federal governments. Monarchy represented one extreme in the forms of government; its opposite was "democracy," which was considered equally undesirable. As Alexander Hamilton observed on the floor of the Constitutional Convention, "the members most tenacious of republicanism . . . were as loud as any in declaiming agst. the vices of democracy." [12] Republican government was thought to be an alternative to these extremes, a middle course between the Scylla of tyranny and the Charybdis of anarchy.

"Democracy," referring to a distinctive form of government, meant the direct, complete, and continuing control of the legislative and executive branches of government by the people as a whole. This was approximated in the New England town meetings, but since no one proposed town meetings for state and national governments, direct democracy

[11] *Dennis v. United States,* 341 U.S. 494, 523 (1951) (concurrence).
[12] Max Farrand, comp., *The Records of the Federal Convention of 1787* (New Haven, 1937, rev. ed.), I, 288 (Madison, 18 June).

fore should reflect the will of the people. Frequently this phrase was merely a rhetorical flourish, but even when so used it implied that the people are the source of all power. Popular sovereignty in turn led to the "agency" concept of government: the people are the principals, their elected representatives the agents chosen to carry out the popular will. The idea was formulated in section 2 of the 1776 Virginia Declaration of Rights, drafted by George Mason: "All power is vested in, and consequently derived from, the people; that magistrates are their trustees and servants, and at all times amenable to them." This did not mean that representatives were to be merely mouthpieces for whatever a numerical majority believed at any one time, but rather that, in the long run, the elected officials, exercising their independent judgment, would reflect what most enfranchised citizens wanted most of the time.[19]

Two delegates to the Philadelphia Convention brought together these various strands of republican thought in precisely articulated definitions. Roger Sherman, who figured largely in the "Connecticut Compromise," believed a republic to be

[19] On the idea of republican popular sovereignty, see Charles Pinckney in the South Carolina ratifying convention (Elliot, *Debates*, IV, 328): in a republic, "the people at large, either collectively or by representation, form the legislature"; James Madison to Thomas Jefferson, 24 Oct. 1787 (Hunt, ed., *Writings of Madison*, V, 28): "The republican principle refers the ultimate decision to the will of the majority"; and Justice James Wilson, in a concurring opinion in *Chisholm* v. *Georgia*, 2 Dall. 419, 457 (U.S., 1793): "My short definition of [a republican] government is, one constructed on this principle, that the supreme power resides in the body of the people." On the agency concept, see Wood, *Creation of the American Republic*, 183–185, and Bailyn, *Ideological Origins*, 162–165.

a government under the authority of the people, consisting of legislative, executive, and judiciary powers; the legislative powers vested in an assembly, consisting of one or more branches, who, together with the executive, are appointed by the people, and dependent on them for continuance, by periodical elections, agreeable to an established constitution; and that what especially denominates it a republic is its dependence on the public or people at large, without any hereditary powers.[20]

Madison's definition in Number 39 of the *Federalist* was similar, though it laid greater stress on the majoritarian principle:

a government which derives all its powers directly or indirectly from the great body of the people; and is administered by persons holding their offices during pleasure, for a limited period, or during good behaviour. It is *essential* to such a government, that it be derived from the great body of the society, not from an inconsiderable proportion, or a favored class of it; . . . It is *sufficient* for such a government, that the persons administering it be appointed, either directly or indirectly, by the people.[21]

Despite the authority of Sherman and Madison, neither definition expresses precisely the elements of republican government assured by the guarantee clause. Yet both recapitulated characteristics of republican government that

[20] Sherman to John Adams, 20 July 1789, reprinted in Adams, ed., *Works of Adams*, VI, 437.

[21] *Federalist* No. 39. Compare this discussion of the characteristics of republican government with those enumerated by Gerald Stourzh in *Alexander Hamilton and the Idea of Republican Government* (Stanford, 1970), ch. 2: lack of hereditary succession, many rulers, rule by majority, representative government, rule of law, and the need for civic virtue in the people.

were widely held at the time and that have survived intact.

Sherman's insistence that a republican government had to be "agreeable to an established constitution" suggests several important limitations on its power. John Adams summarized these in the phrase from James Harrington's *Oceana* that was incorporated into Article XXX of the 1780 Massachusetts constitution: a republican government was "a government of laws and not of men." By emphasizing the primacy of a constitution and laws, Sherman, Adams, and their contemporaries meant three things. First, the "natural law," conceived of as the law of God or principles inherent in nature, set limits to all earthly laws and powers. A legislature, for example, might expropriate a person's property without compensation, but that would be neither just nor legitimate because it violated the supreme natural law. Second, they demanded that the powers of government be delineated in a written constitution, which no legislature could transgress. Third, they insisted that the state exert its powers only through laws properly enacted by the legislature, that is, in conformity with the higher laws of God and the constitution. No government could be republican that did not respect the natural rights that derived from the law of God, that did not function under a written constitution superior to ordinary laws, and that did not act through valid statutory law.[22]

[22] See Adams as "Novanglus" (1776) in Adams, ed., *Works of Adams*, IV, 106; "Thoughts on Government," *ibid.*, IV, 195; James Harrington, *The Commonwealth of Oceana* (London, 1887 [first ed. 1656]), 25–29. Harrington's contribution to American political thought is summarized in George H. Sabine, *History of Political Theory* (New York, 1937), 496–508; Edmund S. Morgan, "The American Revolution Considered as an Intellectual Movement," in Arthur M. Schlesinger, Jr., and Morton White, eds., *Paths of*

The influence of one other European thinker besides Harrington contributed substantially to American concepts of republican government. Montesquieu, in *The Spirit of the Laws*, had stated that a republican form of government was not suitable for a large territory because in the conflict of many interest groups the public good would be submerged in the scramble for private objectives. In a different form, this was the critical problem Madison dealt with in *Federalist* Number 10. Montesquieu also insisted that in a confederation all governments had to be republican because in a mixed confederacy a monarchy would swallow up its republican neighbors. These two problems, faction and republican homogeneity in federated governments, were debated at length from 1787 to 1789 before the ratification of the Constitution. Supporters of the Constitution suggested the guarantee clause as a remedy for both.[23]

Republicanism was, in the late eighteenth century, a "revolutionary ideology" that was to bring about a "radical transformation of American society."[24] The guarantee

American Thought (Boston, 1963), 14, 24; and John R. Howe, Jr., "Republican Thought and the Political Violence of the 1790s," *Am. Q.*, XIX (1967), 147–165 at 157. Handlin and Handlin, *Popular Sources*, 26, mention that a delegate to the 1780 Massachusetts constitutional convention proposed changing the name of the commonwealth to "Oceana."

[23] Montesquieu, Charles de Secondat, Baron de, *The Spirit of the Laws* (New York, 1966 [first ed. 1748; first English ed. 1750]), books 2, 8, 9. On the influence of Montesquieu's thought in America, see Paul M. Spurlin, *Montesquieu in America, 1760–1801* (Baton Rouge, 1940), chs. 6 and 8.

[24] Gordon S. Wood, untitled speech at the Organization of American Historians convention, April 1967, reprinted in John R. Howe, Jr., ed., *The Role of Ideology in the American Revolution* (New York, 1970), 83–91.

clause was not adopted to assure every ingredient of this revolutionary ideology. Some, like the notion of popular republican virtue, cannot be restored by statute or bayonet, and the guarantee clause can only be precatory or monitory. Even for other, more tangible, elements in the republican ideal, such as structural arrangements, the impact of the clause is problematical. Bicameralism, for example, was central to the republicanism of the founders, yet Nebraska was allowed to adopt a unicameral legislature. Nor has the republican idea of judicial independence impeded some states from making their judges elected by the people and subject to popular recall. The clause did explicitly oblige the federal government to take some action with respect to the states, but its force is not necessarily attenuated by its imprecise wording. It merely passes on to succeeding generations the responsibility of constantly redefining the republican ideal, of determining what parts are enforceable by federal action, and of deciding how they are to be enforced.

Possibly the republican impulse, grounded on shifting theories about the nature of government, would not alone have been sufficient to bring about the adoption of the guarantee clause, certainly not in its final form. To understand why the federal government was enjoined to guarantee republican government to the states, we must turn from abstract theorizing and investigate an incident that contemporaries thought posed a deadly danger to republican government—Shays's Rebellion. Madison and other nationalists both in and out of the Philadelphia Convention were troubled by the threat of internal "commotions" well before the Shays's affair.[25] A fear of rebellion and violent overthrow

[25] Nathan Dane, for example, wrote Rufus King, 8 Oct. 1785, suggesting changes to be made in the Articles of Confederation,

of the state governments dogged these men and prompted them to arrange the Philadelphia Convention. Shays's Rebellion confirmed beliefs the nationalists had long harbored that the Articles of Confederation were radically deficient in not giving adequate authority to the national government; it also provided an opportune occasion for convincing others that the federal system had to be altered.

A new constitution was not of itself sufficient to allay their fears. They needed, in addition, an explicit assurance that a threatened state could look to the national government to put down rebellion. Madison therefore inserted into the original Virginia plan a guarantee of a republican government. Those two words, "republican government," do not suggest an immediate and necessary connection with the Shays's Rebellion, but two succeeding guarantee formulas composed and offered by Madison resolve the ambiguity. When he sought a guarantee of "a republican constitution, and its existing laws," or "the constitutional authority" of a state, Madison had in mind federal protection against uprisings like Shays's. Probably the Constitution would have emerged when it did and in the form it did even had Shays's Rebellion not occurred,[26] but this is not true of the guarantee clause. The Rebellion and fears of similar occurrences in the future made Madison insist that the federal government underwrite state authority in these protoclauses.

Political unrest was endemic along the frontier from

---

one of which was in providing "the mode of suppressing revolts in the respective [state] Governments, &c." King, ed., *Life and Correspondence of Rufus King*, I, 67–70.

[26] This is the argument of Robert A. Feer, "Shays's Rebellion and the Constitution: A Study in Causation," *New Eng. Q.*, XLII (1969), 388–410.

Maine to West Florida after the Revolutionary War. In Massachusetts it erupted even before the peace with Britain was concluded. In 1782 veterans of the continental and state armies were dissatisfied with the remote maturity date of their pay certificates; speculators were buying up these certificates; creditors anticipating financial stringency were bringing numerous actions of debt in the lower courts. The farmers' obvious hostility to the distant state government in Boston and to courts and lawyers in general was already disturbing observers on the scene. Into this turmoil stepped a born agitator, Samuel Ely. He insisted that those who were being fleeced by court fees forcibly shut down the courts. Extralegal county conventions were called at his urging. The late revolutionaries in control of the Massachusetts legislature found all this uncomfortably reminiscent of the events of 1765–1776. They suspended the writ of habeas corpus, denounced the would-be insurgents, and modified the rigor of the fee table and the legal tender laws. Agitation subsided, Ely disappeared, and the western pot merely simmered for four years more.[27]

The general court had only temporized in 1782. Its palliatives did not touch the roots of discontent in western Massachusetts. The frontier economy continued to stagnate and did not profit from the slow upturn in export earnings

[27] Early western Massachusetts unrest is delineated in a letter of Major Joseph Hawley of Northampton to Ephraim Wright, a delegate from that town to the general court, 16 April 1782, reprinted in E. Francis Brown, ed., "Shays' Rebellion," *Am. Hist. Rev.*, XXXVI (1931), 776; Robert E. Moody, "Samuel Ely: Forerunner of Shays," *New Eng. Q.*, V (1932), 105–134; Robert J. Taylor, *Western Massachusetts in the Revolution* (Providence, 1954), ch. 6; George R. Minot, *History of the Insurrections . . .* (Worcester, Mass., 1788), 25–26.

in the 1780s. The fluidity of post-Revolutionary society exacerbated the economic cleavage between town and countryside, prosperous seaboard and impoverished Berkshires, stagnant West and rebounding East. High prices, high taxes, and speculation in land and public paper all added to frontier woes. The postwar recession, a highly fluctuating and scarce currency, and private debt intensified the economic plight of those who made their living in the nonmarket economy. Yet in the western farmers' complaints, frightened conservatives foresaw only agrarian communism. Demands for abolition of public and private debt would lead to "a general Distribution of Property," conservatives believed.[28]

Added to all this was the farmers' persistent hostility to courts, sheriffs, and lawyers because of distraint sales and the still-exorbitant fee table. Executions on farmers' real and personal property were particularly obnoxious because the property was usually sold for less than its market value

[28] For a consideration of the frontier economy in this period, see Douglass C. North, *Growth and Welfare in the American Past: A New Economic History* (Englewood Cliffs, N.J., 1966), 59. Political ideologies are discussed in Oscar Handlin and Mary F. Handlin, "Radicals and Conservatives in Massachusetts after Independence," *New Eng. Q.*, XVII (1944), 343–355. The conservative reaction may be seen in Benjamin Lincoln to George Washington, 4 Dec. 1786, in the George Washington papers, Library of Congress (Presidential Papers microfilm collection; hereafter cited as GW Papers, LC); Charles Pettit to Benjamin Franklin, 18 Oct. 1786, in Edmund C. Burnett, ed., *Letters of Members of the Continental Congress* (Washington, 1921–1936), VIII, 487. See also Taylor, *Western Massachusetts*, chs. 6 and 7; Richard B. Morris, "Insurrection in Massachusetts," in Daniel Aaron, ed., *America in Crisis* (New York, 1952); Marion L. Starkey, *A Little Rebellion* (New York, 1955), 17 ff., 233.

to eastern speculators or creditors. These economic grievances were easily translated into political terms.

After the Massachusetts general court disbanded in the
early summer of 1786, calls for county conventions were
issued throughout the state. Bristol, Hampshire, Worcester,
Berkshire, and Middlesex successively called conventions
that were well attended and that passed resolutions detailing
their inhabitants' grievances. Thus began an ominously
familiar pattern that had accompanied the Revolution a
decade earlier. The dissidents did not limit themselves to
passing resolutions. They began to form mobs which prevented the quarter sessions courts from sitting, most notably
at Northampton. When a mob, partly under the command
of Daniel Shays, prevented the courts from sitting in Springfield, Massachusetts had a crisis on its hands.

Alarmed because the insurgents' officers were Revolutionary War veterans and spurred on by the rumor that
British agents and unregenerate Tories were aiding the
rebels, the general court reconvened in October. It immediately attempted to put down the rebellion by a combina-
tion of suppression and appeasement. It passed a riot act,
suspended habeas corpus, and authorized preventive arrests
by state warrant, while trying to relieve some of the grievances by minor debtor relief measures, by an "Address to
the People" that explained the costs and problems of the
state government, and by a postponement of the Hampshire
and Berkshire court sessions.

The sword and olive branch proved unavailing. In December the insurgents improved their organization, disci-
pline, and coordination; they now controlled an effective
paramilitary force. To add to the confusion and difficulties

of the government, the Shaysites began to receive assistance from sympathizers in Maine, New York, Vermont, Rhode Island, and New Hampshire, the last of whom staged their own minor rebellion.[29]

The Massachusetts state government now found itself in an embarrassing predicament. It could not rely on the militia, especially in the western counties; it could not afford to raise a special force of volunteers; and Congress was niggardly about coming to its aid. A solution of sorts was reached by a congressional subterfuge and by Major General Benjamin Lincoln's shakedown of wealthy Boston merchants, which provided funds for raising a mercenary expeditionary force. Shabby as these expedients were, they succeeded in collecting a force powerful enough to ease Shaysite pressure on the United States arsenal at Springfield and to force a general dispersal of the insurgents.[30]

This show of strength by the government forced fragments of Shays's army into Vermont, New York, and Connecticut. The remainder, exhausted by forced marches and hopeless skirmishes, surrendered and availed themselves of Governor James Bowdoin's amnesty proclamation. The Rebellion collapsed by early February 1787, and the rebels' grievances were partly assuaged by wholesale pardons, a revised fee table, and the defeat of Bowdoin, who emerged

[29] Starkey, *A Little Rebellion,* and Taylor, *Western Massachusetts,* ch. 7, both contain good summaries of the details of the Rebellion.

[30] Lincoln's account of the shakedown may be read in Lincoln to George Washington, 22 Feb. 1787, GW Papers, LC; General William Shepard to Bowdoin, 26 Jan. 1787, and Lincoln to Bowdoin, 28 Jan. 1787, both in Joseph P. Warren, "Documents relating to Shays Rebellion," *Am. Hist. Rev.,* II (1897), 693.

as something of a scapegoat despite his relative moderation, in the 1787 gubernatorial elections.

Shays's Rebellion occurred at a watershed in the history of civil unrest in early America. The characteristics of the Rebellion—purposiveness and responsibility—made it a typical example of mob action in the eighteenth century. Yet where earlier mobbings had been tolerated or even connived at by civil officials as serving a useful function not legally attainable, beginning with Shays's the authorities took a harsh and repressive attitude toward mob actions. Since independence, it was felt, the interests of the government and the people were identical, so there could be no valid reason for extralegal violence. The American experiment in republicanism was considered fragile and chancy; therefore mobs had to be put down in the new republic. The guarantee clause and the domestic violence clause were products of this new attitude.[31]

The Rebellion was responsible for the adoption of the guarantee clause in two ways. First, it stimulated the exertions of those who believed that the Articles of Confederation had to be scrapped in favor of a more vigorous central government having power to suppress local insurrections. Second, it proved to Madison and other nationalists the need for inserting into the new Constitution an express authorization for such intervention. These effects occurred through a revealing interplay of local and national politics.

Early in October 1786, as the general court was convening, it became obvious to Governor Bowdoin and his ad-

---

[31] On the changing attitudes toward mobs in the 1780s, see Pauline Maier, "Popular Uprisings and Civil Authority in Eighteenth-Century America," *Wm. & M. Q.*, XXVII (1970), 3–35.

visors that the state did not have enough funds to pay loyal troops to crush the insurrection. They decided to seek assistance from the Confederation Congress because the governors of the surrounding states were either sympathetic to Shays, indifferent to Massachusetts' problems, or besieged by their own minor insurrections. This aid should have been easy enough to arrange, since Congress' Secretary of War, Henry Knox, a native of Massachusetts, was in his home state observing affairs in a quasi-official capacity; but constitutional and political problems supervened.

In the first place, the Confederation Congress had no constitutional authority to act. The only provision of the Articles that sanctioned intervention of any sort was the third, and this limited the power to act to other states, not the central government:

The said States hereby severally enter into a firm league of friendship with each other, for their common defence, the security of their liberties, and their mutual and general welfare, binding themselves to assist each other, against all force offered to, or attacks made upon them, or any of them, on account of religion, sovereignty, trade, or any other pretence whatever.

Even if this provision could be stretched to cover wholly internal insurrections, it was merely a mutual guarantee among the states and gave no power to the national government. This was confirmed by the "expressly" restriction of the second Article, which limited national power vis-à-vis the states: "Each State retains its sovereignty, freedom and independence, and every power, jurisdiction and right, which is not by this confederation expressly delegated to the United States, in Congress assembled." Article III was a dead letter since Massachusetts' neighbors were either unwilling or unable to come to her aid.

The sixth Article forbade Massachusetts to aid herself: "Nor shall any body of forces be kept up by any State, in time of peace, except such number only, as in the judgment of the United States, in Congress assembled, shall be deemed requisite to garrison the forts necessary for the defence of such State." Articles II, III, and VI produced a perfect impasse: Massachusetts could not raise troops; neighboring states were unable to come to her aid; Congress was constitutionally impotent.

Even if enough state and national officials could be found to connive at a violation of the Articles, neither Massachusetts nor Congress could accomplish anything effective because the treasuries of both were nearly empty. If money to pay the troops was to be had at all, it would have to come through requisitions from other states, a solution that posed its own political difficulties.

Governor Bowdoin therefore proposed a ruse: Congress should raise troops to quell an Indian uprising on the northern frontier, securing men chiefly from Massachusetts and her neighbors, and march them through western Massachusetts. The possibility of an Indian uprising was real enough, but those not originally in on the secret soon saw the real use to which the troops would be put.[32]

Congress proved amenable to the suggestion. Knox had written to Congress in September, pointing out the danger to the national arsenal at Springfield and urging that a de-

[32] Joseph P. Warren, "The Confederation and Shays Rebellion," *Am. Hist. Rev.*, XI (1905), 42–67 at 47.

tachment be sent to guard it. He also alluded to a problem that was to prove persistent by cautioning Congress against embodying any troops it could not pay. Congress immediately appointed a committee, which soon turned in a report that reiterated the Indian danger, recommended Bowdoin's ruse, recited the danger to the Springfield arsenal, and predicted civil war and anarchy if Congress did not act. It urged that Congress "extend such aid to the state of Massachusetts as may be necessary to restore the government to the full exercise of its constitutional authority." [33]

This committee report indicated that state and national authorities looked to the national government as a bulwark against anarchy and insurrection, and that Congress was willing to play such a role if its finances permitted, but that it could do so only through subterfuges. The Articles of Confederation, to the extent that they prevented national action, would be ignored. The nationalists found this intolerable. A constituent instrument that prohibited self-preservation by the states and national assistance to repress insurrections was worse than useless.

On the day the committee reported, Congress secretly enacted a resolution that recited the need for national aid to Massachusetts but warned that

in the present embarrassments of the federal finance, Congress would not hazard the perilous step of putting arms into the hands of men whose fidelity must in some degree depend on the faithful payment of their wages, had they not the

[33] Knox to Congress, 28 Sept. 1786, in Ford, ed., *Journals,* XXXI, 676. See William Grayson to James Monroe, 22 Nov. 1786, in Burnett, ed., *Letters,* VIII, 516. *Secret Journals of the Acts and Proceedings of* [the Continental and Confederation] *Congress* (Boston, 1821), I, 268–269.

fullest confidence, from authentic and respectable information, of the most liberal exertions of the money holders in the state of Massachusetts and the other states in filling the loans authorized by the resolve of this date.[34]

The humiliation could not have been greater: the Congress of the United States could not raise an army to preserve internal peace for fear the troops would mutiny at the first missed pay date; Congress had to beg private financiers for loans to preserve peace; and it virtually had to threaten the other states with the bogey of Massachusetts' anarchy in order to get an advance on unpaid requisitions. We can easily imagine the emotions of the nationalists as they listened to this singular resolution.

The nationalists left behind a volume of correspondence that shows how they reacted to the Shays uprising and how they hoped to resolve the problems posed by the weakness of Congress under the Articles of Confederation. The Rebellion produced among them a sense of impending catastrophe and opportunity. "Present appearances portend extensive national calamity," gloomily wrote Virginia's congressional delegate Henry Lee; "a continuance of our present feeble political form is pregnant with daily evils and may drive us at last to a change." Rufus King of Massachusetts echoed Lee: "Events are hurrying to a crisis; prudent and sagacious men should be ready to seize the most favour-

[34] *Secret Journals*, 269. Lynn Montross, *The Reluctant Rebels: The Story of the Continental Congress, 1774–1789* (New York, 1950), 390, sees the resolution as a not-too-subtle hint to the states to pay back-due requisitions. The hint had its desired effect, according to James Madison; Virginia paid its requisition on the understanding that it would be used to finance an expedition against the rebels. Madison's "Notes of Debates," 19 Feb. 1787, reprinted in Ford, ed., *Journals*, XXXIII, 719–722.

able circumstances to establish a more permanent and vigorous government." [35]

Lee and others believed that weak state governments invited subversion and rebellion. Mixed with their rhetoric about anarchy and a division of property were reports that British agents were fomenting the insurrection from Canada. The weakness of a single state like Massachusetts, especially one so close to Lower Canada, was seen as a danger to the rest, even to one as remote as Virginia.[36]

Soon, however, a more positive note crept into the letters. Hamilton's call for a federal convention had gone out from Annapolis on September 14th, and prospects of a change in government emboldened the nationalists. To some, like Stephen Higginson, wealthy Massachusetts merchant-capitalist, it was the answer to four years of prayer:

> You will endeavour no doubt to draw strong Arguments from the insurrection in this State in favour of an efficient General Government for the Union. As all the states are at least equally exposed with this to such commotions, and none of

[35] Lee to James Madison, 25 Oct. 1786, in Burnett, ed., *Letters,* VIII, 492; Lee to Washington, 11 Nov. 1786, *ibid.,* 506; King to Elbridge Gerry, 11 Feb. 1787, *ibid.,* 539. See also Washington to Humphreys, 22 Oct. 1786, in John C. Fitzpatrick, ed., *The Writings of George Washington* (Washington, 1934–1941), XXIX, 26 (hereafter cited as GW *Writings*); Washington to Madison, 5 Nov. 1786, *ibid.,* 50. Henry Lee, nicknamed "Light-Horse Harry," an ardent nationalist, should be distinguished from his cousin Richard Henry Lee, also a Virginia delegate to the Continental Congress, who became an Antifederalist.

[36] Henry Lee to Washington, 8 Sept. 1786, Burnett, ed., *Letters,* VIII, 463; Henry Lee to Washington, 17 Oct. 1786, GW Papers, LC. On the rumors of British meddling, see also John Jay to Thomas Jefferson, 14 Dec. 1786, in Boyd, ed., *Papers of Jefferson,* X, 596; Edward Carrington to Virginia's Governor Edmund Randolph, 8 Dec. 1786, Burnett, ed., *Letters,* VIII, 516.

them are capable of the exertions we have made, ["we" here meaning Massachusetts "money holders"] they will have reason to fear the worst consequences to themselves, unless the Union shall have force enough to give the same effectual aid in a like cause.[37]

As others picked up the theme, there emerged the notion that the national government should assume ultimate responsibility for repressing insurrections in the states. Henry Lee broached the idea early in a letter to Madison, thereby planting a seed that was to bear fruit in half a year's time. Writing in disgust at the helplessness of Congress, he lamented: "The United States who ought to be able to aid the government of particular states in distresses like these are scarcely able to maintain themselves." [38]

The new Congress that convened in January 1787 included James Madison as a delegate from Virginia. He was aware of the sorry performance of the previous Congress through his correspondence with Lee, who had sat on the secret committee. Perhaps, though there is no direct evidence, he had read the committee's report urging national aid to Massachusetts "to restore the government to the full exercise of its constitutional authority." In any event, he soon had an opportunity to offer his thoughts on the role the national government should play in quelling internal disorder.

In compliance with the Bowdoin ruse, Congress had au-

[37] See Higginson's letters to Knox, 12 Nov. 1786, 25 Nov. 1786, 8 Feb. 1787, 13 Feb. 1787, and to Nathan Dane, 3 March 1787, in J. Franklin Jameson, ed., "Letters of Stephen Higginson," Am. Hist. Assn., *Annual Report*, 1896, 704, 742–752, and the editor's introduction, 705–712. See also Washington to Lafayette, 25 March 1787, in GW *Writings*, XXIX, 183.

[38] Lee to Madison, 19 Oct. 1786, Burnett, ed., *Letters*, VIII, 489.

thorized the enlistment of a federal contingent to be used against Indians on the northwest frontier. By February 1787 the enlistment quota remained unfilled, the national treasury was empty, and Congress realized that it would have to stop enlistments immediately or face the prospect Knox had warned of, a mutinous, unpaid army. Rufus King, then representing Massachusetts in Congress, urged that both troops and money be raised nonetheless to deter "similar calamities" in other states. Madison immediately rose to support King. He

admitted that it appeared rather difficult to reconcile an interference of Congs. in the internal controversies of a State with the tenor of the Confederation which does not authorize it expressly, and leaves to the States all powers not expressly delegated; or with the principles of Republican Govts. which as they rest on the sense of the majority, necessarily suppose power and right to be on the same side.

He went on, however, to urge that troops be kept up.[39]

Madison was much taken with this idea and with his first-hand experience of Congress' debility. He saw that the defect was structural: Congress was not unwilling to suppress the insurrection; the weakness lay in the Articles of Confederation. Several months' reflection prompted him to draw up a brief pamphlet, the "Vices of the Political System of the U. States," an eleven-item catalogue of the great defects of the Articles. The sixth "vice" was the "Want of Guaranty to the states of their Constitutions & laws against internal violence." Repeating a thought from his February speech, he explained: "According to Republican Theory,

[39] Madison's "Notes of Debates," 19 Feb. 1787, Ford, ed., *Journals*, XXXIII, 719–722.

Right and power being both vested in the majority, are held to be synonimous. According to fact and experience a minority may in an appeal to force, be an overmatch for the majority." [40]

With remarkable perception, the "Vices" pointed out three ways in which the minority might destroy the majority rule that Madison considered essential to republican government. First, the minority might comprehend "all such as possess the skills and habits of military life." Second, "one-third of those who participate in the choice of rulers may be rendered a majority by the accession of those whose poverty excludes them from a right of suffrage, and who for obvious reasons will be more likely to join the standard of sedition than that of the established Government." Last, and most foreboding, "where slavery exists the republican Theory becomes still more fallacious."

From pointing out the defects of the Articles to suggesting how they might be remedied was only a short step for Madison. On 8 April 1787 he wrote a long letter to Virginia's Governor Edmund Randolph, outlining his thoughts on what must be done at the upcoming Convention. This letter marks the birth of the Virginia Plan and the guarantee clause. Although a "consolidation" that would abolish the states was "inexpedient," Madison wrote Randolph, "an individual independence of the states is utterly irreconcilable with the idea of an aggregate sovereignty." As part of his program for restricting the independence of the states, Madison suggested that "an article ought to be inserted expressly guaranteeing the tranquillity of the states against internal as well as external danger. . . . Unless the

[40] "Vices of the Political System of the U. States," in Hunt, ed., *Writings of Madison*, II, 363 ff.

Union be organized efficiently on republican principles innovations of a much more objectionable form may be obtruded." Welding these two ideas, Madison and Randolph produced a part of the earliest version of the guarantee clause: "a Republican Government . . . ought to be guaranteed by the United States to each State." [41]

To the extent that the guarantee clause and its section 4 companion, the domestic violence clause, were intended by their drafters to authorize repression of insurrections, they were parts of a contemporaneous process of delegitimizing the resort to violence by the people as an extralegal means of defending the community interest when government failed to do so. In this aspect, the guarantee protected republican government from the people. But the threat to republicanism came not only from below; there was also a threat *de haut en bas*. Republican government had to be protected from kings.

Shays's Rebellion was connected with another set of events that goes far toward explaining why Madison insisted that the new national government be organized "on republican principles." The "innovations of a much more objectionable form" he mentioned in the Randolph letter referred to rumors then being bruited about that there was a conspiracy afoot to set up an American regency—that the United States might soon come under the rule of a king or prince.

For a decade Americans had agreed on at least one characteristic of their government: there would be no king or nobles. Beginning in early 1787, this consensus was shaken. Rumors circulated and increased as the year wore on: the

[41] Ibid., 336 ff. See also Madison to Washington, 16 April 1787, *ibid.*, 344 ff. for comparable ideas.

popular Prince Henry of Brandenburg or perhaps the Bishop of Osnaburgh might be induced to accept an American regency. No one advocated a regency publicly; the only surviving records of the scheme denounce those who were suspected of loyalist or monarchic sympathies. But if the regency was illusory, the rumors and the fear they inspired as the Philadelphia Convention met were not. When the delegates insisted on writing in a guarantee of republican government, they were acting on fears that were real to them. The guarantee clause was designed in part to destroy forever the idea of an American king or lords.

Even after one hundred eighty years, the American regency remains shadowy. German, British, Canadian, and American archives have been gleaned for tangible evidence that someone, somewhere, at some time, actually did propose the regency to one of Europe's princelings. Nothing has turned up, yet the tantalizing question remains—was there some fire under all the smoke? But for an understanding of the origins of the guarantee clause, it is the smoke not the fire that is important.

The subject of an American monarchy had been a touchy one since 1776. It aroused a latent xenophobia in many otherwise levelheaded Americans because it seemed that aliens had been most forward in proposing quasi-monarchical schemes. The Count de Broglie, with the support of Baron Johann de Kalb, had proposed to Silas Deane in 1776 a plan for a generalissimo of the American armies that smacked strongly of monarchy. At the close of the Revolutionary War, Colonel Lewis Nicola, an Irishman who had won the respect of Washington for his efficiency as a military administrator, suggested to his commander in chief that a monarchy would prove the only feasible form of government for the United States. Such proposals were doomed because of the fervid antimonarchic sentiment Americans cherished after the Revolution, and nothing more was heard of them till the time of Shays's Rebellion.[42]

Suddenly in the autumn of 1786, as many Americans became apprehensive over the Massachusetts disturbances, the banked fires of xenophobia were rekindled by an odd indiscretion by the ebullient Frederick William von Steuben. Steuben's peacetime retirement had been unhappy. His personal ambition and wounded pride, combined with his disgust at the inefficiency of popular government, led to his disenchantment with republican America. He insensitively joked about the prospects of a king in the United States, a subject which Americans did not think at all funny. But he seems to have sympathized at heart with the downtrodden, and he was outraged by the Bowdoin ruse for getting national troops into Massachusetts to suppress the Shaysites. He vented these feelings in an anonymous letter signed "Bellisarius" and published in the New York *Daily Advertiser,* exposing the Bowdoin scheme. The authorship of "Bellisarius" quickly became common knowledge.[43]

The irony of the "Bellisarius" letter was that Steuben,

[42] The de Broglie, Nicola, and other proposals are examined in detail in the foremost study of monarchical sentiment during and after the Revolution, Louise B. Dunbar, *A Study of "Monarchical" Tendencies in the United States from 1776 to 1801* (Urbana, 1922), chs. 2–3.

[43] See John M. Palmer, *General von Steuben* (New Haven, 1937); Friedrich Kapp, *The Life of Frederick William von Steuben* (New York, 1859); and Steuben's letters to Richard Peters, "end of 1783," and Baron von der Goltz, ? 1785, reprinted in Kapp, 688, 698; to William North, 17 Sept. 1786 and 29 Oct. 1786, reprinted in Palmer, 337–338. "Bellisarius" is reprinted in Palmer, 339–340.

whose contempt for republicanism at times seemed real enough, argued that republicanism was threatened by the repression of the Shaysites. He asked indignantly: "If however the numerous militia should coincide in sentiment with the malcontents, and a very small number of respectable gentlemen only, should be interested in keeping up the present system of administration, would Congress dare to support such an abominable oligarchy?" Congress, of course, intended to do just that; but its members thought it outrageous that the suspect alien, Steuben, should accuse them of crushing a popular republican movement. This letter stirred up a hornet's nest of rumor, much of which assigned Steuben a central role in a regency conspiracy. Rufus King, who backed the Bowdoin ruse so strongly that Steuben thought him the inventor of it, wrote Elbridge Gerry in a letter seething with xenophobia that Steuben proposed to make himself a Prussian-style military dictator in America by riding on the backs of the Shaysites.[44]

By early 1787 two variant regency rumors were making the rounds. Those who shared King's reaction seized on one that linked Steuben with a Prussian regency plot. According to this version, Nathaniel Gorham, president of Congress in 1786, became so depressed by the feeble showing of Congress in the Shays matter that he wrote to Prince Henry of Brandenburg offering him the American regency. This letter was supposedly sent through Steuben, who endorsed it. Prince Henry did later write to Steuben, stating in broad and vague terms that some proposal of Steuben's (in a letter now lost or not yet found) would be impracticable. Steuben's loose talk to friends about the need for

[44] King to Gerry, 5 Nov. 1786, Burnett, ed., *Letters*, VIII, 496; see also Henry Lee to Washington, 11 Nov. 1786, GW Papers, LC.

a good stiff Prussian autocrat in America corroborated this rumor.[45]

The second regency rumor involved a prince of the Hanoverian line, the second son of George III, who was the Bishop of Osnaburgh, a secular office. The origins of this rumor, which was not linked to Steuben, remain unknown. The Osnaburgh rumor, though not as popular among contemporaries, is of greater significance than the Brandenburg one for the origins of the guarantee clause. It connected American desires for a regency to clandestine contacts with the British throne. This, in turn, reminded everyone that at the outbreak of Shaysite disaffection in the summer of 1786, rumors attributed the agitation to the activities of British agents filtering down through Vermont, where sentiment for union with Lower Canada was common. There is no doubt today that Guy Carleton, First Baron of Dorchester and governor of Lower Canada, willingly fished in troubled waters by placing agents or informants in New England. Their number was exaggerated, but they were there. One of these, in a report that Dorchester transmitted to his superior, Lord Sydney, stated that monarchic inclinations were extensive throughout America and that the cryptomonarchists favored the Hanoverian line. Sydney took the reports seriously, and in his reply to Dorchester stated that "should an application of that nature be made, it will require a very nice consideration in what manner so important a subject should be treated." [46]

[45] Richard Krauel, "Prince Henry of Prussia and the Regency of the United States, 1786," *Am. Hist. Rev.*, XVII (1912), 44–51; Dunbar, *Monarchical Tendencies*, ch. 4. Both authors believe that the rumor was substantially accurate.

[46] Dorchester to Sydney, 10 April 1787, in Douglas Brymner, ed., *Report on Canadian Archives, 1890* (Ottawa, 1891), ser. Q27-1,

Other rumors attributed monarchic sympathies to specific persons or groups. David Humphreys believed that Josiah Meigs, editor of the New Haven (Connecticut) *Gazette*, was favorable to the Osnaburgh scheme. This, Humphreys thought, was a result of weak government since men would seek desperate expedients to avoid the dangers of anarchy. The contemporary historian of Shays's Rebellion, George Minot, agreed with Humphreys:

There began also to arise another class of men in the community, who gave very serious apprehensions to the advocates for a republican form of government. These, though few in number, and but the seeds of a party, consisted of persons respectable for their literature and their wealth. They had seen so much confusion arising from the popular councils, and had been so long expecting measures, for vindicating the dignity of government

that they began to consider a counterrevolution and military dictatorship. Rumors like this provoked Washington's melancholy comment: "What astonishing changes a few years are capable of producing. I am told that even respectable characters speak of a monarchical form of government without horror. From thinking proceeds acting, thence to acting is often but a single step." [47]

97–99. Sydney to Dorchester, 14 Sept., 1787, in Farrand, *Records*, III, 80–81.

[47] Humphreys to Alexander Hamilton, 1 Sept. 1787, Harold C. Syrett, ed., *The Papers of Alexander Hamilton* (New York, 1961—), IV, 241; Minot, *History of the Insurrections*, 61–62; Washington to John Jay, 1 Aug. 1786, GW *Writings* XXVIII, 501. For other corroborations of the influence of the rumors, see Madison to Washington, 21 Feb. 1787, Hunt, ed., *Writings of Madison* II, 315–316; Madison to Edmund Pendleton, 24 Feb. 1787, Burnett, ed., *Letters*, VIII, 547; Rufus King to Jonathan Jackson, 3 Sept.

That "persons respectable for their wealth" should have been guilty of promonarchical backsliding would have been no surprise. But such sympathies also existed in the poor subsistence-farming region of the Massachusetts Berkshires. In the Massachusetts ratifying convention, Jonathan Smith of Lanesborough, Berkshire County, who described himself as "a plain man" and a farmer, flatly stated: "Our distress [during the Shays's Rebellion] was so great that we should have been glad to snatch at anything that looked like a government. Had any person, that was able to protect us, come and set up his standard, we should have all flocked to it, even if it had been a monarch; and that monarch might have proved a tyrant." So it appears that "Camillus," writing in the Boston *Independent Chronicle* some time in 1787, was not wrong when he said that both the "common people" and "men of speculation and refinement" found popular government unstable and "raved for monarchy." [48]

Rumors of a monarchy persisted through the summer of 1787 and plagued the Philadelphia Convention. They were so embarrassing that delegates found it necessary to deny that they were engaged in a closed-door cabal the outcome of which would be a monarchy. "We are informed," said

---

1786, *ibid.*, 459; Rufus King to James Madison and William Grayson (the Virginia delegates to Congress in 1787), *ibid.*, 55; William Grayson and James Madison to Rufus King, 11 March 1787, *ibid.*

[48] Elliot, *Debates*, II, 102–103. Elliot does not identify the "Smith" quoted. His identity can be determined from internal evidence in the quoted speech by a comparison of the Smiths listed in *Debates and Proceedings in the Convention . . . in . . . 1788* (Boston, 1856). "Camillus" is reprinted from the *Independent Chronicle* in the Philadelphia *Daily Packet*, 13 June 1787.

a source in the Philadelphia *Pennsylvania Journal,* "that many letters have been written to the members of the federal convention from different quarters, respecting the reports idly circulating, that it is intended to establish a monarchical government, to send for the Bishop of Osnaburgh, &c., &c.,—to which it has uniformly been answered . . . we never once thought of a king." Delegates Alexander Martin of North Carolina and Abraham Baldwin of Georgia both denied rumors that the Convention was toying with the Osnaburgh scheme. The attitude of the Convention delegates was well summed up in a *ben trovato* anecdote about Benjamin Franklin related by James McHenry, a Maryland delegate: "A lady asked Dr. Franklin Well Doctor what have we got a republic or a monarchy— a republic replied the Doctor if you can keep it." [49]

The rumors of an American regency reinforced the nationalists' reaction to Shays's Rebellion by confirming their belief that weak government, state as well as national, invited rebellion; that rebellion produced anarchy; and that, once anarchy triumphed, the republican experiment was lost and order could be restored only by a conspiratorial counterrevolution or a military coup, either of which might end in monarchy. Madison summed it up late in his life when he tried to explain the motives of those in the 1780s who hoped for a dismemberment of the Confederation:

[49] The Philadelphia *Pennsylvania Journal and Weekly Advertiser,* 22 Aug. 1787; Alexander Martin to Governor Caswell of North Carolina, 20 Aug. 1787, in Walter Clark, ed., *The State Records of North Carolina* (Goldsboro, 1902), XX, 763–764; conversation of Abraham Baldwin with Ezra Stiles, 21 Dec. 1787, recorded in Franklin B. Dexter, ed., *The Literary Diary* [of Ezra Stiles] (New York, 1901), III, 294; James McHenry, "Anecdotes," in Farrand, *Records,* III, 85.

"Either from a better chance of figuring on a Sectional Theatre, or that the Sections would require stronger Govts. or by their hostile conflicts lead to a monarchical consolidation." [50]

Thus from the turmoil of the Confederation years emerged the desire for assuring the republican character of the states in the American federal union. Sentiment for some assurance of republican government was common even before the incidents of 1786–1787; the "republican" requirement in the Virginia territorial cession and in the 1787 Northwest Ordinance evidence that. Before 1786 such a clause in a new national constitution would have been thought desirable; after the Shays insurrection it became a necessity.

[50] Madison, "Preface to Debates in the Convention of 1787," in Farrand, *Records,* IV, 549.

2

Drafting and Ratification

Delegate James Madison arrived in Philadelphia in May 1787 convinced that the upcoming convention would "decide forever the fate of republican government." [1] As the Convention was called to order on May 25, he was busily caucusing with the Virginia delegation, working out the details of the blueprint for the constitution known as the Virginia Plan. Drawing on his experience in the Continental Congress, his pamphlet on the "Vices" of the Articles of Confederation, and his letter of April 8 to Edmund Randolph, Madison hammered out the earliest formulation of the guarantee clause. His April suggestion of "an article . . . expressly guaranteeing the tranquility of the states against internal as well as external danger" took form as section 11 of the Virginia Plan. It read: "Resd. that a Republican Government & the territory of each State, except in the instance of a voluntary junction of Government & territory, ought to be guaranteed by the United States to each state." [2]

[1] Charles Warren, *The Making of the Constitution* (Boston, 1928), 82.

[2] Farrand, *Records*, I, 22 (Madison, 29 May). It is not known with certainty who actually drafted the plan presented by Ran-

ware on June 9. They proposed redividing the whole area comprising the thirteen states into new states of equal size. Pressing the advantage given them by shock, Read specifically objected to the territorial guarantee and urged that the states themselves be done away with and all American territory be united into "one great Society" or a "hotchpot." [6]

The proposal's sponsors probably did not expect it to be taken seriously; it was a stalking-horse for the Paterson plan. Since it had no chance of adoption, it was likely proposed to fend off immediate action on the Randolph plan and to give the small states bargaining leeway. It had its intended effect. Randolph's section 11 was replaced, by unanimous vote, with a substitute formula moved by Madison and seconded by Randolph: "Resolved that a republican constitution, and its existing laws ought to be guaranteed to each state by the United States." [7]

The abortion of the territorial guarantee and the significantly different wording of the substitute shifted the focus of debates to the problem of the requisites of republican government. With the territorial guarantee out of the way, the delegates were free to decide whether they wanted a guarantee of a "republican" government, and if so, what this would entail.

At this point Madison's and Randolph's recorded thoughts on the need for a guarantee of republican government or "existing laws" assume vital importance since the two men had drafted and sponsored the guarantee's original versions. Both were quite explicit about what they expected of the clause. Madison in the "Vices" and Ran-

[6] *Ibid.*, 202 (Madison, 11 June).
[7] *Ibid.*, 193–194 (Journal, 11 June), 206 (Yates, 11 June).

dolph in his "Letter on the Federal Constitution" saw the clause principally as a remedy for the weakness of the Articles of Confederation.[8]

The "domestic tranquility" so ardently desired by the framers could be endangered in two ways, as Randolph pointed out when he introduced the Virginia Plan: either by "quarrels between the states" or by "a rebellion in any [state] not having constitutional powers" to suppress it. The remedy was his section 11, guaranteeing a republican government to the states. Madison fully agreed. In the "Vices" Madison had insisted that the states were vulnerable to internal violence like Shays's Rebellion because the central government lacked power to guarantee the state constitutions and laws. Hence, in the mind of its authors, the guarantee of a republican government was to be a grant of power to the federal government to suppress insurrections. This original intent was ratified when the Convention later approved a syntactical welding of the guarantee clause to the invasion and domestic violence clauses.

But the guarantee was to be more than an assurance of domestic tranquility; it was also a prohibition of monarchies. When Randolph rose to support the Madison amendment on June 11, he said not a word in objection to the abandonment of the territorial guarantee. Both he and Madison saw that there was far more at stake than a mere federal underwriting of the large states' western lands. Whereas to Madison it was a question of achieving the *sine qua non* of successful government, internal peace, to

[8] Randolph's "Letter on the Federal Constitution" is reprinted in Paul L. Ford, ed., *Pamphlets on the Constitution of the United States* (Brooklyn, 1888), 267.

Randolph it was a matter of preserving republican governments in the new nation. He supported the amendment, as New York delegate Robert Yates noted, "because a republican government must be the basis of our national union, and no state in it ought to have it in their power to change its government into a monarchy." [9] Rather than restrict popular government, the Virginia Plan was meant to assure it, and section 11 was part of this assurance. Thus the guarantee prohibited monarchical forms of government and assured that the powers of the national government would be used to proscribe them.

The Madison-Randolph guarantee implied the supremacy of the federal government over the states. "It was a primary article in [Madison's] creed," said Alexander Hamilton, "that the real danger in our system was the subversion of the National authority by the preponderancy of the State Government." Madison therefore insisted that the federal government needed some coercive authority over the states. He argued at one point that the states were mere corporations, implying that effective sovereignty resided in the federal government and that the states were its creatures. Madison repeatedly urged national intervention in state affairs to preserve the rights of the people and the form of republican government. His insistence on the necessity of this power led one commentator to state that section 11 "was the capstone of the nationalist effort to establish a dominant central government." [10]

The Convention, sitting as the Committee of the Whole,

---

[9] Farrand, *Records*, I, 206 (Yates, 11 June).

[10] Hamilton to Edward Carrington, 26 May 1792, Harold C. Syrett, ed., *The Papers of Alexander Hamilton* (New York, 1961—), XI, 438. For Madison's reference to the states as corporation, see Farrand, *Records*, I, 471 (Yates, 29 June), 479 (Paterson,

approved Madison's amended version of the clause as part of its "Report" of June 13. Nothing more was heard of it in the critical five weeks that ensued because the delegates were preoccupied with hammering out a compromise between the small and large states on the question of representation in Congress. On July 17 the great compromise was worked out, and the convention was free to turn to what had been, for over a month, subordinate matters.

The delegates soon fell to wrangling over Madison's guarantee formula. The attack on it came from an unexpected quarter and for unexpected reasons. Gouverneur Morris of Pennsylvania pointed out that the federal government would be bound to guarantee "such laws as exist in R. Island," something that no one foresaw or wanted. But James Wilson and George Mason immediately pointed out the real purpose of the clause, which was concealed by its somewhat euphemistic wording. "The object is merely to secure the States agst. dangerous commotions, insurrections and rebellions," explained Wilson, and Mason added that the power was necessary for the federal government to protect itself, as well as the states, against sedition. Randolph, however, insisted that while this was indeed one of the purposes of the clause, there was another: "To secure Republican Government." Madison, recognizing the validity of both the objection and the defenses, moved another amendment: "That the Constitutional authority of the States shall be guaranteed to them respectively agst. domestic as well as foreign violence." [11]

29 June); Clarence C. Ferguson, "The Inherent Justiciability of the Constitutional Guaranty against Domestic Violence," *Rutgers L. Rev.*, XIII (1959), 407–425 at 409.

[11] Farrand, *Records*, II, 47–49 (Madison, 18 July).

Madison's new proposal had two defects, both of which were noticed immediately by the delegates. It might be construed as a guarantee of existing constitutions, laws, or governments and might thereby discourage rather than permit change. Second, it did not explicitly condemn monarchy or other forms of tyrannical government. Delegates as disparate in their views as Luther Martin and Nathaniel Gorham perceived the causal connection between the inability to change government, sedition, and tyranny, though their prescriptions for avoiding all three naturally differed. Neither Martin's demand that the states be left to suppress rebellions themselves nor John Rutledge's belief that the federal government had an inherent though not explicit power to suppress them commanded support. The Shays's Rebellion was obviously on the minds of most of the delegates, and Gorham probably expressed the fears of all when he noted that "an enterprising Citizen might erect the standard of Monarchy in a particular state, might gather together partizans from all quarters, might extend his views from State to State, and threaten to establish a tyrany over the whole." To allay these fears and objections, James Wilson offered this amendment: "That a Republican form of Governmt. shall be guaranteed to each State & that each State shall be protected agst. foreign & domestic violence." It was immediately adopted, 9–0. The guarantee clause and the remainder of section 4 had now emerged in substantially their final form. This formulation, together with the rest of the document as approved by the Committee of the Whole, went to the Committee of Detail.[12]

The debates of July 18 confirmed the earlier Randolph-

[12] *Ibid.*

Madison interpretation of what the Convention was about when it accepted the guarantee clause in embryonic form. A simple territorial guarantee had been rejected in favor of a broad guarantee of republican government that would, first, secure one of the Convention's principal objectives, internal order; second, prevent the establishment of autocratic governments in the states; and third, give broad powers to the federal government over the states to achieve the first two objects. All this is obvious enough from the debates. But Randolph's insistence that some independent phrase guaranteeing a "republican government" be included along with the clause protecting states against internal commotion remains unexplained.

This problem is resolved if the guarantee of republican government is read in the context formulated by Wilson, that is, as the first half of an inseparable commitment to the people of the states. The second half comprises the protection against "foreign & domestic violence," which is a negative or repressive guarantee with overtones threatening the use of armed force. The guarantee of republican form of government, on the other hand, was a positive, prophylactic guarantee, to be secured by the civil branches of the federal government. The violence clause contemplated that the federal government, acting through the armed forces, would undo something that had been done or begun. The republican government clause, on the other hand, permitted federal authority to take action before violence erupted. As subsequent events bore out, the violence clause was a warrant for military action, whereas the broader and more generalized guarantee clause could be read as an authorization for Congress, the President, or the courts to act. This is reinforced by the inclusion in Article I of an explicit power for Congress "to provide for calling forth the Militia to execute the Laws of the Union, suppress Insurrections and repel Invasions." Had the Convention meant to restrict power to act under the guarantee to any one branch of government, it would have relocated the clause in Articles I (Congress), II (President), or III (courts).

The Wilson clause, as it went to the Committee of Detail, contained the substance of the guarantee clause. All changes made in committees and on the floor merely refined the phrasing or qualified the sweep of the amendment. But the Committee of Detail did reject several suggested changes that throw some light on what the delegates thought might be accomplished by the clause. The Committee rejected the guarantee formula of the "Pinckney Plan," a draft by Charles Pinckney, which merely repeated the unworkable Article III of the Articles of Confederation: "The said states of N.H. &c. guarantee mutually each other and their Rights against all other Powers and against all Rebellions &c." The nationalists who dominated the Committee of Detail were determined that the new guarantee would be more effective than the old, would assure republican government, and would add to the federal government's power.[13]

The workings of the Committee and the intentions of its members can be inferred to a great extent from the Randolph-Rutledge working outline that guided the Committee in preparing its drafts for submission to the Convention. From this document it appears that the Committee intended the guarantee clause to be a grant of power to the federal government, not dependent on the will of the state governments, and that the clause was a substantive

[13] *Ibid.*, II, 137 (papers of the Committee of Detail).

addition to its companions in section 4, not mere verbal surplusage. The draft reads:

The guarantee is
   1. to prevent the establishment of any government, not republican:
   2. to protect each state against internal commotion: and
   3. against external invasion.
   4. But this guarantee shall not operate in the last Case without an application from the legislature of a state.[14]

The Randolph-Rutledge draft outline also included, in its Article I, an independent grant of power to Congress "to subdue a rebellion in any particular state, on the application of the legislature thereof." This draft clause for the first time contained the proviso that any federal suppression of insurrections required the consent of the state legislature. This proviso was probably inserted to placate Charles Pinckney and other likeminded delegates who saw too much exaltation of federal over state power, but its inclusion did not dampen the enthusiasm of nationalists. Benjamin Rush expressed the feelings of these men when he gleefully wrote to Timothy Pickering: "The new federal government like a new Continental wagon will overset our State dung cart, with all its dirty contents (reverend, and irreverent) and thereby restore order and happiness to Pennsylvania." [15]

In the Committee, Wilson was instrumental in getting his formulation changed to: "The United States shall guaranty to each State a Republican form of Government; and shall protect each State against foreign Invasion, and, on

14 *Ibid.*, IV, 49 (original numeration).
15 Rush to Pickering, 30 Aug. 1787, *ibid.*, IV, 75. See Warren, *Making of the Constitution*, 602, 604.

the Application of its Legislature against domestic Violence." In this form it was reported out on August 6. Two days later Rufus King pointed out that the guarantee against sedition might someday be used to force the northern states to help the South suppress slave uprisings. In an embittered and disillusioned attack on the refusal of the southern delegates to set a date for prohibiting the slave trade, King reiterated, as one of the basic objects of the new government, the need to suppress "internal sedition." But the importance of this observation for the guarantee clause, when King linked it to the possibility of slave insurrections, escaped the notice of the delegates. The clause underwent minor emendations on the floor and in the Committee of Style and was agreed to in its present form on September 15.[16]

The guarantee clause was not meant to solidify republican government in the mold of existing political institutions. It obviously could not, if only because the state governmental structures in 1787 were too varied and too changing to share any but the broadest common characteristics. In the clause's negative thrust, it was designed to prohibit monarchical or aristocratic institutions in the states. What began simply as a revulsion, grounded in experience and necessity, against rule by kings became transformed into a pledge of popular government. In its positive aspects the clause assured that innovation would be possible within a republican framework. It was more than

[16] Farrand, *Records,* II, 159 (Committee of Detail, Wilson draft); 188; 220 (8 Aug., Madison). See also debates on the "subdue a rebellion" clause of Wilson's draft, 17 Aug., *ibid.,* 316–317 in Madison's notes, where the importance of federal suppression of insurrections was reiterated. For changes in the clause's phrasing, see *ibid.,* 459 (Journal, 30 Aug.), 578 (Committee of Style), 621 (Journal, 15 Sept.).

the Philadelphia Convention's benediction on the extant state constitutions; it looked to the future, insuring that state governments would remain responsive to popular will.

The same ideas and events that produced the guarantee clause (fears of splitting the Union, Shays's Rebellion, frontier unrest, territorial disputes, rumors of monarchy) were responsible for other nationalizing features of the Constitition. The powers of Congress to lay taxes "to pay the Debts and provide for the common Defence and general Welfare of the United States," to regulate commerce, to control the militia for purposes of enforcing federal law and suppressing insurrections, to enact "necessary and proper" laws for carrying out granted powers, together with the supremacy clause of Article VI, were all products of the same desires that created a strong central government to forge a nation from a confederacy.

Our understanding of the framers' intent is derived not only from the Philadelphia Convention records, but from contemporary debates over the proposed Constitution in newspapers, pamphlets, and the state ratifying conventions. Antifederalist polemical writings and the ratification debates contribute little about the framers' intentions since their allusions to the guarantee clause are almost always tangential. In the most celebrated of the pro-Constitution newspaper essays, *The Federalist*, however, the clause is discussed at length and interpreted in the light of Madison's and Hamilton's varying conceptions of republican government.

In the treatment of the guarantee clause, as elsewhere in *The Federalist*, Publius emerges as a "split personality." [17] In describing republican government, Madison stressed its

[17] Alpheus T. Mason, "The Federalist—A Split Personality," *Am. Hist. Rev.*, LVII (1952), 625–643.

representative or delegative nature and the need for wide-spread popular participation in governmental decision-making through frequent elections and direct or indirect control of all branches of government. Hamilton, on the other hand, dwelt on the negative sense of republican—nonmonarchical. Madison strove to show his readers the need for representative government and its adaptability to an extensive territory. Hamilton sought primarily to assure that the new federal government could not degenerate into a monarchy.[18]

As to the role of the clause in securing republican governments, Hamilton wrote with an eye on the latter part of section 4, emphasizing the need to suppress insurrectionary faction and foreign invasion. Madison viewed the clause in its positive aspect, as a guarantee of responsive, broadly representative government. In *The Federalist* Hamilton looked to the past and to Europe for examples of what republican government should not become. Madison looked to the future and to the conditions of America to see what the United States could become.[19] Madison's views are of far greater importance for this study, partly because he played so large a part in the clause's creation (Hamilton had no role at all), partly because Hamilton's emphasis was on the latter two parts of section 4 rather than the guarantee clause, and partly because the clause developed more along the lines envisioned by Madison than those of Hamilton.

[18] A useful elaboration of Hamilton's conception of republican government is contained in Gerald Stourzh, *Alexander Hamilton and the Idea of Republican Government* (Stanford, 1970).

[19] Compare Nos. 6, 21, and 25 (Hamilton), stressing the need for suppressing insurrections, with Nos. 10 and 14 (Madison), where Madison elaborates his theory of republican government.

Madison's expostulation of section 4, as it relates to republican government, was most thorough in Number 39 where he defined a republic as a "government which derives all its powers directly or indirectly" from the majority of the people. By this definition, the federal government and all the state governments were republican, despite the variety of their forms. Republicanism, however, did not imply "democracy" in the eighteenth-century sense to Madison. In Number 14 Madison recapitulated the virtues of republican, that is, representative government in large territories as contrasted with the evils of democracy, which he saw as impracticable for either a large or a federated government. The guarantee was of government, to use James Wilson's favorite metaphor, in which the people form the base of the pyramid. It was, in this sense, popular government, but it was not wholly "democratic." [20]

In Number 10, dealing with faction and representative government in extensive territories, Madison contrasted direct democracy, where the citizens all gather together to act as a do-it-yourself legislature, with a representative republic. When he pointed out that direct democracy was not feasible for an area as large as the United States, Madison posed the dilemma: must a government of a large territory be despotic (not subject to the popular will) because the citizens cannot gather in some large field to adopt laws? Or, by being truly "democratic," must it be impossible? Must the people choose between power and self-government? Obviously not, Madison replied: a way out

[20] For a fuller discussion of this distinction, see Gaetano Salvemini, "The Concepts of Democracy and Liberty in the Eighteenth Century," in Conyers Read, ed., *The Constitution Reconsidered* (New York, 1968), 105–107.

of the dilemma can be found by having the people select agents—representatives—to perform their legislative duties.

Up to this point Madison had done little more than recapitulate Montesquieu. What gives his analysis its striking originality is the way in which he showed the added advantage of large republican government for suppressing faction.[21] Faction throve in small territories, he believed, because there it had the best chance of acquiring sympathetic adherents and becoming a majority. Large territories, with their multiplication of factions, prevent a local majority from dominating the whole, and a perversion of republican majoritarianism will thereby be prevented.

When Madison came to an exposition of section 4 itself in Number 43, he again followed Montesquieu in insisting that monarchies and republics could not coexist in a confederation. To prevent "aristocratic or monarchical innovations," the guarantee clause insured the continuation of republican institutions. Madison assured his readers that all extant state governments were republican and would be guaranteed in their continuance, or in any republican modification, by the federal government. Federal intervention to suppress domestic violence, he argued, would tend to prevent bloodshed and should be most useful in suppressing usurpations of power by minorities in the states. He darkly hinted at the possibility that slaves or persons who were disqualified from voting because they were too poor or were aliens might join a minority to overthrow

---

[21] Any claim for the originality of *Federalist* 10 must be qualified by a recognition of Madison's debt to David Hume, as Douglass Adair demonstrated in "That Politics May be Reduced to a Science: David Hume, James Madison, and the Tenth *Federalist*," *Huntington Lib. Q.*, XX (1957), 343–360.

the state government. The guarantee, as an assurance of majoritarian rule, would be, as he insisted in Number 41, "as much leveled against the usurpations of rulers as against the ferments and outrages of faction and sedition in the community."

Because Alexander Hamilton by contrast stressed the repressive and combative character of section 4, he tended to view the guarantee clause primarily as a justification for federal suppression of insurrections. In Number 21 he suggested that the guarantee clause was designed only to prevent violent changes in republican institutions. Section 4 "could be no impediment to reforms of State Constitutions by a majority of the people in a legal and peaceable mode. This right would remain undiminished. The guarantee could only operate against changes to be effected by violence." Here Hamilton misunderstood the clause because he needed to assuage his readers' fears of federal military power. His repeated references to the Shays uprising suggest that either he was obsessed with it or that he was playing on the fears of his New York readers. Elsewhere (Numbers 6, 22, 34, and 84), Hamilton iterated his "non-monarchical" conception of republican government, contrasting republics with monarchies, not with democracies. In the final Number of *The Federalist*, 85, he concluded by citing the guarantee of republican governments as one of the principal advantages to be derived from the federal union.

The guarantee clause emerged from the pages of *The Federalist* with its assurance of popular control of government, rule by majorities in the states with safeguards for the rights of minorities, and emphasis on the substance as well as the form of republican government enhanced and more explicit than in the Philadelphia debates. It did not, however, reassure Antifederalist opponents of the Constitution, nor did it convince them that the clause was a substantive safeguard of republican ideals.

The real and deeply felt division of opinion between Federalists and Antifederalists in the newspaper and convention debates over ratification tended to obscure for them as well as for us their underlying consensus on essentials. They were in basic agreement on the character of republican government, though they differed markedly on the value of the clause guaranteeing it. All agreed that state and federal governments must be republican and that this required direct or indirect popular control of the legislative, judicial, and executive branches of both governments. In all shades of opinion there was a fear of irresponsible power, though Antifederalists more than their opponents tended to fear a concentration of this power in the federal government and therefore supported the diffusion of power among the states. Federalists were concerned about the concentration of power at the state level, either in the hands of a popular demagogue or in one of the branches of the legislature.

The finest defense of the Constitution in the state ratification conventions was James Wilson's presentation of the Federalists' case at the Pennsylvania convention. Wilson had to meet a vigorous attack on the Constitution directed by John Smilie, an unlettered but intelligent frontiersman who later appeared as a prominent supporter of the Whiskey Rebels. Smilie struck early in the convention with the usual Antifederalist argument that the Constitution was inimical to popular sovereignty because it tended to concentrate power in the national government. Fortunately for the Federalists, Wilson's espousal of popular sovereignty was no less complete than his devotion to the nationalizing Constitution, and he was able to parry Smilie's attack effectively by showing that the greatest potential threats to popular rule were the state governments themselves. He refuted Smilie's criticism by insisting that the Antifederalists were wedded to state, not popular, sovereignty.

Pressing the advantage of his counterattack, Wilson buttressed these arguments by linking the issue of electoral qualifications with the guarantee clause:

In this system [the Constitution] it is declared that the electors in each state shall have the qualification requisite for electors of the most numerous branch of the state legislature. This being made the criterion of the right of suffrage, it is consequently secured, because the same constitution guarantees to every state in the Union a republican form of government. The right of suffrage is fundamental to republics.

Wilson thus assumed that control of the government by the people was elemental in republics and saw the guarantee clause as assuring it.[22]

The clause received only passing mention in the convention debates of other states.[23] It was debated extensively but

[22] The Pennsylvania debates remain today one of the best reported of all the state conventions, thanks to the efforts of John Bach McMaster and Frederick D. Stone, *Pennsylvania and the Federal Constitution* (Lancaster, 1888), 302, 319, 345. Wilson's devotion to the cause of popular government is effectively presented in Charles P. Smith, *James Wilson: Founding Father* (Chapel Hill, 1956), chs. 15–18, as well as in Robert McCloskey's introduction to *The Works of James Wilson* (Cambridge, Mass., 1967).

[23] See Elliot, *Debates*, III, 424 (George Nicholas in Virginia on slave uprisings); IV, 195, and II, 126 (James Iredell in North

inconclusively in newspapers and pamphlets. The Constitution's supporters echoed Madison's emphasis on the constructive possibilities of the clause. Its assurance of popular, responsive government was stressed by Tench Coxe, pamphleteering under the *nom de plume* "An American Citizen." In his fourth essay he alluded to the danger that the "rich or powerful" might rise in the state, "whereby the powers thereof shall be attempted to be taken out of the hands of the people at large." Coxe took the guarantee so seriously that he argued that such a seizure of power would be treasonable. The wealthy businessman-historian James Sullivan, writing as "Cassius," carried Coxe's point further, arguing that a bill of rights was unnecessary because the guarantee clause "provides for the establishment of a free government in all the states." [24]

The Antifederalists remained unimpressed. Whatever their specific grievances, they were united in believing that the new Constitution imperfectly guaranteed republican government. William Grayson, Samuel Bryan of Pennsylvania, and the anonymous author of the "John De Witt" letters all detected "aristocratic" tendencies in the national government and inveighed against the structure and terms of the Senate and the Presidency. Patrick Henry, not to be outdone, saw the President as a cryptomonarch be-

---

Carolina and James Bowdoin in Massachusetts, respectively, on republican homogeneity in federations); and II, 521–530 (William Grayson in Virginia on republican government for extensive territories).

[24] Coxe's essays are reprinted in Paul L. Ford, ed., *Essays on the Constitution of the United States* (Brooklyn, 1892), 145–146. Sullivan's articles in the Boston *Massachusetts Gazette*, 25 Dec. 1787, are in *ibid.*, 43–44.

cause of his powers, especially his control of the "standing army" authorized by the Constitution.[25]

The most common ground of Antifederalist criticism of the guarantee clause was that it was meaningless. Alexander Hamilton's erstwhile colleagues at Philadelphia, Robert Yates and John Lansing, after declaiming against the power of the federal government over the states, inconsistently objected to the guarantee clause on the grounds that it did not go far enough since it assured only the form, not the substance, of republican government to the states. Mercy Otis Warren, who was deeply bothered by the new central government's taxing powers, was not at all assuaged by the guarantee clause. To her it was a "delusory promise. . . . If the most discerning eye could discover any meaning at all in the engagement" it would still not prevent federal "monopoly" of tax revenues.[26]

John Adams agreed that the clause had little specific

[25] For Henry and Grayson, see Elliot, *Debates*, III, 43–64, 521–530; Bryan, writing as "Centinel" in the Philadelphia *Independent Gazette*, 5 Oct. 1787, is cited in McMaster and Stone, *Pennsylvania*, 569. "John DeWitt," in the Boston *American Herald*, 5 Nov. 1787, reprinted in Cecilia M. Kenyon, ed., *The Antifederalists* (Indianapolis, 1966), 106–108. Miss Kenyon's introduction to this collection and Jackson T. Main, *The Antifederalists: Critics of the Constitution* (Chapel Hill, 1961), are two excellent introductions to the thinking and fears of the Antifederalists.

[26] Yates, Lansing, and other New York Antifederalists signed the eighteenth-century equivalent of today's full-page newspaper ad, calling it the "Albany Manifesto" and publishing it in the New York *Journal*, 26 April 1788, reprinted in Kenyon, *Antifederalists*, 360. Mrs. Warren's diatribe was "Observations on the New Constitution, and on the Federal and State Conventions," reprinted in Lawrence W. Towner, ed., *Old South Leaflet No. 226* (Boston, 1955).

meaning in 1787. But he saw, as the Antifederalists seemingly did not, that this would leave it open to construction by later generations. In 1787 no man could predict with certainty how the clause would evolve. Adams, in 1807, perceived this clearly: "But I confess I never understood it [the guarantee clause] and I believe no man ever did or ever will. . . . The word [republic] is so loose and indefinite that successive predominant factions will put glosses and constructions upon it as different as light and darkness." [27]

Federalists and Antifederalists agreed on the desirability of republican government for the United States and the separate states, and they agreed on its basic characteristics. With a few exceptions, most of which can be dismissed on the basis of opportunism or local peculiarities, the opponents of the Constitution agreed with its supporters that a republican government was characterized by representation, bicameral legislatures, a separate executive, a written constitution, mixed and balanced government, an independent judiciary, explicit guarantees of the rights of the people, and limitations on the exercise of governmental power. The Antifederalists generally were willing to accept a restricted franchise, a different mode of election to the upper house and a different form of representation in it, and some strengthening of the central government. The principal point of difference was whether the proposed Constitution effectually achieved what all conceded to be desirable. The Antifederalists were instinctively more sus-

[27] Adams to Mercy Warren, 20 July 1807, in "Correspondence between John Adams and Mercy Warren relating to her 'History of the American Revolution,'" Mass. Hist. Soc. *Collections*, 5th ser. (Boston, 1878), IV, 352 ff.

picious of the centralization of power and hence concluded that the Articles, which provided for a feeble central authority, were preferable to the proposed Constitution.

In the Confederation period the inchoate concept of republican government began to coalesce so that by 1787 it had some definite content. A republic was, at least, the antithesis of a monarchy or an aristocratic form of government. The guarantee clause was designed to put the desirability of establishing monarchic or aristocratic governments forever beyond the range of debate.

Necessity, as much as inclination, forced the new states and their confederation to adopt nonmonarchical and nonaristocratic forms of government. Montesquieu had taught and most Americans concurred that in a confederation, which the new nation plainly had to be, all component governments should be republican. This meant that the American empire was to be republican throughout. But the transforming effects of the American Revolution were immediately at work to replace this negative meaning of "republican" with something else, positive and forward looking.

With the king and nobility abolished, the questions naturally arose: Who was to govern? And for whose benefit? And how? A republic, almost by definition, had to be a government of more than one or a few, for the benefit of more than one or a few; it had to be a government of and for the many—the people.

Americans saw that for the new *res publica*—the public thing—to remain of and for the people, it would have to function under a constitutive charter that guaranteed the rights of the people. It must be, as Harrington and Adams said, "a government of laws and not of men."

As the issues of the War for Independence were settled

on the field and in Paris, Americans realized that their primitive formulations of the republican concept would not do. They had reached important basic agreement on the great issues of control and benefit—by and for the people. But they quickly saw that if they were not to exchange one form of tyranny for another, they would have to come to grips with the challenge and the opportunity of controlling power. The use of power had been legitimized by the drafting of state constitutions, but it had to be channeled and controlled. Since it could be abused by groups as well as individuals, the institutional wielders of power had to check each other to prevent any one of them from grasping the totality of the state's power.

This was done by preserving a "mixed" government. Legislative, executive, and (later) judicial functions came to be separated, and each was given its share of power. This internal control was an institutional supplement to the external control of the written constitution. The negative implications of antimonarchical government were thereby transmuted to the positive promise of responsible government.

But if government was to be responsible, it had to be responsive. Only some form of representative government could harness the new nation's resources. Since the states and the central government could not be "simple democracies," republicanism required that they be fully representative. The people had to control their agents by frequent elections, by a closeness of the representative to his constituents, by a free press.

Thus the constitutive document that created the government had to provide for change. Not only the governor and the legislature, but even the state constitution, had to be subject to change when demand was widespread enough. Massachusetts and New Hampshire went so far as to guarantee in their constitutions the right of revolution. But this was extreme; the goal was peaceful and orderly change. Supporting the notion that the wielders of power had to be restrained by each other was the additional belief that the people had to be protected, if necessary, from their government. This was the impetus for the bills of rights.

The character of the American republics—not monarchical, but not "simple democracies"—raised the problem of the relationships of minorities to majorities, something implicit in the concept of a bill of rights. The majority had to be protected from the tyranny of a minority, but it also had to be restrained from oppressing the minority. This, too, was a new challenge to the infant republic.

The above were some of the characteristics of "a republican form of government" that section 4 obliged the United States to guarantee to the states. From the Philadelphia and ratification debates, certain other and more specific meanings can be drawn. Section 4 is actually two discrete promises: of a republican government and of protection. The meaning of the protection clause was clear enough; but the ambiguity of the word "guarantee" and the phrase "republican form of government" was so great that they, like the clause itself, were blank checks to posterity.

The guarantee was seen in two aspects. In its positive sense it was preventive. The people of the states were to be secured in their control of government so that the negative side of the guarantee, the promise of armed intervention made explicit in the protection clause, would not have to be resorted to. In its negative sense the guarantee was a warning to any who would think of seizing power beyond the control of the people that the United States would step in to restore popular control of government.

The clause was obviously a broad grant of power to the federal government. The protection clause, at least as to "domestic violence," left the decision to call in federal force up to state officials. This was not true of the guarantee clause. If the decision to intervene was left to the power that was to do the intervening, the federal government could ultimately define republican government, determine when state government lapsed from its standard, and decide upon a means of restoration.

Another important feature of the guarantee clause, obvious from the Philadelphia debates, was that it ensured dynamic, not static, government. Earlier versions of the clause, guaranteeing the "territory," the "constitutions," and the "laws" of the states were all rejected. Only the "form of government" was assured. Thus was the need for orderly change secured.

Responsibility for enforcing the clause was not limited to any one branch of the government, so that federal courts, as well as Congress and the President, in the future might implement it. Admittedly, the delegates to the Philadelphia and ratifying conventions did not make this explicit; no one specifically claimed that the courts could exercise this power. From what we can infer from the debates, the delegates do not seem to have given the question any thought, but they in no way denied such a power. With only one inconclusive exception, no delegate at Philadelphia ever implied that the guarantee clause was the responsibility of Congress alone or that the courts should not participate. The exception was Edmund Randolph. In his September 10 speech outlining his objections to the Constitution in its final form, he implied that enforcement authority for the domestic violence clause (not the guarantee clause) rested with "the General Legislature." The other delegates, when speaking of the guarantee clause's enforcement authority, used the terms "the General Government" or "the United States." [28]

The phrasing of the clause and its context and location support the conclusion that it might be enforced by all branches of the government. It appears in Article IV, a catchall article of provisions relating to relations between the states *inter se* and between the states and the Union, rather than in Article I, which dealt with the powers of Congress and with limitations on federal and state authority, or Article II, which dealt with the powers of the President, or Article III, which dealt with the powers of the federal courts. Further, the delegates chose the term "the United States," rather than "Congress" or "the President" as the agent for enforcing the clause. This may not wholly remove the ambiguity, but it does suggest a nonrestrictive responsibility resting on all three branches of the government for implementing the clause.

This was the "original understanding" of the guarantee clause. Its promise was to be ignored or evaded often in the next 175 years, but it was to remain, even if dormant, a guarantee of popular government.

[28] Farrand, *Records*, II, 563 (Madison, 10 Sept.).

3

Domestic Violence

The guarantee clause was first invoked in response to a series of rebellions against state or national authority between 1793 and 1843. Presidents and Congresses responding to these upheavals read the clause in the context of the entire section 4, so that it was first seen as an adjunct to the domestic violence clause. The guarantee clause thus took on a repressive cast developing along the lines sketched by Hamilton. Because the clause was used to suppress violent change, those who later opposed change of any kind saw it as a guarantee of the *status quo*.

The Whiskey Rebellion of 1794 in Pennsylvania affected the guarantee clause in an indirect but important way. Neither Congress nor President George Washington referred to the clause as authorization to put down the Rebellion since the domestic violence clause provided authority enough; but the statutes enacted to implement federal power under the domestic violence clause suggested an allocation of authority among the three branches of the federal government that spilled over to cover the guarantee clause as well. None of the issues raised by the Whiskey Rebellion was precisely in the domain of the guarantee clause. Rather, they concerned the assertion of federal authority to enforce federal laws despite the recalcitrance of one adversely affected section. The relevant constitutional text was the clause in Article I, section 8, empowering Congress "to provide for calling forth the Militia to execute the Laws of the Union, suppress Insurrections and repel Invasions." Nevertheless the interrelation between the insurrections, domestic violence, and guarantee clause was so intimate that precedent under one has affected interpretation of the others.

The western frontier of Pennsylvania was in political ferment in the early 1790s. As in Massachusetts a decade earlier, the harsh conditions of a frontier economy were aggravated by a drain of specie to the East. The four western Pennsylvania counties had only one profitable export, whiskey, the principal source of cash and their only effective tie to a market economy. The British presence in frontier outposts of the Northwest Territory contributed, at least in the settlers' minds, to the receding but still-present Indian threat. Land engrossment by nonresident speculators and threats to unimpeded navigation of the Mississippi contributed to disaffection among Pennsylvania frontiersmen.[1]

Added to these tangible sources of dissatisfaction were two psychic ones, the frontiersman's ambivalence toward the "city" (in this case the frontier village of Pittsburgh) and the westerner's suspicion of the East and of distant federal authority. These produced embryonic political divisions, soon to appear in the emergent Federalist and Republican parties. Because they were sensitive about being considered uncivilized yokels, envious of the political and eco-

---

[1] The most extensive secondary account of the Whiskey Rebellion, emphasizing economic sources of frontier agrarian discontent, is Leland D. Baldwin's *Whiskey Rebels* (Pittsburgh, 1939), chs. 1–3.

nomic power of the East, nostalgic for urban comforts, and resentful of the eastern "oligarchy's" lack of sympathy with frontier needs, western Pennsylvanians were in a mean temper by 1791.[2]

Congress in that year, acceding to Secretary of the Treasury Alexander Hamilton's request, repealed an excise on imported liquors and imposed it instead on domestically produced whiskey. This statute immediately provoked noisy opposition from the western Pennsylvania farmers, who justifiably saw the measure as a transfer of the tax burden from wealthy eastern consumers of imported spirits onto the single cash "crop" of the frontier. In response, Congress enacted the Militia Act of 1792, providing:

That whenever the laws of the United States shall be opposed, or the execution thereof obstructed, in any state, by combinations too powerful to be suppressed by the ordinary course of judicial proceedings. . . . [§2] [and] in case of an insurrection in any state, against the government thereof, it shall be lawful for the President of the United States, on application of the legislature of such state, or of the executive (when the legislature cannot be convened) [§1]

to call out the militia of that state or any adjoining states to suppress the insurrection or resistance to federal laws. The Militia Act of 1792 expired by its own terms in 1794. Congress, unwilling to dispense with such a useful statute, reenacted its substance with some important changes as the

[2] Russell J. Ferguson, *Early Western Pennsylvania Politics* (Pittsburgh, 1938), 126, 128, emphasizes the social and political base of disaffection. See also Harry M. Tinkcom, *The Republicans and Federalists in Pennsylvania, 1790–1801* (Harrisburg, 1950), 75–90, 94–95, who presents both economic and political interpretations of the Rebellion.

Enforcement Act of 1795. The change in popular names is significant: the original statute grew out of attempts at enacting uniform militia legislation, but the experience of the Whiskey Rebellion demonstrated to Congress and particularly to the Federalists the utility or necessity of providing the ultimate sanction of military force for the execution of federal laws. The Enforcement Act of 1795 was supplemented by an 1807 statute authorizing the President to use regular army forces as well as the federalized militia for law enforcement purposes. The acts of 1795 and 1807 remain in the United States Code today, virtually unaltered from their original form, as the basic authority for federal control of state military forces.[3]

The Militia Act affected the guarantee clause in two ways. First, it was the principal statutory source of federal authority to put down violent challenges to republican government in the states. It was this act that lent a repressive aura to the clause. Second, it could be interpreted (and was in *Luther* v. *Borden*) as a delegation of congressional power to the President to enforce at least part of section 4's guarantee. Although it was based only on the domestic violence clause, Chief Justice Roger Taney read this statute as if it also controlled the allocation of authority under the guarantee clause.

[3] Act of 2 May 1792, ch. 28, 1 Stat. 264; Act of 28 Feb. 1795, ch. 36, 1 Stat. 424; Act of 3 March 1807, ch. 39, 2 Stat. 443; 10 U.S.C. §§ 331, 332 (1964). Two useful surveys of the implementation of this authority are Bennett M. Rich, *The Presidents and Civil Disorder* (Washington, 1941), and U.S. Senate, "Federal Aid in Domestic Disturbances 1903–1922" [the period covered is actually 1789–1922], 67 Cong., 2 sess., ser. 7985, doc. 263. For congressional intent in enacting the 1792 statute, see *Annals of Congress* (1792), 574–577.

In 1792, acting under this new statutory authorization, President Washington issued the first of his insurrection proclamations, ordering the disaffected frontiersmen to dissolve any combinations opposing the execution of federal law. Whether from respect for Washington or fear of the threat implied by the proclamation or for purely local reasons, the proclamation was effective and resistance to the whiskey excise subsided for a time. This, however, was merely the lull before the storm. In 1794, when western fears had built up unendurably over the progress of John Jay's negotiations in London over navigation of the Mississippi and the whiskey excise began to be enforced, the farmers acted. After they roughed up a federal marshal, militiamen from the western counties gathered in force and armed at Braddock's Field to demonstrate their opposition to the excise and to listen to radical harangues. Disorganized, largely leaderless, yet with a sense of grievance that was no less forcible for being unarticulated, the Pennsylvania farmers defied federal authority.[4]

Washington, Hamilton, and Congress reacted sharply. Before these disturbances erupted, Congress had authorized the President to order the governors of all states to have eighty thousand militiamen ready to march anywhere "at a

[4] Washington's proclamation may be found in James D. Richardson, comp., *A Compilation of the Messages and Papers of the Presidents* (New York, 1897–1917), I, 116–117. For details of the Braddock's Field muster, see Hugh H. Brackenridge, *Incidents of the Insurrection* . . . (Philadelphia, 1795), book I, ch. 8; James Carnahan, "The Pennsylvania Insurrection of 1794, Commonly called the 'Whiskey Insurrection,'" N.J. Hist. Soc., *Proceedings* VI (1853), 115, 126–127. On the role of the state militia at Braddock's Field, see *Pennsylvania Archives*, 2nd ser. (Harrisburg, 1876), IV, 11. The militia had been called up for an Indian campaign.

moment's warning" to cope with Indian troubles on the frontier. Hence Washington had the necessary military force on call. But he scrupulously conformed to the procedures specified in section 3 of the 1792 Militia Act before calling them up. First, Associate Justice James Wilson of the United States Supreme Court submitted his certification that federal laws were being opposed in Washington and Allegheny counties by combinations beyond the controlling power of judicial process. Washington issued his second proclamation on August 7 ordering the insurgents to disperse. He covered the mailed fist with a velvet glove, though, by appointing three commissioners, United States Attorney General William Bradford, United States Senator from Pennsylvania James Ross, and Pennsylvania Supreme Court Justice Jasper Yeates, to work out a settlement with the insurgents. Their powers were broad, but they had to secure an assurance that the farmers would submit to the whiskey excise. This done they were authorized to promise, on Washington's behalf, that militia would not be sent to the disaffected counties.[5]

The commissioners failed to secure a satisfactory promise of compliance with the federal laws. They reported to Washington that the excise statute was unenforceable and that "some more competent force" would be necessary to give federal officials "and well-disposed citizens that protection which it is the duty of Government to afford." This report exhausted Washington's willingness to compromise

---

[5] Wilson's certificate is reprinted in *American State Papers, Miscellaneous* (Washington, 1834–1862), I, 85. Washington's August proclamation is in Richardson, *Messages*, I, 150–152. The terms of the Ross-Yeates-Bradford commissions are in *Am. S.P., Misc.*, I, 86 (5 Aug. 1794), and 87 (8 Aug. 1794).

the matter peacefully. He ordered the Pennsylvania, New Jersey, Maryland, and Virginia militia, between thirteen and fifteen thousand men, to march to the western counties.[6]

The frontiersmen's resistance collapsed, extremist leaders fled, and moderates like Albert Gallatin, Hugh Brackenridge, and William Findley undertook the thankless job of reconciling the farmers and the national government. Party development was enormously stimulated by western hatred for the excise and its author, Hamilton. A mildly conservative reaction set in in Pennsylvania politics and the proto-Jeffersonian Democratic societies of Pennsylvania were crushed, chiefly because of Washington's condemnation of them. This in turn abetted Madison's rise as an opposition congressional party leader. Above all, Washington's insistence that change must be peaceful and that redress must be sought by ballot not bullet was vindicated. The promise of a republican form of government—responsive government, whose policies might be altered but only by peaceable measures—was firmly restated.

When Chief Justice Taney, in *Luther* v. *Borden*, was asked to decide which government in Rhode Island was legitimate in 1842, he refused to do so. One of his grounds

[6] The commissioners' report is in *Am. S.P.*, *Misc.*, I, 87 ff. See William Findley, *History of the Insurrection in the Four Counties of Pennsylvania* (Philadelphia, 1794), chs. 2–3, a reasonably moderate account, but with an acerbic anti-Hamiltonian bias. Support for Findley's view may be found in Henry M. Brackenridge, *History of the Western Insurrection* . . . (Pittsburgh, 1859), ch. 11. Presidential discretion in deciding when an emergency is sufficient to call up militia was affirmed in *Martin* v. *Mott*, 12 Wheat. 19 (U.S., 1827). The *Martin* case is an important precedent of *Luther* v. *Borden* for its approval of wide executive discretion under section 4.

was that this function had been committed by the domestic violence clause and the 1792 Militia Act to the President in the first instance. He applied similar reasoning to the guarantee clause, stating that it was not part of a court's function to determine which government is republican. In this way, the Whiskey Rebellion and congressional response to it affected later development of the guarantee clause.

The Rebellion, by emphasizing the repressive aspect of section 4 and the need for the federal government to exert itself vigorously to preserve internal peace and governmental authority, also made it appear that the clause's primary function was to assure a tranquil society. The clause was urged by many as a guarantee that the *status quo* should not be disturbed. This view was later adopted by two groups in the United States, Whig conservatives who tried to resist the reform movements of the Jacksonian era and defenders of slavery.

Between 1794 and 1842 several brief episodes of violence flared up in the states, chiefly the Fries Rebellion (1798, Pennsylvania), the Nullification crisis (1832, South Carolina), and the Buckshot War (1838, Pennsylvania). Each of these events reinforced the lessons of the Whiskey Rebellion: that enforcement of the domestic violence clause is primarily a presidential responsibility under the Militia Act of 1792 and that the guarantee clause and its section 4 companions could be put to repressive use, particularly when national authority is challenged by nonpeaceful opposition. The culmination of these local upheavals, the Dorr Rebellion of 1842, had a different and more powerful impact on the subsequent development of the clause.[7]

[7] See Rich, *The Presidents and Civil Disorder*, 21–54.

The Dorr Rebellion would have been no more significant for the development of the guarantee clause than the Buckshot War of five years earlier but for two things. First, both factions in the Rhode Island controversy implicated the clause in their appeals to President John Tyler and both eventually relied on it to support their position. This produced an extensive debate over the meaning of the guarantee of republican government between conservative Whigs and "Radical" Democrats and forced the President to articulate a rationale for his inaction. Both the Whig arguments and Tyler's apologia have since provided doctrinal justification for a constrictive reading of the clause.

Second, seven years after the Dorr Rebellion was put down its issues were revived in a new forum, the United States Supreme Court. Chief Justice Taney's opinion in *Luther* v. *Borden* has had a greater effect on the development of the guarantee clause than any other single event in its history. Taney simultaneously placed primary responsibility for the clause's enforcement on Congress and the President and, by the doctrine of "political questions," withdrew the courts from playing any role in its enforcement.

In 1842 Rhode Island was in the anomalous position of being the only state in which the people had not drafted or ratified their own constitution. The royal charter granted by King Charles II in 1663 had been retained as the state constitution in 1776. Since 1663 no important changes had been made in the charter.[8]

The charter restricted the suffrage to "freemen," who by statute were defined as the owners of $134 worth of real

[8] The 1663 charter is reprinted in Francis N. Thorpe, ed., *The Federal and State Constitutions* (Washington, 1909), VI, 3211–3222.

property, together with their eldest sons. It also provided that the lower house of the General Assembly should be composed of two representatives from each town, except that Newport returned six and Providence, Portsmouth, and Warwick, four each. As a result of the dynamic expansion of Rhode Island's population and economy in the half-century after the Revolution, both provisions created disfranchisement and malapportionment that were severe even by early nineteenth-century standards. The appearance of large urban manufacturing centers in the northeastern corner of the state was accompanied by the growth of a city population that did not own land and was therefore disfranchised. Further, some towns quadrupled their population while others stagnated or lost residents without a change in the allocation of seats in the house. As a result, by 1840 the General Assembly was controlled by a rural minority. As examples of malapportionment and disfranchisement, in 1840 Smithfield, represented by two delegates, had a population of 9,534; Portsmouth, with four delegates, numbered 1,706 inhabitants. Providence had a population-per-delegate ratio of 5,793:1; Jamestown's was 182:1. Other complaints about the charter included the excessive powers of the General Assembly, the judiciary's relative lack of independence, and the absence of a bill of rights.[9]

Malapportionment and disfranchisement were aggravated by ethnic and economic tensions. Catholic Irish and French-Canadian immigrants were beginning to congregate in the

[9] The figures are from Peter J. Coleman, *The Transformation of Rhode Island* (Providence, 1963), 220, 256. See also Charles E. Gorman, *An Historical Statement of the Elective Franchise in Rhode Island* (pamphlet, n.p., n.d., a written statement submitted 1 Nov. 1879 to the U.S. Senate Committee on Election Frauds).

cities, together with some Yankees who had given up hard-scrabble farming for industrial employment. This intensi-fied the mistrust of farmers for the city dwellers. While the farming areas stagnated economically, the cities felt the im-pact of the industrial revolution, with its attendant low wages, long hours, unemployment, and slums.[10]

Because the General Assembly could amend the charter by statute, it was the target of efforts to mitigate disfran-chisement and malapportionment. At first the reformers' demands were quite modest. They asked either that the franchise be extended to all taxpayers and militiamen or that a convention be called to consider the question. The General Assembly, a principal beneficiary of both evils, refused to take any action on such demands in 1811, 1821, 1822, 1823, and 1830. When in 1824 it did submit the ques-tion of calling a convention to the freemen-voters, they rejected the proposal resoundingly.[11]

After the voters rejected another such proposal in 1834, the previously moderate suffrage reform party, called the "Constitutionalist movement," disintegrated and was re-placed by a new organization, the Rhode Island Suffrage Association, which proved to be a good deal more radical in both its objectives and its methods. The Constitutionalists had sought only taxpayer-militia suffrage and had contented

[10] Joseph Brennan, *Social Conditions in Industrial Rhode Island* (Washington, 1940), ch. 6; Chilton Williamson, *American Suffrage from Property to Democracy* (Princeton, 1960), 242–244; Cole-man, *Transformation*, 231–233.

[11] For the reformers' objectives, see Thomas W. Dorr and others, *An Address to the People of Rhode Island* (Providence, 1834), and Jacob Frieze, *A Concise History . . .* (Providence, 1842), 27–28. Cf. Chilton Williamson, "The Disenchantment of Thomas W. Dorr," *R.I. Hist.*, XVII (1958), 97–108.

themselves with petitioning the General Assembly, but the Suffrage Association insisted that a majority of the male adults in a state had the right to change or abolish their government if it was oppressive. The reformers now advocated a type of majoritarian democracy, at least for the original ratification of a new state constitution.[12]

The radicalization of the suffragists' objectives was accompanied by a radicalization of their methods. They suggested that the "people," disfranchised white adult males as well as freeholders, should call a convention, elect delegates by traditional town-meeting procedures, adopt a new constitution, submit it for ratification, and, if the document received more favorable votes than the total cast at the last preceding national election, proclaim it as the state constitution. Elections were to be held as soon as possible under the new instrument, and they hoped the old government would submit with good grace to its successor.

This plan succeeded splendidly in 1841 for several reasons. The hotly contested 1840 presidential campaign had

---

[12] Arthur M. Mowry, *The Dorr War* (Providence, 1901), is the best extant treatment of these events, but it is badly dated. For a somewhat different emphasis on the radicalism of the Dorr Rebellion from that in text, see Marvin Gettleman, "Political Opposition and Radicalism in the Dorr Rebellion," unpublished paper read at Organization of American Historians Convention, 1969. The formation of the Rhode Island Suffrage Association was encouraged and perhaps originally suggested by a New York City Locofoco organization, the "First Social Reform Society of New York." Charles Carroll, *Rhode Island. Three Centuries of Democracy* (New York, 1932), I, 480; Arthur M. Mowry, "The Constitutional Controversy in Rhode Island in 1841," Am. Hist. Assn., *Annual Report*, 1894 (Washington, 1895), 363–364. See also Robert L. Ciaburri, "The Dorr Rebellion in Rhode Island: 'The Moderate Phase,'" *R.I. Hist.*, XXVI (1967), 73–87.

left Rhode Islanders with a taste for political action. The suffrage and malapportionment grievances were too pressing to be ignored any longer. Most important, radical and moderate suffragists joined in a marriage of convenience and found cooperation congenial, the moderates supplying prestige and numbers, the radicals rhetoric and ideas.

Suffragist pamphleteers insisted that the exclusive suffrage and malapportionment of Rhode Island under the charter made that government "unrepublican." William Goodell, the prolific New York editor, author, and reformer, went so far as to argue that adoption of the guarantee clause nullified the 1663 charter. Most suffragists, however, simply argued that the people were masters of the government, not the reverse, and that they could change it when they wished. The issue, as an anonymous suffragist saw it, was "whether all power is embodied primarily in the people, or in the instruments of their creation." [13]

The increasing strength of the Suffrage Association prompted the General Assembly to offer some concessions

[13] William Goodell, "The Rights and Wrongs of Rhode Island" (Whitesboro, N.Y., 1842), issue no. 8 of the *Christian Emancipator*, Goodell's short-lived antislavery newsletter; Anon., *Facts Involved in the Rhode Island Controversy* (Boston, 1842), 3; "A Member of the Boston Bar" [John A. Bolles], *The Affairs of Rhode Island* (Providence, 1842), 11; Amos Kendall, *Kendall's Expositor*, 14 April 1842. The best summary of the Suffrage Association theory is contained in its "Declaration of Principles," 7 Feb. 1841, reprinted in U.S. Congress, House of Representatives, *Rhode Island—Interference of the Executive in the Affairs of*, 28 Cong., 1 sess., ser. 447, doc. 546 (1844). See also speech of Dorr, 18 Nov. 1841, *ibid.*, 851 ff. This last-cited document is most commonly known by the name of the chairman of the House Select Committee on Rhode Island (1844), the New Hampshire Radical Democrat, Edmund Burke, and will hereafter be cited as *Burke's Report*.

to its demands. The assembly called a constitutional convention and even reapportioned the delegations to come a bit closer to an equitable allotment, though it insisted on the restricted freeholders' suffrage for both election and ratification. This convention met in November 1841 and was known as the "Freeholders' Convention," its product as the "Freeholders' Constitution." The suffragists called their own convention the "People's Convention"; it produced the "People's Constitution."

Both constitutions were submitted for ratification, the People's without electoral restrictions (except for sex, race, and citizenship qualifications) and the Freeholders' to the enfranchised voters only. The People's was ratified, 14,000 to 52; the Freeholders' was rejected, 8,689 to 8,013. Opposition to the Freeholders' constitution and support for the People's constitution centered in the expanding industrial towns of the north and east. The suffragists expectably showed their greatest strength in the industrialized areas and were weakest in rural areas.[14]

The strong showing of the suffragists provoked a rash of pamphleteering by their opponents, who will be called, for convenience, the Freeholders. The Freeholders, identifying republicanism with legitimacy, condemned the theory and the procedures of the suffragists. Emphasizing the need for "stability" and "law and order," deprecating "anarchy" and "revolution," the conservatives expressed horror at the sug-

[14] Coleman, *Transformation*, 274–277; Mowry, *Dorr War*, 137; *Burke's Report*, 18, 119, contain statistics, tables, and maps supporting the generalization of the text paragraph. The two constitutions were remarkably similar, the Freeholders' being slightly more liberal than the Peoples' on suffrage questions and the Peoples' more generous to urban areas in its reapportionment provisions.

gestion that republican government required that "the whole legislative power would be exercised by the representatives of mere numbers." As to the argument that government was the servant of the people, the antisuffragists admitted the proposition but insisted that "the people" meant those who had the vote.[15]

Herein lay the basic difference between the reformist and conservative positions in the controversy, a difference that is often overlooked or misunderstood. Both factions would agree with the proposition that, as Chief Justice Taney put it in 1849, "according to the institutions of the country, the sovereignty in every State resides in the people of the State, and that they may alter and change their form of government at their own pleasure." They could agree only because the statement was a truism that left unanswered the basic questions: Who are the people and how may they exercise their sovereign will? Suffrage reformers in 1841 thought it axiomatic that "the people" meant every sane white adult male, period, while their Freeholder opponents insisted that "the people" comprised only those who had traditionally and legitimately exercised political power, that is, those given the vote under the charter of King Charles.

The second question, how the sovereigns exercise their

[15] Quotations are from William G. Goddard, *An Address to the People of Rhode Island* (Providence, 1843), 29–39. See generally Charles O. Lerche, Jr., "The Dorr Rebellion and the Federal Constitution," *R.I. Hist.*, IX (1950), 1–10; also the "Opinion of the Justices" of the Rhode Island Supreme Court, denouncing the suffrage movement as illegal in both its ends and its means, reprinted in Carroll, *Rhode Island*, I, 488. See also John Whipple, *Address of John Whipple, to the People of Rhode Island* (Providence, 1843).

power, produced a comparable split of opinion. Suffragists believed that any reasonably honest nose count of the adult males would be a proper expression of the sovereign will, particularly where this nose count was proclaimed to be for a constituent act as it was in the 1841 elections. Freeholders, with their abhorrence of extralegality, insisted that the will of the people could be ascertained only through procedures that had received the sanction of time and tradition, had been granted originally by the King of England, and had received the approval of Rhode Island's legislative bodies for nearly two centuries. As Justice Joseph Story, who sympathized with the Freeholders, indignantly asked, "what is a Republican government worth if an unauthorized body may thus make, promulgate, and compel obedience to a constitution at its own mere will and pleasure?" [16] Of course, each side saw the other's position as an abomination, suffragists accusing Freeholders of perpetuating ancient inequities out of a selfish lust for power, Freeholders claiming that suffragists were enemies of stability using reform as a mask for revolution.

Freeholders criticized the idea of government by simple numerical majorities. Their ablest spokesman was Elisha Potter, a lawyer who was to become a Whig congressman in 1843. He argued that pure majoritarianism characterized only democracies, not republics, and that the representative nature of republican government was not sullied by the malapportionment and suffrage abuses that existed in Rhode Island. Potter's position reflected in part the concept of representation classically stated in Edmund Burke's speech

[16] Joseph Story to John Pitman, 10 Feb. 1842, in William W. Story, ed., *Life and Letters of Joseph Story* (Boston, 1851), II, 416.

to the Bristol electors, namely, that a representative must think for himself and if his ideas are not consonant with those of his constituents, so much the worse for the constituents. Potter, in setting forth the conservative position on the nature of representative government, also believed that representation in a republic did not require that all men, or even a majority, exercise political power. The "people" might be so circumscribed as to constitute only a numerical minority, but so long as the representatives reflected their will the government was republican. Republicanism was destroyed only when the constituency decreased to an unspecified number small enough to justify labeling the government an aristocracy or oligarchy. To the suffragist argument that a person without a vote was not represented because he had no way of making his opinions felt, the conservatives replied that the legislative and executive branches represented the whole polity, those without political power as well as those with the vote. This was uncomfortably close to the theory of virtual representation that earlier justified rotten boroughs and the disfranchisement of entire cities in England. As to the guarantee clause, Potter pointed out that Rhode Island's government was considered republican at the time it was admitted to the Union and that what was adequately republican for 1790 remained so in 1842.[17]

To this argument, Thomas Wilson Dorr, leader of the Rhode Island Suffrage Association, replied that the constitution cannot be superior to the sovereignty that inalienably resides in the people:

We contend for [the people's] absolute sovereignty over all

[17] Elisha R. Potter, *Considerations on the Questions of the Adoption of a Constitution, and Extension of Suffrage in Rhode Island* (Boston, 1842).

Constitutions and prescribed modes of amendment, with the limitations only that are established in the Constitution of the United States. The establishment of any mode of convenience, for amending a Constitution through the action of the Legislature, cannot impair the general unalienated & inalienable right of the People at large to make alterations in their organic laws in any other mode, which they may deem expedient; Constitutions and plans of government not being barriers against Popular Sovereignty, by the theory of our institutions, but forms of expressing, protecting & securing the Rights of the People, intended to remain in use until the People shall otherwise indicate and direct.[18]

After the ratification of the People's constitution and the rejection of the Freeholders', Rhode Island careened on to crisis. The existing state government passed a law designed to prevent the establishment of a government under the People's constitution. Suffragists dubbed this the "Algerine" law after the harsh regime of the Dey of Algiers. The suffragists held elections for the new state government in April 1842, but the Algerine law had its effect: less than 6,500 persons turned out. They elected Dorr the new People's governor. The People's legislature met in an unused Providence foundry for two days and adjourned, *sine die* as it turned out.[19]

In spite of bombast and belligerent posturing on both

[18] Dorr to Nathan Clifford, 24 Jan. 1848, in C. Peter Magrath, "Optimistic Democrat: Thomas W. Dorr and the Case of Luther v. Borden, *R.I. Hist.*, XXIX (1970), 94–112 at 100.
[19] The Algerine law is reprinted in *Burke's Report*, 816. For contemporary evaluations of Dorr and his objectives, see "A Rhode Islander" [Frances G. McDougall] *Might and Right* (Providence, 1844), 230–231, and Dan King, *The Life and Times of Thomas Wilson Dorr* (Boston, 1859), 286–290.

sides, there was little disagreement on the need for suffrage reform. Except for a few extremists, by May 1842 Freeholders were ready to concede some sort of reform, but refused to do so under the threat of armed force. John Whipple, one of Freeholder Governor Samuel King's emissaries to President Tyler, wrote the President before his interview that he understood Tyler to feel that

free suffrage must *prevail*. Undoubtedly it will. That is not the question. The freeholders of Rhode Island have yielded that point; and the *only* question is, between their constitution, providing for an extension of suffrage, and ours, containing *substantially* the *same* provision. Whether their constitution shall be carried out by *force of arms, without* a majority; or the present government be supported *until* a constitution can be agreed upon that will command a majority. . . . Nearly all the leaders, who are professional men, have abandoned them, on the ground that a majority is not in favor of their constitution.

Elisha Potter, another of King's representatives, agreed:

The only objection made [to the immediate call of a constitutional convention by the Freeholders] was, that they did not wish to concede while the People's party continued their threats. All allowed that the concession must be made. . . . If two or three noisy folks among the suffrage party could only have their mouths stopped for a week or two, a reconciliation could be brought about at any time.

The *sine qua non* of the Freeholder conservatives, however, was legality: reforms were conceded, however reluctantly, but they could be brought about only in a legitimate way. United States District Court Judge John Pitman, who sympathized ardently with the Freeholders, put it thus: "We shall have to give up our freehold qualification, but our reforms will be made if at all I trust by a legal convention and voted for by the people in a legal way." But after they were frightened by the bombast of New York radicals and by Dorr's increasing intransigence, the Freeholders concluded that stability and the assertion of the legitimate government's authority must precede compromise and reform at all costs.[20]

While the Freeholders' government marshaled its forces after their Governor Samuel King's inauguration on 5 May 1842, the People's government dissolved. In an attempt to stave off the inevitable, Dorr and some of his supporters went to Washington to secure either the assistance or the neutrality of President John Tyler. Details of the Tyler-Dorr interview remain unknown. Apparently Tyler was originally not hostile to the objectives of the Dorrites, but the three-man Freeholder delegation headed by Elisha Potter had got his ear first and persuaded him to adopt their "legitimist" viewpoint. In any event, Dorr could not allay Tyler's suspicions of his movement when they met.[21]

[20] Whipple to Tyler, 9 April 1842, in *Burke's Report*, 669; Potter to Tyler, 15 May 1842, *ibid.*, 677; Pitman to Joseph Story, 26 Jan. 1842, in Joseph Story Papers, William L. Clements Library, University of Michigan. For accounts of other compromise efforts, see letter of Burrington Anthony, undated, to *People's Democratic Guide*, June 1842; "A Massachusetts Man Resident in Rhode Island," *The Close of the Late Rebellion* (Providence, 1842), 18. For Freeholder recognition of the need to conciliate suffragists, see Elisha R. Potter to Tyler, 2 June, 6 June, 10 June 1842 (initialled copy); John Brown Francis to Potter, 7 June 1842; William Sprague to Potter, 10 June 1842, all in Elisha R. Potter papers, Rhode Island Historical Society, Providence, R.I.

[21] King, *Dorr*, 125; [McDougall], *Might and Right*, 79; *Kendall's Expositor*, 14 April 1842. For early pro-Dorrite contacts with Tyler, see William Allen to Dorr, 15 April 1842, and John A.

Dorr left Washington dispirited, intending to return to Rhode Island. During a stopover in New York City, however, he was feted by the leading Locofocos, lionized by the radical Democracy, and promised military aid by some impetuous colonels of the New York militia. Dorr recovered his habitual optimism and returned to Providence determined to reassert the authority of his government.[22] The Freeholders' government responded vigorously. Spurred by a fear that Dorr would take his own belligerent oratory seriously, Governor King became increasingly stiff-necked. Dorr did rally a handful of followers for an attempt to seize the Providence arsenal, but this, like the cannon hauled in for the occasion, misfired. Dorr then fled the state and his support in Providence collapsed.

At this point, the baneful influence of Tammany reappeared. The New Yorkers persuaded Dorr to return to Rhode Island and organized some support for him from sympathizers in neighboring Connecticut and Massachusetts, where his cause was popular. Dorr and these supporters, together with a brace of Rhode Islanders, regrouped in the hamlet of Chepachet, Rhode Island. Alarmed, King called out the militia, which rallied without exception to his government. Before the militia reached the Chepachet for-

Brown to Dorr, 5 May 1842, in Dorr MSS., Rider Collection, John Hay Library, Brown University, Providence, R.I.

[22] Arthur M. Mowry, "Tammany Hall and the Dorr Rebellion," *Am. Hist. Rev.*, II (1898), 292–301. See also testimony of William G. McNeil, 2 May 1844, in the treason trial of Dorr, in George Turner and W. S. Burges, *Report of the Trial of Thomas Wilson Dorr* (Providence, 1844, reprint of proceedings as published in the Providence *Republican Herald*). A valuable compilation of expressions of support or sympathy for the suffragists is the New York *People's Democratic Guide*, Oct. 1842, a monthly Locofoco paper.

tifications, Dorr's little band dispersed, and he fled to New Hampshire. Dorr's travels provoked the New York *American* to quip: "Why is Suffrage Governor Dorr tossed to and fro like a shuttlecock? Because he is not a battle-Dorr." [23]

After Dorr's threat was liquidated, the moderate suffragists who had rallied to the loyalist standard insisted on constitutional revision. They now enjoyed the support of conservatives who had refused to consider suffrage reform while the Dorr menace loomed. Only a few die-hards refused support for the new constitution ratified in November 1842. Unlike the People's and the Freeholders' constitutions, the new constitution provided for taxpayer-militia suffrage, but did not restrict it to whites. Representation was dealt with in a brief paragraph providing that the house should always consist of seventy-two members, "constituted on the basis of population," that is, apportioned pro rata on the basis of census enumeration, but with each town assured at least one representative and no town allowed to have more than twelve.

Dorr and his sympathizers had lost the battle but won the war. This gave little consolation to Dorr, who considered his defeat a triumph of force over righteousness, particularly after his nemesis in the Democratic party, James Fenner, was elected governor in 1843. Crushed, Dorr gave up the struggle, returned to Providence, and was tried for treason by vindictive political enemies. He was convicted in 1844 and sentenced to life imprisonment. This pointless and brutal act roused considerable support for reversal of the conviction, New Yorkers again taking the lead by encour-

[23] The *American*'s witticism is quoted in Nathaniel Weyl, *Treason* (Washington, 1950), 196.

aging the formation of a Dorr Liberation Society. An attempt to have the United States Supreme Court issue a writ of habeas corpus failed, but the liberationists' efforts were rewarded when Governor Charles Jackson, elected on a "Liberation" ticket, released Dorr. He was amnestied in 1851, and the Rhode Island legislature reversed his conviction for the record in 1854. Dorr died ten months later.[24]

When Governor King requested federal assistance from President Tyler to quell a domestic insurrection, he raised guarantee clause issues that drew all three branches of the federal government into the Rhode Island dispute. The Dorr Rebellion was thus a climacteric in state-federal relations in the early nineteenth century.

It may have been unavoidable that the President of the United States should be urged to involve himself in the Rhode Island suffrage dispute, but it is one of the ironies of our history that the man occupying the White House in 1842 should be one who, by inclination and background, would be extremely loath to do so. John Tyler had treated Andrew Jackson to a stern lecture on meddling in South Carolina's internal affairs during the Nullification crisis ten years before. In some ways an old Republican who had outlived his era, Tyler found the Democracy uncongenial when Martin Van Buren assumed party leadership in 1837. Seeking a political environment more compatible with his economic conservatism, Tyler became a pseudo-Whig in time to balance the 1840 Whig ticket. President William Henry Harrison's unexpected death thrust him into the White House, and Tyler speedily made it clear that he

[24] Ex parte *Dorr*, 3 How. 320 (U.S., 1845); Anon., *The Conspiracy to Defeat the Liberation of Governor Dorr* (New York, 1845).

intended to be more than a caretaker "acting President." [25]

Tyler's attempts to please Whigs and states'-rights Democrats succeeded only in alienating both. For his troubles he was read out of his newly adopted party and threatened with both censure and impeachment in the House. As a result of his frustration in trying to ride two party horses at once and because of his ideological commitments, Tyler later tried to form a third party that would combine respect for southern slavery and sectional interests with a program of certain types of government aid to promote national economic development. He eagerly exploited splits in the Democracy on the Texas problem by wooing New York's Hunkers and a Tammany faction while freezing out ex-President Martin Van Buren's Barnburners.

Into this political turmoil came Governor Samuel King's letter to Tyler of 4 April 1842 (one month before the inauguration of the People's government) requesting "the protection which is required by the Constitution of the United States" because Rhode Island was threatened with "domestic violence" and "revolutionary movements." King's specific request was moderate enough: he wanted a proclamation from Tyler (contents unspecified) and one United States Army officer. King seemed to have felt that a mere gesture of support by the President would be enough to persuade the Dorrites to disband. One crucial problem faced King, however, that proved insuperable: there had

[25] See Robert Seager, *And Tyler Too* (New York, 1963), chs. 3–9; Lyon G. Tyler, ed., *The Letters and Times of the Tylers* (Richmond, 1884–1896), II, *passim;* Oliver P. Chitwood, *John Tyler, Champion of the Old South* (New York, 1939), chs. 14–24; Robert J. Morgan, *A Whig Embattled: The Presidency under John Tyler* (Lincoln, Neb., 1954), 95–105.

not yet been armed resistance to his government. Because the Dorrites did not match their deeds to their declamations, President Tyler refused to take any overt action to help the Freeholders' government. King unsuccessfully tried to get around this difficulty by urging Tyler to take "precautionary measures" under the federal "power to prevent, as well as to defend us from, violence." [26]

Although Tyler was at first not hostile to the objectives of the Dorrites, he would have had difficulty in taking any decisive action one way or the other. His devotion to state autonomy and hostility to the expansion of federal power would have made him reluctant to intervene in state political disputes. Furthermore, in 1842 Tyler still believed he had a political future; he should not antagonize any faction unnecessarily. But if someone's feelings had to be hurt, from Tyler's point of view it might as well have been the Radical Democrats, who, in the persons of New York's Locofocos, were enthusiastically supporting Dorr. If Tyler's political instincts dictated any course, it would have been one of inaction while the Freeholders continued to hold the upper hand.[27]

These considerations prompting inaction were abetted by Tyler's two bedrock characteristics: he was a conservative and a southerner. He well knew that, though southerners looked to the federal army for suppression of possible slave insurrections, they resolutely opposed any federal actions that might suggest that the southern state governments were insufficiently republican. As a conservative Tyler abhorred

[26] The King-Tyler correspondence is in *Burke's Report*, 652–690, with related documents.

[27] Tyler to Governor John Floyd of Virginia, 16 Jan. 1833, in Chitwood, *John Tyler*, 113.

civil disorder, particularly when it had the undertones of class war, as the Rhode Island affair did in the current propaganda.

Tyler's difficulties were not made easier by the conflicting advice he received. Some southern conservatives urged support of the Freeholders. They saw the Dorrites as "mad leaders . . . bringing on anarchy and bloodshed." The New Orleans *Commercial Bulletin*, the organ of that city's business community, urged intervention on the side of the Freeholders to preserve American credit abroad. On the other hand, the Richmond *Enquirer* insisted that Tyler abstain from the dispute. It may have been the advice of Secretary of State Daniel Webster, to whom Tyler still turned in 1842, that was decisive with the President, especially since it harmonized with his conservative instincts. The federal government, Webster believed, must "maintain the existing constitution and laws, till regularly changed." This was the heart of the Freeholder position; if change must be made, it could come about only through constitutional methods. The Dorrite direct-action procedure was extraconstitutional and therefore revolutionary.[28]

Similar views were offered by the three commissioners sent by Governor King to entreat with Tyler in person,

[28] The views of the *Enquirer* and the *Commercial Bulletin* are cited in Mowry, "Tammany Hall," 294. Webster's views and advice in April 1842 must be reconstructed by conjecture and *post hoc* evidence since no record survives of his communications to Tyler in that month. For his attitude in May 1842, see Webster to John Whipple, 9 May 1842, in James W. McIntyre, ed., *The Writings and Speeches of Daniel Webster* (Boston, 1903), XVIII, 127. There is no reason to believe that Webster felt differently a month earlier. His later fulsome praise of Tyler's conduct suggests that the President's acts were fully in accord with Webster's feelings. Webster to Tyler, 18 April 1844, *ibid.*, 189–190.

Elisha Potter, John Whipple, and John Francis. Their mission was highly successful. First, they dispelled any sympathy for Dorr that might have lingered in Tyler's mind. Further, in a "Statement of Facts," they supplied Tyler with the rationale that he used to justify his policies. The Freeholders' government, they insisted, was *the* government of the state, accepted *de jure* and *de facto* by the federal government at the time of its admission. It was therefore the only government entitled to protection under the provisions of the guarantee and domestic violence clauses. Tyler must treat the Dorrites as a rebellious faction.[29]

Tyler replied to King's requests soon after his interview with Whipple, Potter, and Francis. In a letter dated April 11, he first denied that the federal government had any power to arbitrate "questions of domestic policy" between citizens of a state. He then rejected King's suggestion that section 4 authorized the President to "anticipate" rebellions; "there must be an actual insurrection, manifested by lawless assemblages of people." If an actual insurrection existed in the state, he as President, acting under the authority of the 1792 Militia Act, would intervene to uphold the legitimate state government. "In such a contingency, the executive could not look into real or supposed defects of the existing government." He must recognize its authority until it is changed "by legal and peaceable proceedings." He concluded by repeating the rationale of the "Statement of Facts," affirming that he would support the authority of King's government.[30]

Some positions taken by Tyler in this letter of April 11 were to remain the basis for all his subsequent actions and

[29] The "Statement of Facts" is in *Burke's Report,* 669–672.
[30] Richardson, *Messages,* V, 2143–2345.

were to become precedents for later chief executives. First, the decision whether or not to suppress domestic violence lies entirely within the discretion of the President after he receives a call for assistance. Second, actual violence, not just the threat of disorder, must have taken place or be unavoidably imminent as a prerequisite of presidential action. Third, the guarantee of republican government extended to the recognized government of a state, not to the faction challenging it. Fourth, as a corollary to the third point, the President is not free to choose the group that he will aid on the basis of his own notions of republicanism.

In a later communication to Congress Tyler insisted that the President was bound to accept a state's admission into the Union and the fact that it had full representation in Congress as conclusive evidence of its republican character. His duty under section 4 and the 1792 Militia Act was not discretionary; if it were otherwise he would be a "constitution-maker" for the states and an absolute despot. Tyler's view of the extent and limitations on executive discretion has prevailed to this day because it is basically sound. For the President to act before civil disorder broke out and on the basis of his individual concept of republican government would be too great a wrench to the federal system and would arrogate to one man more power than could be safely given.[31]

Tyler's April letter left matters at a standstill for a month. Immediately after the inauguration of the People's government on May 4, King wrote again to Tyler. This time he passed on a resolution of the Freeholders' legislature requesting federal intervention. King's new tactics were no

[31] Tyler's letter to the House Select Committee on Rhode Island, 9 April 1844, in *Burke's Report*, 652–655.

more successful than the old. Tyler again refused. In his reply, dated May 7, he tried to calm King by reminding him that the People's government was collapsing and suggested that a conciliatory attitude might end the whole controversy. But he also reassured King that if the civil authority was insufficiently powerful to suppress violence, the federal government would enforce section 4's guarantee. In a "private and confidential" letter sent with the first the President emphasized the need for concessions to the suffragists' demands, as well as a general amnesty. And there the matter rested, as far as Tyler was concerned, for several weeks.[32]

Meanwhile, Dorr had gone to Connecticut to consult with sympathizers there. This threw the Freeholders into a panic because they assumed Dorr was trying to raise a military force. Just when they thought they had the domestic situation well in hand, the prospect of a "foreign invasion" loomed. King immediately (May 25) wrote again to Tyler, insisting that the need for federal troops was greater than ever. Tyler was not to be budged. He wrote King, stating that an invasion was unlikely, but that, should it occur, he would act under his statutory authority, presumably by calling up the Connecticut and Massachusetts militia and by sending in federal troops. He did take the precaution of ordering the War Department to undertake secret intelligence operations to estimate the size of the threat. He had also increased the detachment at Fort Adams near Providence. So matters stood for another month.[33]

At last, toward the end of June, the possibility of armed invasion that had so agitated the Freeholders materialized

[32] Richardson, *Messages*, V, 2146–2147; *Burke's Report*, 672–674.
[33] *Burke's Report*, 681–682.

in the forlorn form of the Chepachet assembly. King again beseeched Tyler for federal troops, and Tyler again temporized, pointing out that the legislature, not the governor, should have made the request. Tyler did draw up a proclamation ordering the mobs to disperse and sent it up by Secretary of War John Bell, who was dispatched to Providence to supervise the activities of federal troops and to keep an eye on developments there. Because Dorr's men were scattered without bloodshed, the proclamation was never published. This ended President John Tyler's involvement in the Dorr Rebellion.[34]

Tyler had acted with balance, firmness, and tact in meeting the challenge of the Dorr Rebellion. He had the satisfaction of seeing his policies of caution and conciliation vindicated at no cost to his consistency or to national stability. His actions during the crisis had set several important precedents for the future of federal-state relations. He confirmed the widely held assumption that responsibility for execution of the dual promise of guarantee and protection might sometimes fall on the President, as commander in chief of the armed forces, rather than Congress. Yet his caution and moderation served as a warning to future Presidents that the great power confided to them was best used with restraint and that the mere threat of action might be more effective than a precipitate dispatch of troops. Tyler's emphasis on his statutory authority as a necessary supplement to the constitutional grant of power underlined this wary exercise of executive power.

Tyler's caution, however, won him no friends among the Dorrites. They attributed the collapse of their movement to his implicit promise of assistance to the Freeholders' gov-

[34] *Ibid.*, 684–685, 688–690.

ernment and bitterly assailed him for protecting it with the federal aegis. Radical Democratic congressmen sympathetic to the Dorr cause refused to let such an appealing issue disappear without making some political capital out of it. Motivated both by sympathy with the suffrage cause and by a desire to use it as a stick to beat John Tyler, Democrats in both the House and the Senate kept up desultory debate in 1842 on Tyler's motives and actions in an attempt to embarrass him politically. They contended that Tyler threatened to use federal troops to put down Dorr's government and that this threat effectively destroyed the suffrage movement. These 1842 debates got nowhere, and the whole issue seemed to lose its point as the suffragist forces were first put down and then conciliated. By late 1842 Congress appeared to have forgotten the whole episode.[35]

Casting about for a more exciting issue for the 1844 presidential campaign than Tyler's ineffectiveness, House Democrats suddenly found one in their lap. Early that year, the Democratic minority in the Rhode Island general assembly addressed a "Memorial" to the U.S. House of Representatives, asking it to "inquire" into the President's power under section 4, to demand all Tyler's correspondence relating to the Rebellion, and to determine whether the representatives from Rhode Island (both ex-Freeholder Whigs) were entitled to their seats. They concluded by vaguely requesting Congress "to execute to this state the guaranty in the national constitution of a republican constitution [*sic*]."[36]

The House appointed a Select Committee on Rhode Is-

[35] *Globe*, 27 Cong., 2 sess., 430 (18 April 1842), 432 (20 April 1842), 438 (22 April 1842), 510 (18 May 1842), 523 (23 May 1842).

[36] See *People's Democratic Guide*, June 1842; The New York *Young Hickory Banner*, 31 Aug. 1844 (the *Banner* was, as its title

land. It held hearings and produced two reports, *Burke's Report* for the Democratic majority on the committee, which condemned Tyler's actions, and a reactionary minority report. The minority argued that the federal government "is to repress, not to sanction or justify, unauthentic popular movements"; that representation in the United States is virtual, "a majority of those legally entitled to vote represent the whole"; and that there is no "natural right" to the suffrage. The minority report was signed by the only southern members of Burke's committee, which had split on sectional rather than partisan lines. It reflected the abnormal southern sensitivity to the possibility of a northern majority using federal power to challenge the peculiar institution.[37]

The majority, in contrast, claimed that the guarantee clause gives Congress "a supervision over all the state Constitutions, so far as the ascertainment of their republican character is concerned," including the power to "set aside" those constitutions not reflective of the popular will. Though Congress cannot dictate the terms of the state constitution, the people (excluding slaves, minors, convicts, lunatics, and "paupers"—women were not mentioned explicitly) "have supreme, unlimited control over their constitutions" and may reform them as they please. Thus the People's constitution was the only one entitled to the protection of the guarantee clause, and Tyler should have been condemned for supporting the extant government.

The committee majority's position did not attract widespread support in the House; the report, after its reading,

suggests, a Barnburner paper written to promote James K. Polk's candidacy in 1844); the "Memorial" is in *Burke's Report*, 2–3.

[37] The minority report, usually known by the name of its principal author, Rep. John M. S. Causins (Whig-Md.), is H.R. Rept. 581, 28 Cong., 1 sess., ser. 447. See Lerche, "Dorr Rebellion," 7.

was never acted upon, and Congress soon forgot about the Dorr Rebellion. As a result, no precedent was set by Congress for later applications of the guarantee, but ideas had been adumbrated that would one day be implemented vigorously to force on a resistant South the social revolution that the committee's southern minority feared.

By 1845 the Dorr Rebellion was a dead issue in national politics, though its effects were to remain potent in Rhode Island for some time to come. The Rebellion had established certain important precedents for subsequent constitutional interpretation. For one, the contention of the radical Democrats that Congress must determine whether a state constitution is republican and take steps of enforcement had been rejected—but only temporarily, as the events of Reconstruction were to prove. For another, Tyler's caution in using his powers under the successors of the Militia Act of 1792 and his determination to support the extant state government irrespective of his opinions as to its republican character would both be difficult for later Presidents to ignore if faced with similar problems. Finally, as a result of these first two effects, the clause came to be associated with the repressive reading that Hamilton had given it in the *Federalist*. The suggestive interpretations of Madison, the alter ego of "Publius," equating republicanism with popular representation in both the states and the federal system, were for a time ignored.

4

Luther v. Borden (1849)

Rhode Island Dorrites remained undaunted by the suppression of their government and the demise of the Rebellion as an issue in national politics. After their sympathizers in Congress failed to censure President Tyler, they
carried their struggle to a different forum—the United
States Supeme Court. They reasoned that even if the new
President James K. Polk was indifferent or preoccupied
(as he was), and resort to Congress was useless, the Court
might uphold their position if they could bring up a case.
Why they should have reached this conclusion remains
unclear. Perhaps they believed that because seven of the
Justices sitting in 1843 were appointed by Democratic
presidents they could get a sympathetic hearing on their
dispute with the Freeholders. There was in fact some
reason for such optimism. Justice Levi Woodbury, a
thoroughgoing Jacksonian, had declared his support for
the Dorr cause before his appointment to the bench. Justices Robert Grier and John Catron were suspected of
being sympathetic to the Dorrites. Dorr himself thought
that Justices Samuel Nelson and Peter V. Daniel would
also be receptive.[1]

[1] A pro-Dorrite statement signed by Woodbury appears in

The idea of carrying a suit up to the Supreme Court to test the legality of either the Freeholders' or the People's governments under the guarantee clause had been broached several times before 1845. The original program of the Suffrage Association assumed that the President had no role in enforcing the guarantee, and that the proper procedure would be to seek redress first from Congress and then from the United States Supreme Court. In its 1841 "Preamble," the Association outlined its proposed course of action: "Our first appeal is to heaven." Should that fail, recourse would be had to more mundane bodies: the people of Rhode Island, then the General Assembly. "These failing, our final resort shall be to the Congress of the United States, . . . and if need be, to the Supreme Judicial Power, to test the force and meaning of that provision in the Constitution, which guarantees 'to every state in the Union a republican form of government.' " [2]

Even persons unsympathetic to Dorr's cause thought that the federal courts were the appropriate forum to resolve guarantee clause issues. Justice Job Durfee of the Rhode Island Supreme Court, who was later to preside over Dorr's treason trial, thought in 1842 that the whole controversy was amenable only to "judicial correction and I query whether the correction should not come from the courts

---

the *People's Democratic Guide*, June 1842. The attitudes of Grier and Catron are discussed in Charles Warren, *The Supreme Court in United States History* (Boston, 1923), II, 462–467; Dorr to Benjamin F. Hallett and George Turner, 2 Feb. 1847, in Magrath, "Optimistic Democrat," 103. See also Levi Woodbury to Dorr, 15 April 1841 [*sic;* actually 1842] in Dorr Mss., Rider Collection, John Hay Library, Providence, R.I.

[2] The "Preamble" is in "A Rhode Islander" [Frances G. McDougall], *Might and Right* (Providence, 1844), 75.

of that power, which has guaranteed to the state its government together with all its constitutional relations, whose entire subversion is threatened." [3] That Durfee should have taken this position in 1842 is ironic, for his instructions to the jury in *State* v. *Dorr* were construed by Taney as a conclusive pronouncement by a state court for federal courts on the legitimacy of the Freeholders' government.

Among various efforts to compromise the controversy was one involving two men who were to appear as counsel in different stages of *Luther* v. *Borden*. In April 1842 two of Dorr's emissaries, Dutee Pearce and Burrington Anthony, met with Daniel Webster and John Whipple in New York and worked out a compromise plan to test the validity of the People's constitution under the guarantee clause by a made-up suit in the federal courts that would be carried to the United States Supreme Court. In exchange Dorr would stay out of Providence so the Freeholders' government could get on with the business of administering Rhode Island. This suggestion never came to anything, but it indicated that both sides had given some thought to seeking a judicial resolution of Rhode Island's difficulties under the guarantee clause.[4]

Dorr's supporters soon found their opportunity in one of the many minor outrages that had occurred when the Freeholders had imposed martial law on the state after the Chepachet scare. Martin Luther, a Warren shoemaker, had violated the Algerine law by serving as a moderator at the People's election. After he fled to Massachusetts Luther

[3] Durfee to Joseph Story, 5 Aug. 1842, in Story Papers, Clements Library.

[4] Letter of Burrington Anthony, undated, to the *People's Democratic Guide*, June 1842.

Borden, at the head of a Freeholders' posse, broke into his house, searched for incriminating evidence, and terrorized Luther's female relatives.

In 1843 Luther brought an action of trespass against Borden in the United States Circuit Court for Rhode Island, over which Justice Joseph Story presided.[5] Tactically, this choice of forum would have been ill-advised had the Dorrites not expected to carry the cause higher because both Story and United States District Court Judge John Pitman, who presided in the Rhode Island District and served with Story on the circuit court, were flagrantly biased against the People's cause. Pitman had even composed and circulated a pamphlet supporting the Freeholder cause, arguing that the "people" of the state are only those who are enfranchised by the state constitution—a staple Freeholder argument. Hence for Pitman the disfranchised had "no right to complain, much less have they a right to force themselves on the body politic." As a consequence of these views, Pitman observed in May 1842 that "I am obnoxious to these men [the Dorrites]." [6] Luther and the interests he represented could not realistically have hoped for even-handed justice at the circuit court level.

At the trial Borden defended himself on the grounds that he acted under the martial law imposed by the King gov-

[5] A United States Circuit Court was then a two-judge court, comprising a justice of the United States Supreme Court on circuit as presiding judge and the judge of the United States District Court for that particular circuit.

[6] For Story's bias, see Story to Pitman, 10 Feb. 1842, in William W. Story, ed., *Life and Letters of Joseph Story* (Boston, 1851), II, 416. For Pitman's, see [John Pitman], *To the Members of the General Assembly* (Providence, 1842), and Pitman to Story, 26 Jan., 4 May, and 7 Nov. 1842 in Story Papers, Clements Library.

ernment. Luther replied that Dorr's was the only valid government of the state at the time and that the acts of the King government were therefore void. On this, issue was joined. Justice Story refused to permit Luther to introduce evidence that Dorr's was the only legitimate government in the state and instructed the jury, *pro forma*, that the Freeholder government's decision to impose martial law was justified. Verdict and judgment therefore went against Luther, and he sought a writ of error from the United States Supreme Court.[7]

Luther's petition came up to the Supreme Court in 1845 when there were two vacancies on it. The case immediately became ensnarled in partisan politics because Whigs charged that President Polk would make two Democratic appointments to the Court in order to get a ruling in Luther's favor. For this reason and because of the illnesses of Justices John Catron, Peter Daniel, and John McKinley, Chief Justice Taney had to postpone argument repeatedly; three years elapsed before the case was argued and decided. By then its waning political significance had been eclipsed by the Mexican War, the furor over the Wilmot Proviso, and the 1848 presidential campaign. When arguments were at last heard, Justices Catron, Daniel, and McKinley did not sit or, apparently, participate in the decision. Hence this critical case was determined by only two-thirds of the full bench.[8]

Both parties commanded the services of distinguished

[7] There is no official report of *Luther* v. *Borden* in the circuit court. The case is discussed in the unofficial report of *Luther* v. *Borden* in the Supreme Court, 12 L.Ed. 581; Warren, *Supreme Court*, II, 460–462; and Mahlon H. Hellerich, "The Luther Cases in the Lower Courts," *R.I. Hist.*, XI (1952), 33–45.

[8] Warren, *Supreme Court*, 460–466.

counsel. Representing Luther were the Dorrite pamphleteer Benjamin Hallett and, strangely, the conservative Democrat who was then Attorney General of the United States, Nathan Clifford. Borden and the Freeholders' position were represented by John Whipple (one of Governor King's commissioners to Tyler) and Daniel Webster. Hallett led off, holding forth for three days in a long disquisition on Dorrite political theory. His fundamental points were that sovereignty resided in the people, who might change their government whenever they wished. He unwittingly gave away his case, though, in attempting to avoid the Rhode Island Supreme Court's determination in *State* v. *Dorr* (1844; the Dorr treason trial) that the Freeholders' government was the only legitimate one in Rhode Island in 1842, wherein Chief Judge Job Durfee charged the jury. "Courts . . . do not count votes to determine whether a constitution has been adopted or a government elected or not. . . . It belongs to the legislature to exercise this high duty. . . . if we did so, we should cease to be a mere judicial, and become a political, tribunal, with the whole sovereignty in our hand." This decision, he argued, did not bind the United States Supreme Court because it was a political, not a judicial, question. Taney was to turn Hallett's sword against him on this point. Whipple followed Hallett with a shorter and undistinguished conservative refutation of the majoritarian view of popular sovereignty.[9]

[9] The quotation from Durfee's charge to the jury is in [Charles S. Bradley], *The Methods of Changing the Constitution of the States* (Boston, 1885), 14. Dorr's treason trial was a case of original jurisdiction in the Rhode Island Supreme Court. *State* v. *Dorr* was not officially reported. But two lengthy unofficial reports were compiled: Joseph S. Pitman, *Report of the Trial of Thomas Wilson Dorr, for Treason* (Boston, 1844), and [George Turner], *Report*

Webster's turn came next. Two-thirds of his relatively brief argument was given over to oratorical nods in the direction of Whig political theory regarding popular sovereignty, where he emphasized the need for legitimacy and regularity in changing a state's constitution. But toward the close of his argument he hammered home his main points, which dealt not with theory but with the question of the Court's jurisdiction to hear the case. Here his florid oratory was perceptibly toned down, as he stressed two basic points: the question presented was outside "judicial cognizance" and abstract questions of right and justice were mooted by the obvious fact that it was impossible to resurrect the long-dead Dorr government. On the jurisdictional issue Webster's argument was at variance with his usual position urging expansion of federal judicial power. Luther's proffered evidence, he insisted, could not be received by any court; judicial bodies must look to the political branches for a determination of which government is to be recognized. He also stressed the impossibility of a court's attempting to count ballots and decide on the validity of election returns. Finally, he emphasized that President Tyler, the Rhode Island Supreme Court, Congress, and the Rhode Island general assembly had determined the legitimacy of the Freeholders' government and the 1842 constitution, and that this determination was binding on the Supreme Court. Like Tyler and the Freeholders, he insisted that section 4 was meant to protect the existing government. Chief Justice Taney's majority opinion approved each of these points

---

of the Trial of Thomas Wilson Dorr, for Treason (Providence, 1844). Hallett's argument was reprinted as *The Right of the People to Establish Forms of Government. Mr. Hallett's Argument in the Rhode Island Causes* (Boston, 1848).

and followed closely Webster's order of presentation.[10]

The case was decided shortly afterward, but Taney postponed announcing the decision until 1849 because of his own illness. Since Taney's opinion (for the six Justices who heard the argument, excepting Woodbury, who dissented only on the martial law point) set by far the most important precedent under the guarantee clause for future state-federal relations, the bases of his reasoning and his assumptions are of continuing pertinence and must be examined with care.[11]

After briefly reciting the circumstances of the Rebellion and Justice Story's disposition of the case in the circuit court, Chief Justice Taney noted that the Freeholders'

[10] Though Webster, Durfee, and Hallett did not cite them, precedents were available for the distinction they drew between political and judicial questions, wherein the political question doctrine was foreshadowed. Excepting English and state court decisions, these included: *New York* v. *Connecticut*, 4 Dall. 4 (U.S., 1799); *Martin* v. *Mott*, 12 Wheat. 19 (U.S., 1827); *Cherokee Nation* v. *Georgia*, 5 Pet. 20 (U.S., 1831); and *Rhode Island* v. *Massachusetts*, 12 Pet. 657 (U.S., 1838) (Taney, C. J., dissenting). See also "One of the Rhode Island People," *A Reply to the Letter of the Hon. Marcus Morton . . . on the Rhode Island Question* (Providence, 1842), 21. Webster's argument was reprinted twice: *The Rhode Island Question. Mr. Webster's Argument* (Washington, 1848); and *The Rhode Island Question. Arguments of Messrs. Whipple and Webster* (Providence, 1848). Hallett foresaw Taney's reliance on a political question rationale; Hallett to Dorr, 11 Feb. 1848, in Dorr MSS., John Hay Library. See Maurice G. Baxter, *Daniel Webster and the Supreme Court* (Amherst, Mass., 1966), 58–64, 242, for an evaluation of Webster's position in *Luther* v. *Borden*. For Webster's notes used in the argument, which highlight his strategy and the points he wished to emphasize, see Samuel P. Lyman, *The Public and Private Life of Daniel Webster* (Philadelphia, 1852), I, 290–298.

[11] *Luther* v. *Borden*, 7 How. 1 (U.S., 1849). The quotations from Taney that follow in the text are from this source, pp. 3–15.

was at all times the *de facto* government of Rhode Island
and that Dorr's "government" never exercised any effective
authority. Further, the constitution of 1842 and the government inaugurated under it in 1843 had ever since been
recognized as exclusively legitimate. This led him to consider the practical consequences of a decision upholding
the Dorrite position:

If this court is authorized to enter upon this inquiry as proposed by the plaintiff, and if it should be decided that the
charter government had no legal existence [after 1842] . . .
then the laws passed by its legislature during that time were
nullities; its taxes wrongfully collected; its salaries and compensation to its officers illegally paid; its public accounts improperly settled; and the judgments and sentences of its courts
in civil and criminal cases null and void, and the officers who
carried their decisions into operation answerable as trespassers
if not in some cases as criminals. When the decision of this
court might lead to such results, it becomes its duty to ex-
amine very carefully its own powers before it undertakes to
exercise jurisdiction.

Taney then noted that if the Freeholder government
were illegitimate after May 1842, the 1842 constitution and
the new government were also illegitimate. Further, since
the Dorr government could never be resurrected, no government could ever be legally inaugurated in Rhode Island
since there was no body—federal or state, political or
judicial—that could call into being a new constitutional
convention. Rhode Island would be condemned to per-
petual anarchy or some form of revolution, its government
overthrown, all for the sake of permitting one action of
trespass to vindicate one disputed theory of government.
It was these practical considerations, set out at the beginning

of Taney's opinion, that were dispositive of the case, not any immutable principles embedded in the Constitution.

Read strictly, Taney's opinion held only that federal courts, circuit and Supreme, were bound by the decision of the Rhode Island Supreme Court in the Dorr treason trial that the Freeholders' and not the Dorr government was legitimate. This one point would have disposed of Luther's petition. Taney based his holding on the observation that state courts had accepted the decision of "the political department," that is, the legislature or the executive, as to whether or not the state's constitution had been ratified. This is what happened in Rhode Island, Taney observed, and since its decision construed the laws and the constitution of the state, it was binding on federal courts.

Taney, however, could not restrain his inclination to deliver himself of dicta on other aspects of the case, an irresistible tendency of his that was to have malignant effects in the later cases of *Dred Scott* and *Ableman* v. *Booth*. A court cannot act, he said, without a law to guide it; it cannot "determine what political privileges the citizens of a State are entitled to, unless there is an established constitution or law to govern its decision."

On this general issue—the nature of the judicial function —Justice Woodbury in dissent was even more emphatic. Though critical of the majority's willingness to countenance the imposition of martial law by the Freeholders' government, Woodbury was at one with them in believing that courts should not decide "questions merely political."

The adjustment of these questions belongs to the people and their political representatives, either in the State or general government. These questions relate to matters not to be settled on strict legal principles. They are adjusted rather by inclination,—or prejudice or compromise, often. Some of them succeed or are defeated even by public policy alone, or mere naked power, rather than intrinsic right. There being so different tastes as well as opinions in politics, and especially in forming constitutions, some people prefer foreign models, some domestic, and some neither; while judges, on the contrary, for their guides, have fixed constitutions and laws, given to them by others, and not provided by themselves.

Judges must confine themselves to deciding questions of "private rights," "what is *meum* and *tuum*"; to venture into political questions would make of the courts "a new sovereign power in the republic, in most respects irresponsible and unchangeable for life, and one more dangerous, in theory at least, than the worst elective oligarchy in the worst of times." This was, if anything, an argument even more forcible than Taney's on the undesirability of judges meddling with decisions that rightly belong to the people and their representatives.

To Taney, courts by the nature of their fact-gathering processes and the scope of their judgments were innately incompetent to settle the question urged by the Dorrites. But the result of *Luther* v. *Borden* did not depend on this alone. The United States Constitution took the matter out of the hands of all federal courts. Section 4 "has treated the subject as political in its nature, and placed the power in the hands of that department." Taney here entered into a construction of the guarantee clause that was to guide judicial action under the clause until our time.

Taney disposed of the guarantee in a paragraph:

Under this article of the Constitution it rests with Congress to decide what government is the established one in a State. For as the United States guarantee to each State a republican government, Congress must necessarily decide what government is established in the State before it can determine whether it is republican or not. And when the senators and representatives of a State are admitted into the councils of the Union, the authority of the government under which they are appointed, as well as its republican character, is recognized by the proper constitutional authority. And its decision is binding on every other department of the government, and could not be questioned in a judicial tribunal.

This dictum removed the guarantee clause from the judicial domain and was cited as the holding of *Luther* v. *Borden* in later years. Along with the concluding paragraphs of the opinion, it was the foremost authority for the proposition that the Court must abstain from political questions and that guarantee clause cases are invariably political question cases. Yet its import remains aggravatingly ambiguous. At least one commentator construes it as an assertion of Taney's nationalism; the question thus viewed is not one of allocating powers between courts and legislatures, but between nation and state.[12] Whatever value this emphasis on Taney's nationalism in 1849 has, it reads the guarantee clause paragraph out of the context of the entire opinion. In *Luther* v. *Borden* Taney was spelling out in detail a current Jacksonian conception of the proper distribution of policy-making power among the branches of government in a democracy rather than endorsing suffragist political theory.

Taney buttressed his arguments by noting that Congress had delegated initial responsibility for enforcement of the

[12] See Michael A. Conron, "Law, Politics, and Chief Justice Taney: A Reconsideration of the *Luther* v. *Borden* Decision," *Am. J. Legal Hist.*, XI (1967), 377–388.

domestic violence and invasion clauses of section 4 to the President by the 1792 Militia Act. Judicial second-guessing of the commander in chief would be especially inappropriate and section 4 would be "a guarantee of anarchy, and not of order." Hence the President must first determine which government in the state is republican before he acts under the domestic violence clause and the Militia Act. This Tyler had done. If the Supreme Court were to countermand his decision seven years later, the state would be plunged into the chaos that the President's action had helped to avoid. But this presidential authority was provisional only, and Congress would have the final word on the republicanism of the state governments.

Taney concluded his opinion by upholding the declaration of martial law as an emergency measure designed to suppress an incipient insurrection. He dismissed Hallett's three-day effort and the whole Dorrite position in a single brief paragraph. Sovereignty undoubtedly resides in the people, he noted, but whether or not it has been exercised cannot be a judicial question. It is "a question to be decided by the political power." The power of judicial review is so great, Taney thought, that the Supreme Court must be extremely cautious in wielding it and may not invade the spheres belonging to other branches.

Its ambiguities notwithstanding, much of Taney's opinion was a defensible handling of the specific issues presented to the Court by the Dorrite petitioners. A ruling favorable to them would have created insoluble confusion in Rhode Island. Further, Taney wrote when the legitimacy of the Dorr government had been moot for seven years. In view of Dorrite acquiescence in the 1842 constitution, the arguments of Luther's counsel seemed hollow and pointless. Why should the peaceful and liberal settlement of the Rhode Island constitutional crisis of 1842 be upset by the Supreme Court for a disputed question of principle, whose vindication was impossible seven years later?

When Taney spoke, the President of the United States had already dealt with the issue in his capacity as commander in chief. Tyler's course was supported by a majority in Congress, and a hostile one at that. To rule for Luther would be to exalt the principles of a faction in one state over the express will of another in that state and elsewhere, and of the President and Congress.

The Supreme Court could scarcely have done anything other than what it did. Essentially, Taney was correct: *Luther* v. *Borden* did present a political question beyond the competence of the Court to decide. But read in the light of its surrounding circumstances, it hardly warrants the weight given it in the twentieth century, where it abnegated the power of the federal courts to participate in the federal government's duty of guaranteeing a republican form of government to the people of the states.

Taney's construction of the guarantee clause was absolutistic, and therein lay its great vice. Hallett's and Webster's arguments left him no latitude to maneuver. Hallett insisted that the Court adopt a theory of republican government that was then sharply debated in political forums and that, if adopted, would have made the Court the arbiter among fundamental political theories. Webster took advantage of this tactical indiscretion to urge total judicial abstention. Neither course was compelling, but Webster's appeared to be the less of two evils, and Taney took it, apparently without considering its implications for the future.

Taney was not wholly wrong in his guarantee clause reasoning. Three of his reasons for declining to pass on the merits of the Dorrite claims would be applicable to many guarantee clause cases. First was his insistence that courts are not proper bodies to choose among competing political theories and impose them on the states. Whether or not republicanism in the 1840s required universal white manhood suffrage was sharply debated by the articulate public, and this division of public opinion found its political expression in competing Whig and Radical Democratic factional alignments in the national and state legislatures. The court would therefore exacerbate rather than settle theoretical and practical issues by aligning itself with one or the other group. In this sense, the *Luther* case can be seen as one part of what a historian of the Taney court has described as an effort "to impose realistic limits on judicial policy-making." [13] The Supreme Court can educate the nation; given the right conditions, it might even mold a consensus on policy issues. But it should not, by judicial fiat, take on issues whose resolution would require means of implementation beyond the control of the courts, particularly in the face of widespread and well-organized opposition.

Second, courts should not act where their action would be futile. No matter where the merits of the suffrage controversy lay in 1842, nothing could undo the course of Rhode Island history since then. If the Court held for the

[13] R. Kent Newmyer, *The Supreme Court under Marshall and Taney* (New York, 1968), 149.

Dorrites, it would sacrifice its prestige and sharpen political conflicts without contributing toward their solution, all for the sake of a gesture. In refusing to act, Taney respected the wise admonition of the common-law maxim, *lex nil facit frustra*—"the law does nothing in vain."

Third, the Court should abstain from acting where its decision would directly conflict with firm and unambiguous policies of the President or Congress. In 1842 Tyler had plainly decided to uphold the authority of the Freeholder regime, as the 1845 publication of *Burke's Report* revealed, and those in Congress who disagreed were not able to command a majority, or even a respectable minority, to override or criticize it. The Court, which depends so heavily on political acceptance of its decisions for their enforcement, would have risked an executive or congressional repudiation of its mandate had it ruled for the Dorrites. Often a clearly articulated presidential or congressional policy decision, especially one that is put into operation without major public obstruction, reflects so wide a political consensus that no court could reverse it or bring about compliance with an order that offended it.

Where none of these reasons for abstention is present—where a decision will not force the judges to take on the role of philosopher-kings, where the Court's decision will be effective, and where it will not conflict with a clear presidential or congressional policy—a guarantee clause case should not be considered beyond the domain of the courts. Contrary to the assumptions of later judges, such cases do not automatically present political questions, and those they do present may or may not be suitable for judicial determination. It is simplistic to assume that classifying a case as one presenting a political question—which is often a purely verbal exercise that disguises an unarticulated decision on underlying public policy questions—of itself dispenses with the need for discriminating thought about the issues presented. Taney himself did not equate political questions with guarantee clause cases; he merely stated that *Luther* v. *Borden* was both. It was left to later judges on the state and federal benches to identify the two. This resulted in a misreading of *Luther* and an unthinking, automatic application of Taney's rationale to cases that did not warrant it. Sensing this, Justice William O. Douglas criticized Taney's opinion in 1962:

> The statements that this guaranty is enforceable only by Congress or the Chief Executive is not maintainable. . . . the abdication of all judicial functions respecting voting rights, however justified by the peculiarities of the charter form of government in Rhode Island at the time of Dorr's Rebellion, states no general principle. . . . Today we would not say with Chief Justice Taney that it is no part of the judicial function to protect the right to vote of those "to whom it is denied by the written and established constitution and laws of the state." [14]

In *Luther*, Taney had refused to act under the guarantee clause because Congress had admitted Rhode Island's senators and representatives to their seats. This alone should not be determinative for a court on the question whether the state has a republican form of government, although a refusal by Congress to seat the members for that reason would so clearly indicate congressional policy that the Court could not disregard it. Congress rarely deliberates on the republicanism of state governments when it passes

[14] *Baker* v. *Carr*, 369 U.S. 186, 242–243 (1962) (concurring).

on the credentials of its new members; usually this is an opening-day formality. The Court should not feel automatically foreclosed from considering guarantee clause issues, especially those that rise after the members have been seated, since Congress cannot realistically be said to have made an explicit determination of the issue presented to the Court.

For the same reasons, congressional resolutions admitting a state to the Union cannot be determinative of all issues under the guarantee clause. This is particularly true of the older states. What was passably republican in the nineteenth century would not necessarily be so today because the standards of republicanism evolve over time. Although the typical authorizing resolution admitting a state contains a declaration that its government is "republican," this usually has little more than ceremonial significance. The phrase merely indicates that at the time of admission the formal structure of state governmental institutions did not deviate so far from contemporary concepts of republicanism that it would be monarchic or despotic.

The Court should not be bound absolutely in guarantee clause cases by actions taken by the President under section 4, unless he should explicitly state that he is acting pursuant to the guarantee clause. No President has ever done this; in all cases where the President has acted to forestall or put down violence the source of his authority has been the domestic violence clause. Confusion between the two arises because the latter half of section 4 is often erroneously referred to as "the guarantee"—as it was by Taney in *Luther v. Borden*.[15] Considerations suggesting that domestic violence clause cases not be decided by courts are not identical

[15] 7 How. 43.

with such considerations under the guarantee clause; the statutory basis for presidential authority (the 1792 Militia Act and its successors) is seldom relevant to modern guarantee clause problems; and the guarantee clause, whether considered in the light of the framers' intentions or of its latter-day evolution, has different objectives from the domestic violence clause. Hence the Court should not assume that the President meant to lay down any policy under the guarantee clause when he has acted under section 4.

Luther v. *Borden* (1849) was the first great turning point in the history of the guarantee clause. Chief Justice Taney's decision foreclosed the possibility of judicial enforcement of the guarantee for over a century. His opinion became the touchstone for later development of the political question doctrine as it related to domestic questions and provided the basis for a greatly expanded growth of the doctrine in the twentieth century. The case proved to be one of the principal obstacles to proponents of judicial activism in reapportionment cases until the decision in *Baker* v. *Carr* (1962).

In addition to taking the courts out of participation in enforcing the guarantee, Taney's *Luther* dicta placed on Congress primary responsibility for its implementation. The consequence of this, unimaginable to Taney at the time, was to leave Congress a free field in reconstructing the southern states after the Civil War. As a result, *Luther* v. *Borden* shaped the course of Reconstruction in a vital way, an irony that Chief Justice Taney surely would not have relished.

PART II

FRUITION

5

Slavery in the American Republic

Chief Justice Taney's *Luther* v. *Borden* opinion was anomalous in one respect. Taney was usually sensitive to the implications of cases before him regarding slavery, so much so that by the late 1840s his opinions reflected an almost morbid obsession with potential constitutional challenges to the states' exclusive control of slavery.[1] Yet in the *Luther* case, Taney entirely missed any such implications in arguments on both sides though they fairly bristled with suggestive analogies to the problems of slavery and racial discrimination.

Although Taney's vigilance lapsed, John C. Calhoun's had not. In 1843 Calhoun perceived more clearly than most the threat posed to slavery as a system of race control by the constitutional issues raised in the Rhode Island controversy. Seizing an opportunity in the form of some queries from William Smith of Rhode Island, Calhoun in mid-1843 tried to impose a definitive interpretation on the guarantee clause that would forever preclude its being used to weaken

[1] See, for example, his strained concurring and dissenting opinions in the License Cases, 5 How. 504 (U.S., 1847), and the Passenger Cases, 7 How. 283 (U.S., 1849), where he doggedly insisted on the

the southern states' control over their peculiar institution. Drafted as a public letter, Calhoun's reply to Smith constituted one of his principal political essays. In his rigidly logical way, Calhoun interpreted federal power under the guarantee clause so as to arrive at conclusions divergent from Taney's.[2]

Calhoun fully perceived the potential of the clause: "There is not another in the whole instrument more important; or, on the right understanding of which, the success and duration of our political system more depend." The republican government guarantee, he wrote, was meant to protect the people of the states "from the ambition and usurpation of their governments, or rather rulers." The President of the United States must, in his discretion, determine whether a state has a republican form of government; if he determines that it does not because of the usurpation of its rulers, he must help the people put down the antirepublican regime. This obviously was an extremely delicate function to entrust to the central government, so Calhoun insisted that the President's determination be restricted by three absolute rules: (1) the President is bound by Congress' determination that a state has a republican form of government as expressed in its admission of the state to the Union; (2) after a state's admission, no change "which does not essentially alter its form" can deprive a state of a republican form of government; and (3) the criteria of re-

---

power of a state to control chattels and persons coming within its borders and elaborated a sweeping concept of state police powers to scotch any potential federal power over the domestic slave trade under the commerce clause.

[2] The Smith Letter is in Richard K. Cralle, ed., *The Works of John C. Calhoun* (New York, 1888), VI, 209–239.

publicanism are to be found in the forms of state government *c.* 1789–1791.

Under Calhoun's interpretation, the President would be
obliged to support any extant legitimate regime. Without
these safeguards no power given to the federal government
"could be more dangerous. Give to the Federal Government the right to establish its own abstract standard of
what constitutes a republican form of government, . . .
and it would be made the absolute master of the states,"
interfering with their institutions on the basis of "caprice,
ambition, party influence, or party calculations of those
who, for the time being, might hold the reins of power."

Applying these principles to the circumstances of the
Dorr Rebellion, Calhoun said that, though he was sympathetic to the extension of suffrage, a numerical majority in
a state had no right to alter the state's constitution except
by the methods prescribed in its constitution. To recognize
such a right would be a long step toward the tyranny Calhoun most dreaded, that of majoritarian democracy: "The
government of the uncontrolled numerical majority is but
the absolute and despotic form of popular governments."
Thus he agreed that Tyler's course of action was correct.
Concluding on a note reminiscent of Hamilton in the *Federalist*, Calhoun stated that the guarantee clause assured
peaceful change through the established amending process
by providing federal protection against revolution or force-
ful overthrow of the state governments.

Throughout the Smith letter there ran an implicit theme
that Calhoun had earlier stated on the Senate floor: once
admit a broad federal power under the guarantee clause
and eventually the northern states would restrict the south-

ern states' control of slavery. When in 1833 Senator John Forsyth of Georgia remarked incautiously that the guarantee clause might have been put to good use to repress South Carolina's resistance during the Nullification crisis, Calhoun was dismayed. Did not the gentleman realize, he scolded, that the guarantee clause "if not rigidly restricted to the objects intended by the Constitution, is destined to be a pretext to interfere with our political affairs and domestic institutions in a manner infinitely more dangerous than any other power which has ever been exercised on the part of the General government"? [3]

Calhoun was not the only Southerner sensitized to federal power under the guarantee clause in the 1830s and 1840s. He was, in fact, reiterating points that had repeatedly been made by slavery's defenders. His narrowly syllogistic reasoning in the Smith letter represented the most explicit statement of the southern position on the clause yet made.

The southerners were not arguing in a vacuum. Northern opponents of slavery had early recognized the possibilities in the guarantee clause for striking at it and had worked out their own theories of the relationship between slavery and republican government by 1820. In its early form, the argument that slavery was inconsistent with a republican form of government was used to restrict its further spread into the territories, but Calhoun in his 1833 rebuke to Forsyth predicted accurately. The clause was soon used to strike directly at slavery in the states themselves. By the time Calhoun replied to Smith in 1843, antislavery thinkers had mounted a direct assault on slavery in the states, using the guarantee clause as one of their primary weapons.

[3] 9 *Congressional Debates* 774 (1833).

Though abolitionists had discovered the guarantee clause somewhat belatedly, the contradiction between republican liberty and American slavery had been noted even before the Declaration of Independence was drafted. Granville Sharp, the great British abolitionist of the late eighteenth century, wrote acidulously of the Americans in 1769:

At New York, for instance, this infringement on civil or domestic liberty [i.e., slavery] is become notorious and scandalous, notwithstanding that the political controversies of the inhabitants are stuffed with theatrical bombast and ranting expressions in praise of liberty. But no panegyrick on this subject (howsoever elegant in itself) can be graceful or edifying from the mouth or pen of one of those Provincials; because men, who do not scruple to detain others in Slavery, have but a very partial and unjust claim to the protection of the laws of liberty. . . . The boasted liberty of our American colonies, therefore, has so little right to that sacred name, that it seems to differ from the arbitrary power of despotic monarchies only in one circumstance; viz. that it is a many-headed monster of tyranny, which entirely subverts our most excellent constitution; because liberty and slavery are so opposite to each other, that they cannot subsist in the same community.[4]

Sharp did not dislike America; within a decade he resigned his post as an underclerk in the War Office rather than order a shipment of munitions to British troops in the revolting colonies. But he perceived, with a detachment difficult for the colonials, that American claims for liberty were belied by slavery.

[4] Granville Sharp, *A Representation of the Injustice and Dangerous Tendency of Tolerating Slavery; or of Admitting the Least Claim of Private Property in the Persons of Men, in England* (London, 1769), 81–82.

The mightiest blow struck against slavery in America before 1863 was the Declaration of Independence, which states:

We hold these truths to be self-evident, that all men are created equal, that they are endowed by their Creator with certain unalienable Rights, that among these are Life, Liberty, and the pursuit of Happiness. That to secure these rights, Governments are instituted among Men, deriving their just powers from the consent of the governed, That whenever any Form of Government becomes destructive of these ends, it is the Right of the People to alter or to abolish it, and to institute new Government, laying its foundation on such principles and organizing its powers in such form, as to them shall seem most likely to effect their Safety and Happiness.

This passage, particularly the phrases "all men are created equal" and "Life, Liberty, and the pursuit of Happiness," became the fundamental text of later abolitionist assaults on slavery. As the embodiment of the Americans' revolutionary ideology, the Declaration immediately raised some embarrassing questions for those who would fight for their own liberty while enslaving others. Eventually Americans would have to repudiate either the Declaration or slavery.[5]

The inconsistency between slavery and the revolutionary ideology was seen by Americans and Britons, Whigs and Tories. Thomas Day, an Englishman sympathetic to the cause of American independence, wrote a young American slaveholder in 1776:

If there be an object truly ridiculous in nature, it is an American patriot, signing resolutions of independency with one

[5] See Bernard Bailyn, *The Ideological Origins of the American Revolution* (Cambridge, Mass., 1967), 232–246; Winthrop D. Jordan, *White over Black: American Attitudes toward the Negro, 1550–1812* (Chapel Hill, 1968), 331–333.

138

hand, and with the other brandishing a whip over his affrighted slaves. . . . You and your countrymen are reduced to the dilemma of either acknowledging the rights of your negroes, or of surrendering your own.[6]

Samuel Hopkins, Rhode Island Congregationalist minister, published his influential *Dialogue Concerning the Slavery of the Africans* in the same year, calling upon the Continental Congress to promote a "total abolition" in the states because of slavery's repugnance to the principles for which Americans had taken up arms.[7]

After independence had been established and the Constitution of 1787 adopted, it became axiomatic among opponents of slavery that, as the preamble to the Delaware Abolition Society's constitution stated, "the free constitutions of the American states suffer fundamental violation by the practice of slavery." The principles they embodied might of themselves destroy slavery; at the very least Americans would sooner or later have to reconcile the professions of the Declaration, the federal Constitution, and the bills of rights in the state constitutions with the continuation of slavery.[8]

[6] Thomas Day, *Fragment of an Original Letter on the Slavery of the Negroes, Written in the Year 1776* (London, 1784), 33–34.

[7] [Samuel Hopkins], *A Dialogue Concerning the Slavery of the Africans; Shewing It to Be the Duty and Interest of the American States to Emancipate All Their African Slaves* (Norwich, 1776), 8–9.

[8] *The Constitution of the Delaware Society, for Promoting the Abolition of Slavery, for Superintending the Cultivation of Young Free Negroes, and for the Relief of Those Who May Be Unlawfully Held in Bondage* (Philadelphia, 1788); Zephaniah Swift, *An Oration on Domestic Slavery* (Hartford, 1791), 19. See also the memorials of the New York, Connecticut, and Baltimore societies in *Memorials Presented to the Congress of the United States of*

The principles of republicanism embodied in the constitutions and Declaration obliquely asserted that slavery could not be tolerated in the American republic. Some Revolutionary era leaders saw a more direct and specific incongruity between slavery and republicanism. Madison had suggested in the "Vices of the Constitution of the U. States" that slavery threatened the future of republican government in the South. But slaves were not the only source of danger. Their masters, whom John Adams disgustedly referred to as the "barons of the South," might also be inimical to a republic because of their "aristocratic" status. Northerners saw their putative opulence and indolence as the products of a way of life out of place in republican America.[9]

Though the antislavery movement grew apace between 1790, when the first petition calling for the abolition of slavery was presented to Congress, and 1819, when the first Missouri debates began, its arguments met with little general response. Apart from the abolition of the foreign slave trade in 1808, Congress showed no inclination to meddle with any of the incidents of slavery in America, such as the interstate slave trade. On the contrary, Con-

---

America, by the Different Societys Instituted for Promoting the Abolition of Slavery, &c. &c. . . . (Philadelphia, 1792); Samuel Miller, *A Discourse, Delivered April 12, 1797, at the Request of and before the New York Society for Promoting the Manumission of Slaves, and Protecting Such of Them as Have Been or May Be Liberated* (New York, 1797); Edward Rushton, *Expostulatory Letter to George Washington* (Liverpool, 1797); John Parrish, *Remarks on the Slavery of the Black People* . . . (Philadelphia, 1806).

[9] On this last point, see the "Essay on Negro Slavery" (*c.* 1789), quoted in Jordan, *White over Black*, 333.

gress enacted a fairly efficient fugitive slave act in 1793 and admitted five new slave states to the Union—Kentucky, Tennessee, Louisiana, Alabama, and Mississippi—with a perfunctory statement in the acts of admission that their governments were "republican in form." [10] Thus antislavery arguments that a slave state was not republican had had no visible impact by 1819.

In that year, however, Northern apathy to the political and constitutional implications of slavery temporarily evaporated. Many persons throughout the nation came to realize that slavery was not a dying institution and that it existed most dynamically in the new southwestern states. Settlement of the western empire was going on rapidly, and many in the northeast saw the expansion of the slave economy as a threat to their interests. They lost their belief that slavery would be abolished as soon as possible by the slaveowners themselves. Opposition in principle to enslavement as an evil per se was still limited to a small group of reformers. Opposition to the economic and political consequences of slavery, however, became widespread. In the South the belief that slavery was an evil, whether religious, ethical, or economic, was sharply attacked well before 1820. But by 1819 the northern states were receptive to antislavery arguments and lacked only an occasion to use them. That occasion was presented when the inhabitants of the Missouri Territory requested admission into the Union as a slave state.

[10] For typical statutory formulas, which have remained essentially unchanged since the late eighteenth century, see resolutions for admission of Indiana and Mississippi, 3 Stat. 399 and 472 respectively.

The Missouri crises originated in congressional debates over the admission of Illinois. In November 1818, between the time Illinois Territory presented its credentials for admission and the time it was admitted, John McLean, the representative-elect of the future state, requested the permission of the House of Representatives to take his seat. Representative George Poindexter of Mississippi made a routine motion that McLean's seating be delayed until the House had determined that the Illinois constitution was republican. The motion carried, a committee was appointed, and the next day it reported that the Illinois constitution was indeed republican. But the delay of a day had given some northern representatives time to inspect that constitution, and they discovered, to their shock, that it permitted indentured labor. This, they believed, violated the explicit prohibition of slavery contained in the Northwest Ordinance of 1787.

Representative James Tallmadge of New York, later famous as the sponsor of the amendment bearing his name in the first Missouri crisis, demanded that Congress require Illinois to delete the offending indenture clause. He argued that because of the guarantee clause, no state, once admitted, could change its republican government into a monarchy. By a parity of reasoning, no state admitted as a free state could later change its constitution to permit slavery. This thought apparently did not impress anyone at the time, and the Illinois constitution was speedily approved. Yet the attention and the conscience or self-interest of northern congressmen had been aroused. Equally important, for the first time the generalities of earlier anti-slavery arguments—that slavery and republican government were antithetical—were tied directly to the guarantee clause. The clause had emerged as a means of attacking slavery.[11]

The Illinois flurry was a precursor of the storm to come. Not quite three months after Illinois' admission, the Missouri storm burst with the introduction of the Tallmadge amendment. Tallmadge hoped to eliminate slavery in Missouri by prohibiting the introduction of new slaves and by freeing the children of slaves already there when they came of age. During the days of heated debate that followed in both houses, the North and the South worked out their basic positions on the relationship of slavery to republican government. The South, at first on the defensive, insisted that slavery could exist in a republican state and that the guarantee clause did not authorize federal interference with the domestic institutions or internal affairs of the states. Northern opponents of slavery tried to read the principles of the Declaration of Independence into the Constitution via the guarantee clause.[12]

Early in the debates Representative Timothy Fuller of Massachusetts set forth the northern argument comprehensively. He claimed first that Congress may impose conditions on states seeking admission as an incident of its power to guarantee them republican governments. Next he argued that "the existence of slavery in any state is so far a departure from republican principles" which he found in the Declaration of Independence. From these premises he concluded that the federal government could prohibit

[11] *Annals,* 15 Cong., 2 sess., 310 ff. (1818).
[12] Summaries of the opposing arguments are in William S. Jenkins, *Pro-Slavery Thought in the Old South* (Chapel Hill, 1935), 174–188, and Glover Moore, *The Missouri Controversy* (Lexington, Ky., 1953), chs. 2, 4.

slavery in a territory seeking admission to the Union as a state. Fuller tried to reassure southerners that he intended no attack on the extant slave states or their peculiar institution, which he regarded as preserved by the compromises of the Constitution.[13]

Fuller was not only the first to resort to the guarantee clause; he was its fullest expositor for the antislavery forces. No one later added anything to the force or the content of his arguments on the clause. Northern spokesmen insisted at wearying length that slavery was incompatible with republican government, that Congress could prohibit slavery in the new states, that the features of republican government were to be defined by reference to the Declaration of Independence, and that an extensive denial of civil and political rights made a state government something less than republican as required by the Constitution.[14]

Partly from a desire to accommodate their southern colleagues, Fuller and other opponents of extension in Congress refrained from exploring some of the more unsettling implications of their argument. Pamphleteers outside Congress could ignore this restraint. Though they did not suggest that the guarantee clause could be used to attack slavery in the extant states, they gropingly worked their way to constitutional positions that would, if generally acknowledged, have that effect. Insisting that the Declaration of Independence was the touchstone of republicanism and "the pillar upon which our republican superstructure is reared," William Hillhouse declared that "no

[13] *Annals*, 15 Cong., 2 sess., 1179–1184 (1819).

[14] See the arguments of Sen. David Morril (N.H.), *Annals*, 16 Cong., 1 sess., 130 (1820); Sen. Benjamin Ruggles (Ohio), *ibid.*, 279; Sen. Jonathan Roberts (Pa.), *ibid.*, 128, 338–339; Rep. John Sergeant (Pa.), *ibid.*, 1190; Sen. William Hendricks (Ind.), *ibid.*, 348–349.

state has a right to claim any thing repugnant to it." Josephus Wheaton asked: "Is it not a first principle of republicanism, that the native rights of men are equal and should be inviolable? How then can he be a republican who tramples upon these rights? . . . The phrase republican slaveholder is a solecism." More explicit than earlier critics of slavery, men like Hillhouse and Wheaton prepared the ground for later arguments that the guarantee clause condemned slavery in the old states as well as the territories. Robert Walsh, editor of the Philadelphia *Gazette*, went a step further; after condemning slavery as a "gross anomaly and incongruity" in the American republic, he insisted that Congress could and should strike a blow at it in the states as well as territories by interdicting the interstate slave trade under its commerce power.[15] Later antislavery theorists took up this suggestion, recognizing that it would go a long way toward destroying slavery.

Antislavery constructions of the guarantee clause were fundamentally simple. Beginning with the earlier premise that slavery was incompatible with republican government, they maintained that Congress should recognize no new states as republican that tolerated slavery. Such an extension of congressional power alarmed southerners. Even if they had been willing to accept slavery restriction in the territories—and they were not—an admission of any con-

[15] [William Hillhouse], *The Crisis, No. 1* [and *No. 2*] *Or, Thoughts on Slavery Occasioned by the Missouri Question* (New Haven, 1820), No. 2, 16; Josephus Wheaton, *The Equality of Mankind and the Evils of Slavery, Illustrated: A Sermon. Delivered on the Day of the Annual Fast, April 6, 1820* (Boston, 1820), 21, 22; A Philadelphian [Robert Walsh], *Free Remarks on the Spirit of the Federal Constitution, the Practice of the Federal Government, and the Obligations of the Union, Respecting the Exclusion of Slavery from the Territories and New States* (Philadelphia, 1819), 5, 21.

gressional power over slavery under the guarantee clause would have ominous consequences as Calhoun later insisted. As a result, southerners worked out a detailed conservative interpretation of the guarantee clause, expressing a reaction to the clause so often repeated in our history that it might be considered perennial. The southerners argued that the clause was not an innovative device, but rather a limitation on federal power. It had to be construed in the frame of reference of 1787; evolving concepts of justice and republican government could not be taken into account. Finally, the guarantee clause was an assurance, not of widening democratic participation in government, but of historical restrictions on it.

Southerners were at first surprised that Representative Fuller should invoke the guarantee clause. Did not slavery exist in at least twelve of the original thirteen states when the Constitution was ratified? Had not Congress admitted new slave states with the explicit declaration that they were "republican in form"? Slavery had no relation to the form of government; it was a creature of police laws and could not affect the republicanism of the state government. The United States Constitution explicitly recognized the existence of slavery in at least three clauses. On the merits of the argument, southerners saw nothing incompatible between slavery and republican government.[16]

As to the issue at hand, southerners insisted that if Congress could restrict slavery in the new states and territories, it could eventually do so in the old states as well. Hence

[16] Delegate John Scott (Mo.), *Annals*, 15 Cong., 2 sess., 1196; Sen. John Elliott (Ga.), *Annals*, 16 Cong., 1 sess., 130 (1820); Rep. Alexander Smyth (Va.), *ibid.*, 993; Sen. William Pinkney (Md.), *ibid.*, 412; Rep. Robert Reid (Ga.), *ibid.*, 1028.

Congress could rewrite the constitution of any state in the Union. Senator William Smith of South Carolina pointed out that the guarantee clause refers to *"every* state"; thus to admit that Congress could strike at slavery in the territories and new states as antirepublican would allow Congress to abolish it in the old states too.[17]

This brought the proslavery argument to its next step: the clause could not be read as a grant of power to the federal government to meddle with the internal concerns of the states. The clause presupposed a republican form of government in the extant states and conferred no power to impose conditions on the new states. This point led southerners back to arguing on the nature of republican government. This, they said, was simply self-government, not imposed by some outside power, but chosen by the people. This insistence on republicanism as self-government for the states, free of federal interference, characterized the position of the South through the end of Reconstruction.[18]

Once this logical point had been reached, the proslavery argument emerged full-blown, principally in extended and repetitious arguments by two of the South's most prominent spokesmen in the Missouri debates, Senators James Barbour of Virginia and William Pinkney of Maryland. One of the ironies of the Missouri debates was that Pinkney should have succeeded to this position, for in 1789 as a

[17] Sen. William Smith (S.C.), *Annals*, 16 Cong., 2 sess., 55 (1820); Rep. Alexander Smyth (Va.), *Annals*, 16 Cong., 1 sess., 1004 (1820).

[18] Sen. James Barbour (Va.), *ibid.*, 323; Rep. Christopher Rankin (Miss.), *ibid.*, 1338; Rep. Alexander Smyth (Va.), *ibid.*, 1006; Rep. Philip Barbour (Va.), *ibid.*, 1226; Rep. John Campbell (Ohio), *Annals*, 16 Cong., 2 sess., 1013 (1821).

Maryland legislator he had strongly condemned the slave trade and by implication slavery itself: "But is the encouragement of civil slavery, by legislative acts, correspondent with the principle of a democracy? Call that principle what you will, the love of equality, as defined by some; of liberty, as understood by others; such conduct is manifestly in violation of it." [19]

Barbour and Pinkney insisted that republicanism did not imply civil and political equality, nor did it exclude caste. After all, the antislavery argument carried to its logical end was ridiculous. Children, lunatics, convicts, and women were all deprived of civil and political rights, so why not slaves and Negroes? Pinkney sneered: "But if the ultra-republican doctrines which have been broached should ever gain ground among us, I should not be surprised if some romantic reformer . . . should propose to repeal our republican law *salique,* and claim for our wives and daughters a full participation in political power." The abridgement or denial of civil and political rights was a characteristic of any well-ordered republic. At their worst, slavery and the status of the free Negro in America were anomalies, exceptions to the otherwise applicable requirements of republican government.

Did the southerners see any positive content in the clause? They did indeed: it was the Constitution's command to the federal government that slave uprisings must

[19] Quoted in Henry Wheaton, *Some Account of the Life, Writings and Speeches of William Pinkney* (Philadelphia, 1826), 8–24. By 1820 Pinkney was widely recognized as the foremost appellate advocate of his day. See Robert M. Ireland, "William Pinkney: A Revision and Re-emphasis," *Am. J. Legal Hist.,* XIV (1970), 235.

be put down. It also extended to "that violence and usurpation by which a member [a state] might otherwise be oppressed by profligate and powerful individuals, or ambitious and unprincipled factions." [20]

Between 1820 and 1860 the conservative southern interpretation of the guarantee clause took five forms: 1) the admission of the state to the Union is conclusive that the state had and has a republican form of government; 2) the definition of a "republican form of government" is the same as it was in 1789; 3) a republic is nothing more than the antithesis of a monarchy, so that any nonmonarchical form of government will satisfy the requirements of the guarantee clause; 4) a republican form of government is one in which the people govern themselves, in the limited sense that some part of the state's residents exercise some choice in deciding who the elective officials of government shall be; and 5) the clause is only a promise of federal protection against usurpation by a faction or an uprising of slaves. These arguments persisted through Reconstruction, and their echoes may be heard today.[21]

The substance of the Missouri controversy was laid to rest by an accommodation between the sections, but the

---

[20] Pinkney, *Annals*, 16 Cong., 1 sess., 409 ff. (1820); Barbour, *ibid.*, 323; see also Sen. William Smith (S.C.), *Annals*, 16 Cong., 2 sess., 56 (1820); Rep. Rankin (Miss.), *ibid.*, 1338; the quotation is from Pinkney's speech. For the debates generally, see George Dangerfield's two excellent studies, *The Era of Good Feelings* (New York, 1952), 208–213, and *The Awakening of American Nationalism* (New York, 1965), 118.

[21] See Charles O. Lerche, "The Guarantee of a Republican Form of Government and the Admission of New States," *J. of Politics*, XI (1949), 578, 580.

points made by Fuller of Massachusetts would not be forgotten. The guarantee clause re-emerged regularly in the next forty years in the arguments both of slavery defenders and of abolitionists.

Among the scholars who commented on the guarantee clause between 1820 and 1860, parts of the conservative position as expressed by the southerners won complete acceptance. Even Joseph Story, certainly no protagonist of slavery, construed the clause as a safeguard against "domestic dangers," hinting that it would be of particular value to the southern states. William A. Duer, judge and president of Columbia College (later University), felt that the clause's requirements would be met so long as the states retained substantially the form of government they had in 1787. He bridged the gap between the southern position outlined above and the Whig views expressed after the Dorr Rebellion by arguing that the guarantee would apply even against a majority of the people of a state "when directed to any object of unconstitutional violence." The ambiguity of this last phrase was resolved when Duer made it plain that he was talking about slave insurrections. Other elements of the southern position were repeated by William Rawle, who insisted that the clause could not prevent secession of a state because republican government meant absolute local self-determination, even at the cost of splitting the Union. The only occasion for federal interference would be "threats to internal peace." George Ticknor Curtis, in his magisterial *History of the Formation of the Constitution* (1865) summed up the viewpoint of the antebellum commentators by insisting that the guarantee was exclusively a means of giving the federal government power to suppress insurrections in the states so as to protect majoritarian government from violence. The clause was simply an antisubversive measure.[22]

Elaboration of the restrictive view of the guarantee clause did not end with the debates on the Missouri compromise. Southern spokesmen in the period between the Missouri debates and the Civil War came to see that it could be much more than an assurance of federal help against slave insurrections, which was the position of the northern constitutional commentators. Southerners began by taking up the dilemma of the Revolution—the coexistence of slavery with America's fundamental republican ideals—a point that antislavery pamphleteers persistently stressed. One of these, James Duncan, a scholarly Indiana minister, in his 1824 antislavery tract, *A Treatise on Slavery*, had noted that "it is impossible to vindicate the practice of slavery without condemning the political government of our nation," which was based on "the fundamental principles of our government, which recognize all men as having a natural right to freedom." [23] Duncan's insight—that

[22] Joseph Story, *Commentaries on the Constitution of the United States* (Boston, 1833), III, 685; William Rawle, *A View of the Constitution of the United States of America* (Philadelphia, 1825); William A. Duer, *The Constitutional Jurisprudence of the United States* (New York, 1843), 265–267; George Ticknor Curtis, *History of the Origin, Formation, and Adoption of the Constitution of the United States; With Notes of Its Principal Framers* (New York, 1865), I, 266; II, 79–84. All the commentators were northerners.

[23] James Duncan, *A Treatise on Slavery. In Which is Shown Forth the Evil of Slaveholding, Both from the Light of Nature and Divine Revelation* (Vevay, Ind., 1824, reprinted by the American Anti-Slavery Society, New York, 1840), 53.

the defense of slavery would require a repudiation of principles embodied in the Declaration of Independence and the entire libertarian impulse of the American Revolution —occurred to the defenders of slavery at about the same time and they acted on it in two interrelated ways. They disavowed the Declaration of Independence, and they argued that slavery was not only compatible with republican government, but even necessary to it.

The first widely publicized statement of this new view was made by Alexander G. Knox, a member of the Virginia House of Delegates, in the 1832 debates of that body on a bill for the gradual emancipation of slaves in Virginia. Knox spoke at length against the bill. Noting that slavery existed in the ancient Greek and Roman republics and implicitly comparing them with Virginia at the time of Nat Turner's insurrection, he declared that it was to slavery "that we may trace the high and elevated character that she [Virginia] has heretofore sustained; and, moreover, that its existence is indispensably requisite in order to preserve the forms of a Republican Government." [24]

Southerners worked out an elaborate defense of this idea, asserting, first, that there was a greater equality among freemen in republican slave societies because they were exempted from degrading types of labor performed for them by slaves. Hence there were no distinctions of rank among freemen. Second, freemen enjoyed greater liberty because they were stimulated to a greater patriotic love for the state. Third, slavery was a conservative force in a republic,

[24] Knox's speech is quoted in Joseph C. Robert, *The Road from Monticello: A Study of the Virginia Slavery Debate of 1832* (Durham, 1941), 85.

uniting the interests of labor and capital and minimizing the size of a free landless proletariat that might introduce turbulence into the state.[25]

No expression of this view was so unsettling to abolitionists as that of South Carolina Governor George McDuffie in 1835 in his annual message to the legislature. Nearly half the speech was a fire-eating denunciation of antislavery efforts; McDuffie urged the legislators to enact the death penalty for disseminating abolition propaganda and demanded that the northern states impose heavy criminal sanctions on speech and publication agitating the slavery issue. Defending slavery as a positive good, McDuffie summed up his views: "Domestic slavery, therefore, instead of being a political evil, is the cornerstone of our republican edifice." [26]

A later South Carolina governor, James Henry Hammond, combined the two strains of southern thought: "I endorse without reserve the much abused sentiment of Governor McDuffie, that 'slavery is the cornerstone of our republican edifice;' while I repudiate, as ridiculously absurd, that much lauded but nowhere accredited dogma, of Mr. Jefferson, that 'all men are born equal.'" Since all societies are divided into those who are poor and ignorant, on one hand, and rich and educated, on the other, Hammond argued that slave states are superior to free states in enslaving most of the poor and ignorant. "Hence," he concluded, "slavery is truly the 'cornerstone' and foundation

[25] These arguments are recapitulated in Jenkins, *Pro-slavery Thought,* 190–199.
[26] Governor George McDuffie, "Governor's Message," *Journal of the General Assembly of the State of South Carolina, for the Year 1835* (n.p., n.d.).

of every well designed and durable Republican edifice." [27]

Given these views, southerners by the 1840s naturally considered the guarantee clause to be an assurance rather than a repudiation of slave society, at least for those states wise enough to adopt the system. At the very least, it obliged the federal government to use all the resources at its command, including regular army, navy, and federalized militia forces if necessary, to suppress slave uprisings that threatened the southern republican edifices. In 1847 Calhoun summed up the arguments of slavery defenders and disposed of the abolitionist axiom that liberty for whites must require liberty for blacks. He reviewed arguments on both sides concerning the requirements of the guarantee clause, noting that they could be reduced to a conflict of two basic values: the right of self-government—for whites only (and not necessarily all of them) including the right to enslave blacks—*versus* the right of republican liberty for Negroes. He candidly concluded that the safety and well-being of the South obliged it to defend the former set of values. [28]

For antislavery theorists, the Missouri debates had only raised questions about the guarantee clause, not settled them. After 1820 some southerners would insist that if the guarantee clause was a warrant for federal power to restrict slavery in the territories and new states, it might just as well be used to strike at slavery in the old states too. Until the late 1830s opponents of slavery doggedly replied that they had no intention of interfering with slavery where it

---

[27] [James H. Hammond], *Gov. Hammond's Letters on Southern Slavery: Addressed to Thomas Clarkson, the English Abolitionist* (Charleston, 1845), 5–6.

[28] *Globe*, 29 Cong., 2 sess., 454 (1847).

existed; they merely wanted to restrict its further spread.[29] This position was crystallized in the 1833 constitution of the American Antislavery Society, drawn up by a committee that included William Lloyd Garrison and Amos A. Phelps. Although the preamble declared that slavery "is contrary to the principles of . . . our republican form of government," Article II of the constitution expressly disavowed any federal power to touch slavery in the extant states: "While it admits that each state, in which slavery exists, has, by the Constitution of the United States, the exclusive right to legislate in regard to its abolition in said state." [30] This was the antislavery position for five years.

This dogma was first publicly challenged in the fall of 1837 by one of the antislavery movement's most fecund theorists, Alvan Stewart, Utica lawyer and president of the New York State Antislavery Society. In a paper read before the New York group and referred by it to the national society, Stewart insisted that slavery did not have a legitimate existence anywhere in the United States because it deprived its victims of their liberty without the "due process of law" mentioned in the Fifth Amendment of the federal Constitution. Stewart at that time relied exclusively on procedural due process arguments and did not refer to the guarantee clause.[31]

[29] See, for example, debates on the admission of new slave states: Arkansas: 12 *Register of Debates*, 1055, 4247, 4269–4272 (1836); Florida: *Globe*, 28 Cong., 2 sess., 284, 378 (1845).

[30] [American Anti-Slavery Society], *Proceedings of the Anti-Slavery Convention, Assembled at Philadelphia, Dec. 4, 5, and 6, 1833* (New York, 1833).

[31] Alvan Stewart, "A Constitutional Argument, on the Subject of Slavery . . . ," in Jacobus tenBroek, *Equal under Law* (n.p., 1965), Appendix B.

At the May 1838 fifth annual meeting of the American Antislavery Society, Stewart, acting on the position broached by him the previous autumn, recommended that the Society strike from its constitution the clause recognizing the "exclusive right" of each state to control slavery within its borders. This suggestion appalled more moderate antislavery men, William Jay saying that any congressional interference with slavery in the states would be "a most wicked and detestable act of usurpation," and James Gillespie Birney lamenting that Stewart's proposition would be "exceedingly prejudicial to the advancement of our Cause." Stewart was regarded as a heretic by his fellow antislavery workers, but this did not deter him from elaborating his constitutional arguments and expanding his original concentration on the due process clause to include other sections of the Constitution, including the guarantee clause. Speaking in mid-1838 at memorial ceremonies after a mob burned Philadelphia's Pennsylvania Hall, an antislavery forum, Stewart defined a republican form of government as that which secures "Equality at birth" and "the universal endowment of the right to life, liberty, and the pursuit of happiness," implying that it was the duty of the federal government under the guarantee clause to see that the states provided such security.[32]

[32] William Jay to Young Men's Anti-Slavery Association, undated, in Bayard Tuckerman, *William Jay and the Constitutional Movement for the Abolition of Slavery* (New York, 1894), 95–96; Birney to George W. Benson, 13 June 1838, in Dwight L. Dumond, ed., *Letters of James Gillespie Birney, 1831–1857* (New York, 1938), 458–459. Stewart's speech is quoted in Samuel Webb, *History of Pennsylvania Hall, Which was Destroyed by a Mob, on the 17th of May, 1838* (Philadelphia, 1838), 101–115.

In taking such a position, Stewart was not really far ahead of the attitudes of other antislavery thinkers. Even Birney, who so deprecated Stewart's action in 1837, had earlier insisted that the guarantee clause, "if literally carried out, would extinguish the entire system of slavery." Since "a majority of the people of South Carolina are slaves; can she be said properly to have a republican form of government"?[33] Stewart was radical only in that he explicitly called for direct federal action against the states; Birney and others had not yet pursued their argument to this logical conclusion.

Once Stewart raised it, however, the idea that the guarantee clause could be used to abolish slavery everywhere, not just prohibit its further spread, became a regular element in antislavery constitutional arguments. In time antislavery theorists relied principally on the due process clause of the Fifth Amendment and on evolving concepts of equal protection of the laws.[34] The guarantee clause approach, however, continued to be persuasive either as an auxiliary to other lines of constitutional attack[35] or as the most convenient and direct way of striking at slavery through congressional or judicial action. Thus in 1841 some of John Quincy Adams' constituents petitioned Congress to abolish slavery everywhere immediately because it

[33] Birney in *The Philanthropist*, 13 Jan. 1837, quoted in Howard Jay Graham, *Everyman's Constitution: Historical Essays on the Fourteenth Amendment, the "Conspiracy Theory," and American Constitutionalism* (Madison, 1968), 231.

[34] See tenBroek, *Equal under Law*, *passim*, and Graham, *Everyman's Constitution*, 152–241.

[35] See an early version of this argument in N. P. Rogers, "The Constitution," *Quarterly Anti-Slavery Mag.*, II (1837), 145–153.

denied to any state a republican form of government. To others the guarantee clause was a call to political action, either establishing implicit antislavery criteria by which each voter should measure a candidate or providing a potential plank for a political party. At times the vagueness and the ingeniousness of guarantee clause arguments justified the taunt of F. A. Ross, a defender of slavery, that abolitionists are "seeking, somewhere, an abolition Bible, an abolition Constitution for the United States, and an abolition God." [36] The taunt was fundamentally correct; antislavery men were seeking an "abolition Constitution," and the guarantee clause looked like one promising part of it.

Alvan Stewart was meanwhile elaborating his theories on constitutional ways to overthrow slavery. In what was perhaps his supreme effort in this cause, Stewart appeared before the Supreme Court of New Jersey as counsel for slaves seeking a writ of habeas corpus to liberate them from slavery as it existed under New Jersey laws of the time. Stewart's long and sometimes rhetorical effort in these arguments was a compendium of antislavery constitutional theory. He insisted not only that the guarantee clause empowered Congress to abolish slavery in the states, but also

[36] *Globe,* 27 Cong., 2 sess., 158 (1841); Gerrit Smith, "To the Friends of the Slave in the Town of Smithfield," 12 March 1844, broadside in the Gerrit Smith Collection, New York State Historical Association, Cooperstown, N.Y. See also James G. Birney's public letter of acceptance of the Albany convention's presidential nomination, 11 May 1840, in Dumond, ed., *Letters of Birney,* 562–574; Gerrit Smith, *Letter of Gerrit Smith to S. P. Chase, on the Unconstitutionality of Every Part of American Slavery* (Albany, 1847); F. A. Ross, *Position of the Southern Church in Relation to Slavery* . . . (New York, 1857), 16.

that the clause by its own force illegitimated slavery, and he invited the New Jersey Supreme Court to so declare.[37]

The 1840s and 1850s saw an outpouring of discussion of the guarantee clause by antislavery polemicists. In the hands of some of them, the clause transcended its mere negative character as a prohibition of slavery and became a guarantee of suffrage for the blacks. George W. F. Mellen's *An Argument on the Unconstitutionality of Slavery* reached this position by starting with the southern premise that the clause assured government by the people, but insisted that the people should include black as well as white human beings. An obscure Wisconsin abolitionist, J. L. Jillson, demanded that Congress refuse to recognize his territory as a state because of its exclusion of blacks from the suffrage.[38]

Lysander Spooner, an eminent if sometimes eccentric reformer of the mid-nineteenth century, popularized many of the guarantee clause arguments in his widely reprinted *The Unconstitutionality of Slavery*. He first demolished the southern interpretation of the clause: "The only proper way of protecting a 'republican' state . . . against 'domestic violence' is to plant men firmly upon one another's necks (about in the proportion of two to one), arm the

[37] The New Jersey argument as recorded by a newspaper reporter is in Luther Marsh, ed., *Writings and Speeches of Alvan Stewart, on Slavery* (New York, 1860), 272–367; allusions to the guarantee clause are on pp. 336–346. The New Jersey court rejected Stewart's arguments.

[38] G. W. F. Mellen, *An Argument on the Unconstitutionality of Slavery* (Boston, 1841), 87 ff. Jillson to editor of the Prairieville, Wisc., *American Freeman*, 17 Feb. 1847, in Milo M. Quaife, ed., *The Struggle over Ratification, 1846–1847* (Madison, 1920), 641.

two with whip and spur, and then keep an armed force standing by to cut down those that are ridden, if they dare attempt to throw the riders." He then argued that the federal government must destroy slavery in the states in order to preserve its own republicanism, thus drawing on ideas of Montesquieu that had influenced adoption of the clause in the 1780s. In Spooner's view the clause was the *sine qua non* for national union.[39]

The foremost antislavery expositor of the guarantee clause was William Goodell, an amazingly prolific author, pamphleteer, and editor.[40] Through a career spanning two decades of tireless antislavery propagandizing, Goodell promoted the guarantee clause as a chief weapon in the antislavery arsenal. In the mid-1850s he became the spokesman and principal theorist for a splinter political group dissatisfied with what it thought was the mealymouthed position of the Republican party on the constitutional remedies for slavery. He remained convinced that Congress must attack slavery directly in the states on the grounds that it existed in violation of the Constitution, and he condemned as inadequate indirect attacks on it, such as the official Republican restrictionist program.

[39] Lysander Spooner, *The Unconstitutionality of Slavery* . . . (Boston, 1845), p. 104. This book went through three editions between 1845 and 1853. A copy of the first edition in the Oberlin College collection contains marginal notations that were probably made by William Goodell, who became the clause's foremost expounder. See Geraldine H. Hubbard, comp., *A Classified Catalogue of the Collection of the Anti-Slavery Propaganda in the Oberlin College Library* (n.p., 1932), 22.

[40] A biography of this giant of American reform is sorely needed. The sketch in *Dictionary of American Biography*, VII, by W. Randall Waterman, is inadequate.

Goodell's attention to the possibilities of the guarantee clause seems to have been first aroused as a result of his fervent polemical writings on behalf of the Dorrite cause in Rhode Island. In a number of his *Christian Investigator* entitled "The Rights and Wrongs of Rhode Island," he perceptively saw, as many of his antislavery contemporaries did not, the connection between the events in Rhode Island in 1842 and the future of slavery:

If popular sovereignty was permitted at the North, the precedent would be dangerous to the South. If the disfranchised majority of Rhode Island could form a constitution without leave of their masters, the disfranchised majority of South Carolina might do the same, and the peculiar institution would be overthrown. The northern laborer must therefore be put down, lest the southern laborer should rise.[41]

Returning to the guarantee clause in 1845, Goodell argued that the Declaration of Independence and the bills of rights in the various state constitutions "make the very pith and essence of a republican government to consist in the protection and security of those rights." He thus saw in the guarantee clause a positive command to the states to protect the freedoms and civil liberties of their people.[42]

In the late 1840s and through the 1850s, Goodell was a spokesman for an antislavery political sect whose name and personnel changed over the years but whose *raison*

[41] William Goodell, *The Rights and Wrongs of Rhode Island* (Whitesboro, N.Y., 1842), 51. See also Rev. Charles Woodhouse to Dorr, 11 June 1848, in Dorr MSS., Rider Collection, John Hay Library, Brown University, Providence, R.I.

[42] William Goodell, *Views of American Constitutional Law, in its Bearing upon American Slavery* (Utica, 1845, 2nd ed.), 49.

d'être remained constant: opposition to the Free Soil–Republican program. The Free Soilers and their successors, the Republicans, generally insisted that they wished only to limit the further spread of slavery and that they had no intention of disturbing it directly in the states where it already existed. They believed, perhaps correctly, that such a course would destroy slavery in the long run. To Goodell and a small but distinguished coterie of like-minded political-action abolitionists, such a program was at best temporizing and at worst evasive. Goodell's "Address of the Macedon Convention" in 1847 affirmed that slavery was "illegal and unconstitutional, and that the federal government is bound to secure its abolition by the guaranty, to every state in this Union, of a republican form of government." [43] The Macedon convention platform was repudiated by the Free Soilers because of its uncompromising insistence on total abolition and its advocacy of a set of radical social reforms unacceptable to most Americans, such as abolition of the army and navy, and because it condoned peaceful withdrawal from the Union by the South. Thus the fissionating tendencies of the abolitionist movement were at work; in 1848 the Free Soilers and Goodell's group split, the latter referring to themselves as the "Liberty Party Abolitionists."

As the Free Soil ideology gradually evolved into the platform of the Republican party and received the allegiance of a majority of antislavery men, Goodell's group preserved their autonomy and doctrinal purity. To the proto-Republicans, the guarantee clause was irrelevant since they did not mean to strike at slavery in the states. To

[43] William Goodell, *Address of the Macedon Convention, by William Goodell; and Letters of Gerrit Smith* (Albany, 1847).

Goodell's die-hards, organized as the "Liberty League" for the 1852 elections, as the "Radical Political Abolitionists" four years later, and as the "American Abolition Society" in 1858, such a position only assured the continuation of a Union not worth saving. Goodell was willing to consider what most non-Garrisonian abolitionists believed to be un-thinkable—disunion. Summing up his critique of the Free Soil stance in 1852 Goodell wrote:

This leaves to the several slave states the right of maintaining slavery as long as they please, yet remaining in the Union, with the right, under modification, of making the free states their hunting ground for fugitives. It concedes the duty of the Federal Government and the free states under the Constitution, to assist in putting down insurrections of slaves. . . . Those . . . who nevertheless cling to the Constitution and cry out against antislavery disunionists, would do well to count the cost of such a contest, which seems to be hasten-ing.[44]

Goodell's group maintained this position right through 1860, appearing then as the "Free Constitutionalists." Their 1860 platform strikingly anticipated the later Radical Re-publicans' citizenship/due process/equal protection/priv-ileges-and-immunities approach embodied in the Four-teenth Amendment. Citing the guarantee clause as a means of asserting federal supremacy over the states, they argued that a republican form of government implies something more than merely representative government; it requires that "at least all the members of the republic shall enjoy the protection of the laws," so that the federal government

[44] William Goodell, *Slavery and Anti-Slavery; a History of the Great Struggle in Both Hemispheres, with a View of the Slavery Question in the United States* (New York, 1852), 569.

is obliged to see to it that each state extends to all its citizens, including the enslaved blacks, the protection of law.[45]

Goodell and the Liberty League/Radical Political Abolitionists thus form a link between the original adumbration in 1838 by Alvan Stewart of an antislavery doctrine that would permit the federal government to attack slavery in the states and the later Radical Republican position that saw in the guarantee clause a justification for using federal authority to maintain equal rights for the freedmen in the states. There was, to be sure, no direct continuity; no one in Goodell's group played any significant role in working out the constitutional doctrines of the Radical wing of the Republican party after 1862. The principal Radical theoreticians like Samuel Shellabarger and Charles Sumner do not seem to have been directly influenced by the sectarian arguments and cryptodisunion sentiments of the Goodell element.

As a political movement, the Free Constitutionalists of 1860 had reached the nadir of their effectiveness and had become an extremist sect obsessed with annihilating their ally, the antislavery Republicans, as an objective more important than destroying their ostensible enemies, the Breckinridge Democrats. In this sense, the theorists who placed their chief hopes on the guarantee clause as a way of

[45] *Address of the Free Constitutionalists to the People of the United States* (Boston, 1860). See also the Goodell-ghosted platform of a group sympathetic to his program, *The Constitutional Duty of the Federal Government to Abolish American Slavery: An Exposé of the Position of the American Abolition Society* (New York, 1859); "exposé" then meant an exposition, not an exposure. Some persons outside the political-action groups reached similar conclusions about the guarantee clause; see Theodore Parker, *The Relation of Slavery to a Republican Form of Government* (Boston, 1858).

destroying slavery in the states were complete failures. Yet after slavery was destroyed by other means—under the war powers of the commander in chief and by constitutional amendment—the Goodell sect's arguments were repeated and echoed by the Republicans they excoriated in the fifties as the constitutional justification for Radical Reconstruction.

6
Reconstruction:
Crescendo, 1861–1867

The attack on Fort Sumter constituted a watershed; after 1861 the constitutional context in which the guarantee clause developed was profoundly altered. There was a gross similarity between the functions outlined for the clause by its libertarian exponents both before and after Sumter: it was to be the vehicle for expansion of federal power at the states' expense, it was to be used to strike down slavery, it was to be an assurance of certain basic civil and political rights for freed blacks. After Sumter, though, the liquidation of slavery and the status of the ex-slaves were only two elements of a larger problem, that of Reconstruction. In working out a policy of Reconstruction, the scope and character of the clause were expanded greatly. It was seen as more than a means of abolishing slavery and insuring fundamental liberties; it became a means of re-creating the Union.

The development of the guarantee clause during Reconstruction (1861–1877) went through two phases. In the first, referred to here as "crescendo," the clause was urged by Republican exponents of a thoroughgoing policy of war and reconstruction to authorize their evolving programs.

Democrats responded with a rear-guard action, attempting to limit the clause's applicability and the federal power by insisting that it did nothing more than assure the integrity of the pre-existing state governments. This first phase culminated in the passage of the first Military Reconstruction Act, 2 March 1867. At no point did congressional Republicans rest their Reconstruction policy exclusively on the guarantee clause; through the crescendo phase the clause was one constitutional text among several that authorized their policies.

Reconstruction did not end with passage of the military reconstruction acts, but the influence of the guarantee clause did. In the second phase, "diminuendo," which began in March 1867 and ended by 1880, the clause ceased to be a major determinant of Reconstruction policies. This did not occur because of changing theories about the powers inherent in the guarantee; indeed the clause did not receive its most radical exposition until after March 1867. Rather the increasing congressional disillusion with Reconstruction caused the clause's diminishing importance. After 1867 turmoil in the states that would have suggested implementation of the guarantee of republican government—the rise of the Ku Klux Klan, political anarchy in various southern states—failed to provoke extensive use of the clause. Violence in the South notwithstanding, the guarantee ceased to be a major influence on state-federal relations for two decades after the beginning of military Reconstruction.

There was no obvious or imperative constitutional solution to the problems of Reconstruction. The Constitution was silent, and solutions had to be improvised to suit circumstances. This meant that certain clauses of the Constitution had to be extended beyond their traditional scope, while others had to be ignored as inapposite. The qualifications-of-members clause, for example, had to be adapted to deal with issues remote from the expectations of its framers; the clauses of Article I that allotted two senators and a varying number of representatives to each state had to be regarded as temporarily irrelevant. But none of this was clear or compelling at the time. The lack of obvious or easy solutions misled both contemporaries and historians who supported one solution or another into believing that their opponents were devious and unscrupulous, when in fact all men were trying to adapt the Constitution to an extraordinary situation that the framers did not foresee.

At the onset of the Civil War the potential applicability of the guarantee clause remained uncertain. Different interpretations of federal power under the clause had been suggested, and some had furnished a rationale for presidential, congressional, and judicial action (or inaction), but the clause remained, as Charles Sumner was soon to call it, the "sleeping giant" of the Constitution.

Such precedent as did exist for implementing the guarantee furnished no clear program for the three branches of the federal government in the unprecedented constitutional crisis that faced them in 1861. Congress had invoked the words of the clause in its statutes admitting new states and had imposed conditions on some states at admission. But to those who were foresighted and optimistic enough in 1861 to think about the problems of postwar restoration of the Union, the guarantee clause afforded little firm precedent. For one thing, it was not clear that national power in admitting new states to the Union could be invoked to "readmit" states that had tried to withdraw. Then too, Congress usually justified its admission policy on section 3 of Article IV, rather than section 4. At best, congressional debates and statutes were fuzzy as to just what powers Congress claimed for itself under section 4. That was unavoidable after 1820, since a too-explicit declaration of national power to guarantee republican forms of government would have clashed with prevalent state-sovereignty concepts of the federal Union.[1]

The previous forty years of slavery debates had not shed much more light on the scope of the clause. The views of national power and policy urged by antislavery men had been rejected, at least temporarily. Congress had not adopted the theories of abolitionists who had seen slavery to be inconsistent with republican government. Yet that might soon change. The foremost advocates of slavery and state sovereignty had withdrawn from the national government; the power of the Democracy was temporarily shattered; and the party that now dominated the national government had proclaimed slavery restriction as the core of its policy. Further, by mid-1862 the proslavery argument—that slavery was fully compatible with republican government, enlightened political policy, and Christian religious principles—was plainly dead, never to be resurrected.

A third precedent for interpreting national power under the guarantee clause, the Tyler-Taney construction of the 1840s, was neither ambiguous like the state-admission precedent nor rejected like the antislavery arguments. Yet

[1] Southern secessionists, who before the war had been the most ardent supporters of the state-sovereignty concept, did not consider the guarantee clause a threat to the new polities they erected. The clause was repeated verbatim in both the provisional and the final Confederate constitutions, reprinted in Charles R. Lee, Jr., *The Confederate Constitutions* (Chapel Hill, 1963), appendices.

it was so negative as to be useless to the statesmen of 1861. Taney, after all, had said only that the Supreme Court would not help to determine which state government was legitimate; he relinquished the problem to Congress, which might delegate it to the President if it wished. Taney, while saying that the judicial branch would follow the decision of either political branch as to which government in a state was legitimate, had elaborated no positive criteria of republicanism to guide either Lincoln or Congress. Tyler's policies of inaction or support of extant governments were not much help. Few in Washington were about to support the secessionist governments of the Confederate states, though the Tyler precedent would justify support of shaky Unionist governments in border states.

In short, the guarantee clause was still largely a clean slate. Theories had been adumbrated, but none had won widespread assent except Taney's judicial abstention and Tyler's justification of inaction, which were not relevant in 1861. The guarantee clause could still be cited to bolster divergent and clashing interpretations.

After the firing on Sumter, the first and most pressing constitutional question raised by secession was whether the Constitution was adequate to deal with the emergency. Could the federal government find in it the sources of power that would enable it to crush secession, fight a civil war, and restore the Union, or would the Constitution have to be set aside to preserve the Union? The latter prospect repelled Unionists of all parties; no one wanted to "Mexicanize" American government, as they expressed it. Thus it was necessary to find in the Constitution latent power to reunite the nation. A short *mauvais quart d'heure* of indecision intervened, but by mid-1861 it was settled that the Constitution would be adapted to the crisis. Thus constitutional questions would play a configurative role in resolving the problems of war and Reconstruction: solutions would be thought of in constitutional terms and tested by constitutional interpretation. The text of the Constitution, including the guarantee clause, thereby took on a dramatically heightened importance.[2]

President Abraham Lincoln was the first to call upon the guarantee clause for solutions to the crisis of Civil War. Less than three months after Sumter, the President in a message to the special session of Congress meeting in the summer of 1861 sought in the clause an authorization for extraordinary national authority to put down the rebellion. For tactical purposes, Lincoln preferred not to rely altogether on the various martial clauses of the Constitution, so as to avoid foreign-policy complications arising from treating the Confederacy as a conventional belligerent. The guarantee clause provided a convenient civilian substitute. Lincoln reasoned that if a state may secede, it may discard the republican form. Thus in order to fulfill the guarantee obligation, the nation had to prevent secession.[3]

Lincoln's message provoked the first congressional debate on Reconstruction policy, and with it a dichotomy in attitudes toward the seceded states. Proponents of what might be called the *status quo ante*—mostly Democrats from border states, with a few maverick Republicans and Unionists—insisted that the status and prerogatives of the

[2] On the configurative character of constitutional questions in national crises like the Civil War, see Arthur Bestor, "The American Civil War as a Constitutional Crisis," *Am. Hist. Rev.*, LXIX (1964), 327–352.

[3] Richardson, *Messages*, VI, 20–31.

southern states had not been destroyed by secession.[4] National policy had to be restricted to restoring federal authority in the South; it could not be used to interfere with slavery or to change in any way the forms of government. Anything more, which deprived the people in the seceded states of the right to self-government, would violate the guarantee of republican government.[5] Thus these men carried over the ante-bellum southern attitude toward the guarantee of republican government—that it assured the continuation of extant state forms and institutions. It was a literally conservative rather than an innovative promise.

Our repugnance to the motives of the *status-quo* advocates should not blind us to one valid point in their argument: they realized that more radical theories of the guarantee clause would somewhat deprive the southern polities of self-government. Their vision was of course flawed by inability to recognize that slavery was the most abhorrent way of denying self-government to men, but their point could not be ignored, then or now, by those who saw the guarantee as authority for fundamentally altering the state governments. How far, or how long, can federal power under the clause be pushed before it encroaches to an unacceptable extent on that elementary characteristic of republicanism, the right of self-government?

In opposition to these men stood the bulk of the Re-

[4] A helpful guide to the make-up of the first Civil War Congress, the Thirty-seventh, is Leonard P. Curry, *Blueprint for Modern America: Nonmilitary Legislation of the First Civil War Congress* (Nashville, 1968), ch. 1 and appendices.

[5] Lazarus Powell, *Globe*, 37 Cong., 1 sess., 69 (11 July 1861); John C. Breckinridge, *ibid.*, 140–141 (16 July).

publican party.[6] They advocated varied proposals for dealing with secession between 1861 and 1867—territorialization, conquered provinces, state suicide, among others—that, despite their multifariousness, shared two characteristics: they envisioned extensive federal interference with the forms and functioning of the state governments and they eventually assumed the forcible abolition of slavery. Both characteristics were unacceptable to the *status-quo* group.

The first Republican Reconstruction proposal was suggested by Senator Edward D. Baker of Oregon, who advocated territorialization, under which the federal government would govern the subdued states as it governed territories.[7] Although he insisted that territorial governments could be as republican as state governments, Baker had to ignore two inconvenient facts that plagued all subsequent Republican Reconstruction theories under the guarantee clause. First, any form of government imposed by Washington against the will of the white majority in the southern states would have to be kept in power by an occupation army. If anything is antithetical to republicanism, it is military government; hence, the dilemma of depriving a state of republican government temporarily in order to assure its restoration permanently. Second, the guarantee applies only to states "in this Union." To treat a state as if it possessed something less than full rights of self-governance is to treat it as less than a "State in this Union," at least compared with states not treated in that way.

[6] An excellent treatment of Republican wartime Reconstruction theories is Herman Belz, *Reconstructing the Union: Theory and Policy during the Civil War* (Ithaca, 1969).

[7] *Globe*, 37 Cong., 1 sess., 43–45 (10 July 1861), 69 (11 July).

Republicans met these dilemmas in differing ways. Some argued that the guarantee clause was irrelevant because the southern states had declared themselves out of the Union; they therefore sought constitutional authority in other clauses. Others, like Thaddeus Stevens, felt that Republicans could have it either way: if the southern states were still in the Union, then the guarantee clause would be applicable. If they were somehow not in the Union, then equivalent federal power could be drawn from the admit-new-states clause. This convenient either-or approach troubled Republicans of more fastidious consistency as long as they insisted on conceptualizing the problem of Reconstruction in states'-rights terms. Representative Alexander Diven of New York spoke for these men: after the rebellion was suppressed, "South Carolina . . . will be South Carolina still, with all the rights which Massachusetts has, or else the Constitution is at an end." [8]

The debates of the Thirty-seventh Congress' 1861 special summer session did not produce any specific policy for Reconstruction, and policy considerations as well as constitutional theory were left to drift for a time. But the debates had found an immediate echo outside Congress in an important speech delivered by Henry Winter Davis, Maryland Unionist, at Brooklyn in November 1861. Like Lincoln earlier that year, Davis sought some civilian substitute as an alternate to the war powers of Congress to authorize military action against the south, and like Lincoln he found it in the guarantee clause. He reasoned that the secession governments of the South were set up in violation of the Constitution, which he saw as depriving them of a

[8] *Globe*, 39 Cong., 1 sess., 72–75 (18 Dec. 1865); *Globe*, 37 Cong., 1 sess., 95 (13 July 1861).

republican form of government. Therefore Congress must use all means at its disposal, including the sword, to restore republican governments to the seceded states. Davis considered the guarantee clause such a sweeping grant of war powers that he viewed the obviously more relevant insurrection clause of Article I as ancillary to the guarantee of Article IV.[9]

Davis' speech is of particular importance because he emerged in the Thirty-eighth Congress as the principal exponent of radical congressional power to supervise Reconstruction. As the author of the Wade-Davis Bill, he led congressional opposition to presidential authority in Reconstruction. In so doing, he relied principally on the guarantee clause and on Taney's dicta in the *Luther* case. His Brooklyn speech indicates that even at the start of the war he was working out the radical position that matured in 1864.

The debates in and out of Congress influenced Senator Charles Sumner, who would tower above all others during postwar Reconstruction as an exponent of unlimited power to restructure the South by the guarantee clause. In the earliest days of the war, Sumner believed that emancipation would have to occur through exercise of the war powers entrusted to the President. He was also hampered for some time by his sincerely held prewar belief that the national government could not touch slavery within the states. Only with difficulty did he become converted during the first year of the war to the more radical abolitionist stance that the nation could strike at slavery in the states, and then only because it seemed to him that Lincoln's cautious approach

[9] J. A. J. Creswell, ed., *Speeches and Addresses of Henry Winter Davis* (New York, 1867), 265 ff.

to abolition might squander the golden opportunity provided by the war.[10]

While his fellow-radicals were considering a policy of territorialization on 12 February 1862, Sumner rose in the Senate to offer nine resolutions on the relations of the Union to "territory once occupied by certain states." These resolutions embodied a "forfeited states' rights" theory of Reconstruction which Sumner abandoned the next day for the more sweeping "state-suicide" theory. He insisted that secession terminated both states' rights and slavery. This being so, it became the duty of Congress under the guarantee clause to assume jurisdiction of the states' territories and re-establish their republican forms of government, especially by protecting all inhabitants, including ex-slaves. Sumner thus provided an alternative rationale to Reconstruction theories based on territorialization concepts, with their dependence on the territories clause of Article I. After the territorialization approach was abandoned, the rationale suggested by Sumner assumed considerable appeal, especially as it omitted the most "radical" feature of that proposal, the theory that states reverted to the status of territories. Proponents of a guarantee clause approach could plausibly argue that the affected states were "in this Union." [11]

Appealing as this idea was to prove later, it did not blunt the acrimony of Sumner's more conservative colleagues toward him. William Pitt Fessenden, Republican from Maine and unofficial spokesman for the less radical element of the party, wrote in June 1862 that "if I could cut the

[10] For Sumner's ideas before 1862, see David Donald, *Charles Sumner and the Rights of Man* (New York, 1970), 17, 29, 54.

[11] *Globe*, 37 Cong., 2 sess., 736–737 (12 Feb. 1862).

throats of about half a dozen Republican Senators, . . . Sumner would be the first victim, as he is by far the greatest fool of the lot." Democratic Senator Garrett Davis of Kentucky, the antithesis of Sumner, quickly offered counterresolutions that would have limited the guarantee clause to conferring war powers for suppressing the armed resistance. Neither his nor Sumner's resolutions was adopted, but the radical potential of the clause had been made explicit.[12]

Important as was Sumner's extension of the possibilities inherent in the guarantee clause, his formulation of policy remained sketchy and opaque. This was quickly clarified by several commentators who expounded the clause at length in debates, pamphlets, and articles suggesting practical modes of implementing the guarantee. The first of these commentaries was an article in the *New Englander* magazine in mid-1862. Its author, Timothy Farrar, took up the adequacy-of-the-Constitution theme that had been broached earlier by Winter Davis. He discussed at some length various clauses of the Constitution that supported the warmaking and military government powers of the federal government, stressing the guarantee clause, which, he argued, insured "the supremacy of the nation, and the subordinate responsible position of the states." The clause, in Farrar's view, not only required national supremacy over the states; it also obliged the federal government to force the states, if need be, to carry on their legitimate governmental functions.[13]

[12] *Ibid.*, 786 (13 Feb. 1862). Fessenden to Elizabeth F. Warriner, 1 June 1862, quoted in Eric McKitrick, *Andrew Johnson and Reconstruction* (Chicago, 1960), 272.

[13] Timothy Farrar, "The Adequacy of the Constitution," *New Englander*, XXI (1862), 51–73.

Farrar was echoed by other commentators. The Harvard Law School professor of constitutional law, Joel Parker, published a pamphlet in which he argued that the guarantee clause could be used to restore legitimate state authority, as well as to keep a state government loyal to the Union. He was reflecting an idea widely held at the time in the North that the secessionist governments of the southern states represented the views only of a minority who forced secession on the Unionist majority. Parker's views were carried forward by another Massachusetts lawyer, William Whiting, solicitor of the War Department, whose 1862 pamphlet, *War Powers,* adopted Sumner's interpretation that the guarantee clause authorized the abolition of slavery. This power, wrote Whiting, belonged to both the President and Congress. In an 1864 pamphlet Whiting adopted the prewar antislavery view of the guarantee clause, which required in the states "a Republican Government, which, by guaranteeing freedom to all, shall be in accordance with the true spirit of the Constitution of the United States." [14]

[14] Joel Parker, *Constitutional Law: With Special Reference to the Present Condition of the United States* (Cambridge, Mass., 1862), 18–19. His pamphlet had earlier appeared as an article in the widely read *North American Review* (April 1862). This Joel Parker should be distinguished from his contemporary namesakes, Joel Parker the Democratic governor of New Jersey and Joel Parker the Presbyterian minister, neither of whom shared his revulsion to slavery. Whiting first published his views in a lengthy pamphlet, *The War Powers of the President and the Legislative Powers of Congress in Relation to Rebellion, Treason and Slavery* (Boston, 1862). He expanded this pamphlet to a book-length treatise, *War Powers under the Constitution of the United States,* which by 1871 had gone through nearly 150 reprintings. His 1864 views and prophecy are presented in a pamphlet, *The Return of the Rebellious States* (Philadelphia, 1864).

The guarantee clause was receiving attention simultaneously in Congress. In the Senate Ira Harris, a New York Republican whose contemporaries considered him a conservative, offered a more acceptable plan for wartime Reconstruction than the various territorialization plans. Explicitly basing his approach on the guarantee clause, Harris suggested that the President be empowered to establish provisional governments in the seceding states,[15] consisting of a governor and three judges, who together would exercise legislative functions and separately would conduct the executive and judicial business of the erstwhile states. Though this resembled the governments of the territories, Harris justified it on the grounds that it was necessary to preserve order until a regular and loyal state government could be reorganized. The bill was a moderate measure, because it assumed that the seceded states were still in the Union and was vague regarding the status of the blacks. Harris considered it more palatable than military government or territorialization because it foresaw speedy restoration of self-government and was designed only for the preservation of order until that occurred.

Despite its moderate tone, the Harris bill was never passed by the Senate. Democrats and Republican conservatives, sensing correctly that the measure would indirectly permit the abolition of slavery, objected to it on the grounds that, as Garrett Davis put it, a republican government "must be made by the people, and the agencies by which that government is carried on and operated must be appointed or elected by them," characteristics that a presidentially appointed interim government would necessarily

[15] The Harris bill is discussed at length in Belz, *Reconstructing the Union*, 88–99.

lack.[16] The Harris bill was offered late in the session and was not acted upon because of the press of last-minute business, but it had at least showed that the guarantee clause provided not only an alternative to territorialization and to military occupation under presidential authority, but also a constitutional approach acceptable to most shades of opinion in the Republican party.

Two proposals in 1863, one offered by Harris and the other by Charles Sumner, illustrate how broad an ideological and policy appeal the guarantee clause might accommodate. In the third session of the Thirty-seventh Congress Harris again offered a Reconstruction bill based exclusively on the guarantee clause, differing from his bill of the previous session only in that it called for the appointment of a provisional civil governor (rather than the territorial-type government of the earlier bill) who could not exercise any legislative power and who could appoint officers recognized under state law at the time of secession. The new Harris bill assumed that the provisional governor would call a state constitutional convention as soon as the armed resistance was put down.[17] Though it was not enacted, its features foreshadowed the policy of the military Reconstruction acts. It looked to the speediest possible restoration of state authority, leaving previous institutions intact except for the abolition of slavery, and thus was as moderate a measure as would have then been acceptable to the bulk of the Republican party.

Sumner at the same time, in an article published in the *Atlantic Monthly*, outlined a more radical approach to Re-

[16] *Globe*, 37 Cong., 2 sess., 3138–3145 (7 July 1862).

[17] S. 538, 37 Cong., discussed in Belz, *Reconstructing the Union*, 122–124.

construction under the guarantee clause, calling for direct federal responsibility to protect individual rights and subordinate the power of the states. The clause, Sumner argued, was a grant of power to Congress to "evaluate" the state constitutions and governments, to abolish slavery, and to administer the territory and government of the erstwhile states until they were restored in republican form. Sumner avoided his earlier emphasis on state suicide, but in other respects did not abandon the basic ideas set forth in his 1862 resolutions; he repeated them in 1863 with greater emphasis. What was new was the force of his attack on presidential Reconstruction. In Sumner's revised view, Reconstruction was exclusively a congressional function, and the military governments then operating in Arkansas, Louisiana, Florida, and Tennessee were only temporary, to be replaced as soon as possible by congressional governments. Sumner argued that congressional power under the guarantee clause was unlimited; the clause gave carte blanche to Congress to do whatever it pleased with the subdued states.[18]

This was a potentially irresponsible position since it would have deranged the balance between nation and states in the American federal system, but three things can be said

[18] Charles Sumner, "Our Domestic Relations: Power of Congress over the Rebel States," *Atlantic Monthly*, XII (1863), 507–529. Sumner's position received some indirect support from the Supreme Court, which in the Prize Cases (2 Black 635 [U.S., 1863]) accorded Congress a great deal of needed flexibility in dealing with the restored southern states, which could be treated as enemy governments or insurrectionary states. Like subsequent judicial comments on Reconstruction, notably *Texas* v. *White*, the Prize Cases signaled a judicial awareness of the need for broad and flexible congressional authority to deal with the unprecedented problems of Reconstruction.

in its favor. First, as southern arrogance in defeat increased within a few months after Appomattox, Sumner's extreme views came to accord more and more with the realities; Congress would need a temporary infusion of greatly expanded power to deal adequately with President Andrew Johnson's obstinacy and the reaction of unregenerate ex-rebels. Second, Sumner served the useful function of a forward assault force. As Charles Francis Adams had observed in his Diary as early as 1847, if Sumner had "not sufficient every day steadiness of mind to do well the work of infantry," he performed "with success as a pioneer." [19] Though ahead of the main corps of Republican opinion, he prepared the way for acceptance of more moderate views. Finally, though Sumner's beliefs about congressional power were extreme, the goals he hoped to advance were not.

The guarantee clause in Reconstruction often became a rationale for expediency. In Sumner's hands it was a constitutional fig leaf covering policies of arguable validity but unquestioned necessity. Use of the clause to lend constitutional sanction to policy objectives does not detract from the value of congressional Reconstruction debates as precedent for construing the clause today. Such a use is natural in the course of American constitutional development. All the clauses of the Constitution are tested and expanded by their use in doubtful circumstances. The commerce clause, for example, is the sweeping grant of federal power that it is today because Chief Justice John Marshall and succeeding statesmen used it boldly to extend congressional control

[19] Adams' Diary entry of 8 March 1847, quoted in David Donald, *Charles Sumner and the Coming of the Civil War* (New York, 1960), 139.

of the national economy in situations where it lent color to constitutionally doubtful policies. If we adhered rigidly only to the obvious literal meaning of all clauses in the Constitution they would have been dead letters long since. The expansion of a clause into an area of dubious applicability is a recurrent process of constitutional evolution.

The generalities of the guarantee clause provided a vessel for any policy argument that suited men's interests. To Democrats during Reconstruction the clause guaranteed self-government to the people of the southern states ("people," as they used the term, being qualified to include only whites). In one of the frequent shifts of ideological position that Lincoln characterized by his "little story" about two drunks fighting and in the process exchanging coats, the Democrats snapped up Daniel Webster's argument in *Luther* v. *Borden* that self-government permitted changes in governmental structure only through established procedures of constitutional amendment by the duly qualified voters. Hence, they concluded, the Republican programs of Reconstruction were radically wrong, both in their objectives and in their methods.

The Republicans, having shed the old Whig coat of orderly change through authorized procedures, found no difficulty in crawling into the old radical Democracy's coat of republican government being equated with universal manhood suffrage, with the significant proviso that this meant scrapping racial impediments. To some Republicans, as to their antislavery predecessors, the phrase "republican form of government" incorporated the ideals of the Declaration of Independence into the Constitution.

Until 1864 Congress left Reconstruction to the President. Lincoln appointed military and civilian governors for the seceded states as they came under the control of Union forces. One of these, Andrew Johnson of Tennessee, realized that the persons governed by his regime would need assurances that his position was constitutional. He found the warrant he sought in the guarantee clause, claiming that it authorized Lincoln's appointment of a military governor as a stop-gap remedy to restore a republican form of government to Tennessee. This position was similar to that of the second Harris Reconstruction bill.[20]

An even more important reference to executive power under the guarantee clause was in President Lincoln's "ten per cent plan" of Reconstruction, embodied in his Proclamation of Amnesty and Reconstruction, 8 December 1863.[21] In that part of the proclamation outlining procedures for readmission of the states to full political privileges, Lincoln urged that 10 per cent of those who had been qualified to vote in 1860 be permitted to reorganize a loyal state government. He required of such a government only that it recognize emancipation under executive order (the Emancipation Proclamation) or congressional statute (the Confiscation Acts of 1862). When such a government was organized, "the State shall receive thereunder the benefits of the constitutional provision which declares that 'The United States shall guaranty [*sic*] to every State in this union a republican form of government.' " Though Lincoln blurred the theoretical issue by his use of the passive voice ("the State shall receive"), he had implicitly claimed that the guarantee clause envisioned presidential enforcement.

[20] See Johnson's speech of 13 March 1862, "Appeal to the People of Tennessee," in 1862 *American Annual Cyclopaedia*, 764.

[21] Richardson, *Messages*, VI, 213–215.

Given the ambiguities of *Luther* v. *Borden,* Lincoln's position was not unwarranted.

Lincoln's assertion of presidential authority did not go unchallenged for long. Increasing Radical disaffection with the President's policies led in 1864 to passage of the Wade-Davis Bill, a direct challenge to presidential Reconstruction authority. On 18 January 1864, Henry Winter Davis, an early exponent of federal power under the guarantee clause, who had been sent to the Thirty-eighth Congress from a Baltimore district, reported out of the House Select Committee on Rebellious States "a bill to guaranty certain states a republican form of government." It provoked a rash of debate that provided a full exposition by congressional Republicans of the powers they claimed for Congress under the guarantee clause. Davis, introducing the bill, said of the clause:

That clause vests in the Congress of the United States a plenary, supreme, unlimited political jurisdiction, paramount over courts, subject only to the judgment of the people of the United States, embracing within its scope every legislative measure necessary and proper to make it effectual; and what is necessary and proper the Constitution refers in the first place to our judgment, subject to no revision but that of the people.[22]

What is most striking about the position of Davis and other supporters of the bill is their vagueness about what specific goals they hoped to achieve by exercising the power they claimed. Davis suggested the extirpation of slavery; George Boutwell went so far as to demand universal free

[22] *Globe,* 38 Cong., 1 sess., App. 82–85 (22 March 1864).

public education and the breakup of southern plantations; but no specific legislative goals were set forth. What was at stake in the Wade-Davis Bill debates was not any particular Republican objective like disfranchisement of ex-rebels or full political rights for the freedmen; the real issue, at least to its supporters, was congressional supremacy over both the President and the Supreme Court in defining and enforcing Reconstruction policy. Lest anyone should fail to get this point, Davis made it blunt: "By the bill we propose to preclude the judicial question by the solution of a political question." He was echoed by Nathaniel B. Smithers of Delaware, who emphasized the plenary grant of congressional power under the guarantee clause, as interpreted in *Luther v. Borden.* However, like previous Reconstruction proposals based on the guarantee clause, the Wade-Davis Bill was not an extremist measure. Its passage by both houses indicates that it had considerable appeal to moderates.[23]

Democrats in the House were at first taken aback by the sweeping powers claimed for Congress under the Wade-Davis Bill, but they soon launched a counterattack, reiterating their concept of the guarantee clause, under which the federal government could only preserve the extant state governments. They pressed the logic of their argument to the nadir of futility, which was expressed by Virginia's Unionist John Carlile in the Senate: the standards of what constitute a republican government were set forth in 1789 and the federal government cannot impose any new requirements.[24]

---

[23] *Ibid.*, 1740 (19 April 1864). For an extended discussion of the bill, see Belz, *Reconstructing the Union*, ch. 8.

[24] Representative Democratic challengers were: James C. Allen,

Lincoln pocket vetoed the Wade-Davis Bill, which forced Davis to elaborate the bill's specific objectives. In the "Wade-Davis Manifesto" and in a letter to the *Nation* written a few months later, Davis insisted that the guarantee of a republican form of government to the states was exclusively a prerogative of Congress. By way of additional support for this point, he argued that the Lincoln governments were not republican because in each the Negro was refused the ballot. This claim carried congressional Republican thought an important step forward. The "Manifesto" and *Nation* letter marked the point where antislavery Republicans passed from their old contention that republicanism forbade slavery to their new belief that republicanism required that the Negro be given the vote. Davis in 1864 was just slightly premature; section 2 of the Fourteenth Amendment was only two years in the future, and the Fifteenth Amendment would be hammered out before the decade was over.[25]

The conversion of other Republicans to this new point of view was demonstrated several times during the Thirty-eighth Congress. In debates on swearing in William Fishback, senator-elect from the Lincoln government of Arkansas, Charles Sumner was joined by Senator Jacob Howard of Michigan in insisting that Fishback was not entitled to his seat because the Arkansas government was not republican, as it represented only a minority of white Ar-

---

Globe, 38 Cong., 1 sess., 1738–1739 (19 April 1864); Francis Kernan, *ibid.*, 2068–2069 (3 May 1864); Fernando Wood, *ibid.*, 2074–2080 (3 May 1864); Samuel S. Cox, *ibid.*, 2097 (4 May 1864); George H. Pendleton, *ibid.*, 2106 (4 May 1864); John S. Carlile, *ibid.*, 3453 (1 July 1864).

[25] The "Manifesto" and the *Nation* letter are reprinted in Creswell, ed., *Speeches and Addresses of Davis*, 415 ff., 589.

kansans. In debates the next session on a joint resolution that would have declared Louisiana "entitled to the guarantee and all other rights of a State government under the Constitution of the United States," Sumner denied that the Lincoln government of that state was republican: "If the loyal men, white and black, recognize it, then it will be republican in form. Unless that is done, it will not be." Thus was Negro suffrage tied in with the Arkansas-debate arguments that reconstructed state governments must represent a majority of the state's inhabitants. Sumner went a step beyond that, however, when he claimed that "it is the bounden duty of the United States [under the guarantee clause] by act of Congress to guaranty freedom to every citizen, and immunity from all oppression, and absolute equality before the law." [26]

At the time of Lincoln's assassination, Davis and Sumner did not yet speak for a majority of their fellow-Republicans. Lincoln's tact, the distraction of other wartime issues, the satisfactory behavior of the new state governments, and the inchoate state of Republican opinion about postwar Reconstruction all prevented issues implicit in the guarantee from coming to a head. Even had all Republicans been as eager as Winter Davis and Sumner to press the guarantee issue, they could not have made much headway with it during the war because they were of two minds as to whether the southern states were in or out of the Union. If they had fully believed that the secessionist states were out of the Union, the guarantee clause would have been irrelevant since it applied only "to every State in this Union." Yet it was apparent that the unoccupied southern

[26] *Globe*, 38 Cong., 1 sess., 2459, 2897, 2899 (25 May, 13 June 1864); *ibid.*, 38 Cong., 2 sess., 1067 (24 Feb. 1865).

states were not really in the Union, at least not in the way that New York, or even Missouri, were. All this left the guarantee of Article IV in a sort of constitutional limbo during the war. Generals Robert E. Lee's and Joseph E. Johnston's surrenders therefore made it imperative that the fuzzy status of the guarantee clause be clarified quickly.

Andrew Johnson indicated a greater interest in the guarantee clause than did Lincoln. What was relevant for Tennessee when Johnson was military governor was relevant for all the other seceded states after he became President. Even in his unfortunate vice-presidential inaugural address, Johnson alluded to the clause, stating that it required the immediate admission of his home state's representatives to their seats in Congress. In a speech to some visiting Hoosiers on 21 April 1865, Johnson referred to the clause as the "great panacea," which would enable the Union to crush the rebellion and restore the states to their rightful relation to the Union. He quickly acted on this theory. His proclamations appointing provisional governors for the occupied states all recited section 4 and continued: "Whereas it becomes necessary and proper to carry out and enforce the obligations of the United States to the people of —— in securing them in the enjoyment of a republican form of government." The proclamations empowered the provisional governors to call constitutional conventions "to enable such loyal people of the state of —— to restore said state to its constitutional relations to the Federal Government and to present such a republican form of government as will entitle the state to the guaranty of the United States therefor." These proclamations summarized Johnson's theory of the guarantee clause: the clause could be enforced by the President without any special authorization of Congress; it operated automatically once the states had presented republican constitutions; and the federal government was obliged to render the guarantee. Johnson's assumptions not only clashed head-on with the Republicans', but also swept under the rug all important questions implicit in the clause.[27]

Although the President's announced policy did not fully embrace the opinion of southerners and their Democratic allies that the states were entitled to immediate and automatic readmission as soon as hostilities ceased, it came uncomfortably close to the Democratic position. Nevertheless, many Republicans whose suspicions of the new President had been allayed by Johnson's loose talk of punishing traitors and making treason odious were content to regard his policy as experimental.

Most Republicans were thrown off their guard in the summer of 1865. Richard Henry Dana, Jr., for one, retained a flexible attitude about the requirements of the guarantee. In his famous "Grasp of War" speech delivered at Faneuil Hall on 21 June 1865, Dana maintained:

We advance no extreme or refined theory as to what may be included within the term "republican form of government." In the exercise of the extraordinary prerogative of the General

[27] Johnson's vice-presidential inaugural address is printed in the 1865 *American Annual Cyclopaedia*, 301. The 21 April 1865 speech is reprinted in Edward McPherson, *The Political History of the United States during the Period of Reconstruction* (Washington, 1880), 45–46. The provisional government proclamations are in Richardson, *Messages*, VIII, as follows: Mississippi, 3512 (13 June 1865); Georgia, 3516 (17 June 1865); Texas, 3519 (17 June 1865); Alabama, 3521 (21 June 1865); South Carolina, 3524 (30 June 1865); North Carolina, 3510 (29 May 1865); Florida, 3527 (13 July 1865).

Government to determine whether a state constitution is "republican" there must be practical wisdom and no refined theories. If the constitutions with which the rebel states now come are not "republican" in such a reasonable and practical sense as nations act upon—if they are so unrepublican as to endanger public peace and the stability of our institutions, then we may treat them as not "republican" in the American sense of the term.

Dana's ambiguity was probably the product of an attempt to evade the embarrassing fact that most northern states denied the ballot to Negroes. The small black population of those states would not prevent them from being "republican in a reasonable and practical sense." Dana's point was sensible, though not admirable. Disfranchising half the population of a state was qualitatively as well as quantitatively different from disfranchising 5 per cent or less. Radicals like Dana, in and out of Congress, saw little to worry about in Johnson's emphatic assertion of presidential power under the guarantee clause.[28]

The Republican attitude of "wait and see" did not last long. As early as May 1865 Carl Schurz voiced some suspicion about Johnson's excessive latitude toward recalcitrant southerners. Schurz's fears were soon justified. In a rash of arrogant and vituperative public statements, ex-rebels defied the magnanimity of the conquerors and claimed for themselves the fruits of victory. A Louisiana Democratic convention claimed that the national Democracy was "the only agent by which radicalism can be successfully met, and this government [the United States] restored to its pristine purity and vigor"; Louisiana's state

[28] Richard Henry Dana, Jr., *Speeches in Stirring Times and Letters to a Son* (Boston, 1910), 243–259.

government was "a government of white people, made
and to be perpetuated for the exclusive benefit of the white
race"; Negroes could not be made citizens because of *Dred
Scott;* compensation must be paid for the "confiscation" of
slaves; and the "Negro problem" could be solved only by
"a levee and labor system . . . [to] relieve the planters
and people at large." Elsewhere minorities of the conventions called by Johnson's provisional governors refused to
repudiate Confederate war debts or ratify the Thirteenth
Amendment. This attitude seemed to infect the entire
South, and the voices of moderate southerners who still
retained a grasp on reality were lost in the swell of captious
insolence spilling out of the former Confederacy.[29]

Southern intransigence had an immediate effect on men
of all shades of opinion. Gideon Welles worried about
what he admitted to be the "arrogant and offensively dic-
tatorial" attitude of the South throughout the summer
months of 1865. Even Welles recognized that federal
policy would depend to a great extent on the attitudes of
the southerners. Less wedded to conservatism than Welles,
James G. Blaine wrote that he quickly became disgusted at

[29] Schurz to Sumner, 9 May 1865, in Frederic Bancroft, ed.,
Speeches, Correspondence, and Political Papers of Carl Schurz
(New York, 1913), I, 255. For the arrogance and vindictiveness of
the ex-rebels, see: statement of Governor James L. Orr of South
Carolina, quoted in Francis B. Simkins and Robert H. Woody,
South Carolina during Reconstruction (Chapel Hill, 1932), 38, 63,
and the authors' comment on South Carolinians' attitudes, 23;
resolutions of Louisiana Democratic Convention, 2 Oct. 1865, in
the 1865 *American Annual Cyclopaedia,* 512; resolution of Georgia
legislature, summer 1865, quoted in Edwin C. Woolley, *The
Reconstruction of Georgia* (New York, 1901); Provisional Governor Lewis E. Parsons to the Alabama legislature, July 1865, in
the 1865 *American Annual Cyclopaedia,* 12.

the "quibbles, captious objections, gross outrages, absurd conditions, lack of tact, willfulness, and astounding effrontery" emanating from the South. He was particularly dismayed at seeing unpardoned Confederate officials claiming seats in Congress. Charles Sumner soon lost what tolerance he had for the President and wrote to Schurz: "Now, to my mind the single point to be reached is the assertion of jurisdiction by Congress. One person will reach this point by one road and another by another road. Provided it is reached, it is not of much importance how this is accomplished." Many did reach the "point" Sumner was referring to, and by divergent roads. Sumner's road is of the foremost importance.[30]

Sumner had been touting the guarantee clause for several years as a source of congressional power over the states, but he had always referred to it in conjunction with other clauses of the Constitution. By late 1865, however, the guarantee clause alone seemed to dominate his thoughts. He was fascinated by his friend Francis Lieber's political writings and used him as a sounding board in refining his thinking. In October he wrote Lieber with suppressed excitement:

Words receive expansion and elevation with time. Our fathers builded wiser than they knew. Did they simply mean a guarantee against a king? Something more, I believe,—all of which was not fully revealed to themselves, but which we must now declare in the light of our institutions. We know more than

[30] Howard K. Beale, ed., *Diary of Gideon Welles* (New York, 1960), II, 248 (entry of 1 Aug. 1865 and *passim* 1865); James G. Blaine, *Twenty Years of Congress* (Norwich, Conn., 1884–1886), II, 86 ff.; Sumner to Schurz, 25 Dec. 1865, in Bancroft, ed., *Speeches of Schurz*, I, 374.

Montesquieu on this question. The time has come to fix a meaning on these words [the guarantee clause]. . . . My point is that liberty, equality before the law, and the consent of the governed are essential elements of a republican government.

By the opening of the first session of the Thirty-ninth Congress, Sumner's ideas had taken final shape. On the eve of the first day of Congress, he again wrote to Lieber: "The debate which approaches on the meaning of a 'republican government' will be the greatest in our history. I shall launch it tomorrow." Launch it he did.[31]

The first day of the Thirty-ninth Congress was auspicious. In the House, newly elected Speaker Schuyler Colfax, a Republican from Indiana, broke with a long-established tradition that would have limited his acceptance speech to a perfunctory expression of gratitude to his party colleagues. Instead Colfax delivered a little discourse outlining Republican objectives for Reconstruction, among which was "protection to all men in their inalienable rights." This was primarily a function of Congress because "representing, in its two branches, the States and the people, its first and highest obligation is to guarantee to every state a republican form of government." Thus early was the guarantee clause pushed to the forefront of the upcoming struggle over Reconstruction.[32]

On the same day in the Senate, Sumner began debates on the guarantee clause, as he had promised Lieber, by intro-

[31] Sumner to Lieber, 12 Oct. 1865 and 3 Dec. 1865, in Edward L. Pierce, *Memoir and Letters of Charles Sumner* (Boston, 1877–1894), III, 258–259, 269.

[32] *Globe*, 39 Cong., 1 sess., 5 (4 Dec. 1865).

ducing a series of bills designed "to carry out the principles of a republican form of government in the District of Columbia" (S.3), "to prescribe an oath to maintain a republican form of government in the rebel States" (S.4), "in part execution of the guarantee of a republican form of government in the Constitution of the United States" (S.5), and "to enforce the guarantee of a republican form of government in certain states whose governments have been usurped or overthrown" (S.7). All these bills were referred to the Joint Committee on Reconstruction a week later. None was ever enacted, but together with Colfax's speech they threw the administration and its supporters into a state of consternation. President Johnson, Secretary of the Navy Gideon Welles, and others became convinced that there was a Republican conspiracy afoot to annoy the administration and defeat its policies.[33]

In the short run, Sumner's resolutions were little more than a gesture, a prod to the thinking of his fellow-Republicans. But they performed the valuable office of alerting moderates to the utility of the clause. One of these men, Representative Samuel Shellabarger of Ohio, quickly took a leaf from Sumner's book to provide the principal defense for the "forfeited rights" theory of Reconstruction that he propounded on 8 January 1866. Shellabarger's theory provided a convenient alternative for that large seg-

[33] On Republican attitudes at the time the Thirty-ninth Congress convened, see Blaine, *Twenty Years*, II, 140. For the impact of the events of 4 December on the administration, see Beale, ed., *Diary of Welles*, II, 387–388 (3 Dec. 1865; obviously a later interlineation), 392 (5 Dec. 1865), 410 (2 Jan. 1866), 452 (10 March 1866). With disarming candor, Sumner posted Welles weekly on his theories and strategy; see *ibid.*, 393 (8 Dec. 1865).

ment of his party unable to accept either Stevens' or Sumner's more advanced theories of Reconstruction. Speaking for this group, Shellabarger argued to a friend:

It is absolutely self-evident that here a thing is still looked at as, and called "a state" which has no government or no republican one—else why talk about giving or guaranteeing to each "state" a republican gov. if there could be no Constitutional possibility as a state having lost such government & why talk about guaranteeing a thing which could not possibly be otherwise than continue to be.[34]

Presenting his theory on the floor of the House, Shellabarger argued that though the states continued to exist, in the sense that their population and territory remained intact, their governments were "overthrown" and therefore did not provide the republican form required by the Constitution. The federal government was therefore obligated to step in to provide the guarantee. He then outlined the characteristics of republican government, including civilian government, self-rule, and control by majorities coupled with protection for minorities.[35]

Meanwhile Charles Sumner's efforts to be named to the Joint Committee on Reconstruction had been rebuffed. His wounded vanity and the obvious hostility of some of the Committee members made it necessary that he ignore the Committee and carry his fight over the guarantee clause onto the floor of the Senate. Accordingly, on 2 February 1866 he introduced a joint resolution (S.R.28) embodying his theory of federal power under the clause. The resolu-

[34] Shellabarger to James Comly, 20 Jan. 1866, quoted in McKitrick, *Andrew Johnson and Reconstruction*, 114.
[35] *Globe*, 39 Cong., 1 sess., 142 ff. (8 Jan. 1866).

tion stated that the southern states had failed to provide their people with republican governments, thus making it necessary for the federal government to enforce the guarantee of section 4. It concluded:

To carry out the guarantee of a republican form of government, and to enforce the prohibition of slavery; Be it resolved . . . that in all states lately declared to be in rebellion there shall be no oligarchy, aristocracy, caste, or monopoly invested with peculiar privileges or powers, and there shall be no denial of rights, civil or political, on account of color or race; but all persons shall be equal before the law, whether in the courtroom or at the ballot box; and this statute, made in pursuance of the constitution, shall be the supreme law of the land, anything in the constitution or laws of any such state to the contrary notwithstanding.[36]

Four days later Sumner defended his resolution in a lengthy speech setting forth his new position that the guarantee clause required Negro suffrage throughout the Union, not only in the South. He insisted that the power to enforce the guarantee was congressional and that it was unlimited. This went so far beyond what more practical Republicans thought desirable or possible that William Pitt Fessenden, chairman of the Joint Committee and possibly the most influential regular Republican in the Senate, rose the next day to condemn the resolution out of hand. Fessenden criticized the resolution as too vague and sweeping, but his most telling point, which effectively killed it, was that the resolution accomplished nothing; it was merely a statement of goals and could not be enforced. As Benjamin Wade commented on another occasion, "it's all very well, Sumner, but it has no bones in it." Fessenden was under-

[36] *Ibid.,* 592 (2 Feb. 1866).

stood to be speaking for his party, and the resolution was thereafter ignored.[37]

Sumner might have harmed a good cause by political ineptitude. He was sound in perceiving that indirect guarantees of political rights for Negroes, like those later embodied in the second section of the Fourteenth Amendment, invited evasion. A clear statement of an absolute and positive right would have provided a firmer assurance of the ballot to the freedman. Yet his resolution was, as Fessenden said, a futility. Even section 2 of the Amendment was better than Sumner's grandiose but empty declaration.

Whatever harm Sumner's maladroit performance did to the cause of Negro suffrage was quickly undone by southern legislators and Andrew Johnson. Democratic oafishness in February 1866 made Sumner's resolution seem politically suave by comparison. On the same day that Fessenden buried S.R.28, Johnson, in a widely publicized debate with a Negro delegation headed by Frederick Douglass, insisted southern blacks should not be given the ballot because of their ignorance and poverty. More to the point, the President vetoed the Freedmen's Bureau Bill on February 19th and the Civil Rights Bill on March 27th, thereby alienating nearly the whole body of the Republican party in Congress. Johnson's gross Washington's Birthday speech brought the executive-legislative split into the open and burned all bridges of possible reconciliation. The consequences of temporizing longer were made unmistakably clear for Congress by resolutions adopted by the Alabama

---

[37] *Ibid.*, 674 ff (6 Feb. 1866), 703 ff. (7 Feb. 1866). For Fessenden's attitude toward Sumner and the resolution, see Charles A. Jellison, *Fessenden of Maine* (Syracuse, 1962), 199. The Wade remark is quoted in Donald, *Sumner and the Rights of Man*, 248.

and Georgia legislatures in February 1866. Alabama's stated:

That Alabama will not voluntarily consent to change the adjustment of political power [the three-fifths clause] as fixed by the Constitution of the United States, and to constrain her to do so in her present prostrate and helpless condition, with no voice in the councils of the nation, would be an unjustifiable breach of faith.

Georgia added insult to injury:

Deprivation of Louisiana's rights must rest solely upon the spirit of revenge and lust of illicit power on the part of the political charlatans and deluded fanatics who have not shared the dangers of the battlefield, nor acquired the wisdom of statesmen, unlearned to appreciate the virtues and magnanimity of either the northern or southern soldiers.[38]

The effect of Johnson's insensitivity and the South's arrogance became apparent immediately. On February 19th Representative John Broomall of Pennsylvania introduced some resolutions that were passed immediately by a strictly party vote, 104–33. The second provided: "That whenever the people of any state are thus deprived of all civil government [by rebellion], it becomes the duty of Congress, by appropriate legislation, to enable them to organize a state government, and in the language of the Constitution, to guarantee to such state a republican form of government." This fell short of Sumner's Senate resolution, but it committed the Republican party to the guarantee clause as a device for reconstructing the South.[39]

[38] Johnson's 7 Feb. 1866 speech is reprinted in the 1866 *American Annual Cyclopaedia*, 749–750. The Alabama and Georgia resolutions appear in *ibid.*, 10 and 448.

[39] *Globe*, 39 Cong., 1 sess., 916 ff. (19 Feb. 1866).

Debates on other issues during the remainder of the first session of the Thirty-ninth Congress indicated that the majority of congressional Republicans were moving toward a conception of the guarantee clause similar to Sumner's. Sumner's unpopularity and advanced thinking made it unlikely that he could bring his colleagues around completely to his point of view, but Johnson and the Democrats were pushing moderate Republicans far beyond their limited original aims for Reconstruction. The most important result of this radical drift was the acceptance of the idea that republican government was impossible where a large minority of a state's citizens were disfranchised. The guarantee clause did not necessarily require the enfranchisement of all Negroes everywhere, but it forbade their wholesale proscription where they were numerous. Representative William Lawrence of Ohio expressed this new viewpoint in debates on passing the Civil Rights Bill over Johnson's veto:

A state which denies to half its citizens not only all political, but their essential civil rights, recognized and confirmed by the Constitution and described in this bill, has ceased to be republican in form, and the Constitution has made it the duty of Congress to "guarantee" such form of government. This it may do by law in this form.[40]

As the end of the first session of the Thirty-ninth Congress drew near, it was obvious that Republican thought on the guarantee clause varied. Sumner, representing the most forward position, would have it prohibit all racial disqualifications; some moderates, like Lawrence, thought only that

[40] *Ibid.*, 1836 (7 April 1866). See also Rep. George Boutwell, *ibid.*, 3976 (20 July 1866); Sumner, *ibid.*, 4207 (27 July 1866).

it became operative on quantitative conditions; others like John A. Bingham of Ohio would have been content if a mere majority of adult males in a state had the vote.[41]

Suddenly at the end of the first session, almost all of these divergent views coalesced. The precipitant was the majority report of the Joint Committee on Reconstruction. This report, drawn up by Fessenden, was so skillfully done that only Sumner on one extreme and the Democrats on the other were excluded from the consensus it produced. It eschewed all explicit theories about the status of the seceded states—"profitless abstractions" the report called them. It then crushed the Democratic argument that the guarantee clause required the federal government to maintain the existing state governments or the state constitutions as they were in 1860:

By withdrawing their representatives in Congress, by renouncing the privilege of representation, by organizing a separate government, and by levying war against the United States, they destroyed their state constitutions in respect to the vital principle which connected their respective states to the Union and secured their federal relations; and nothing of those constitutions was left of which the United States were bound to take notice.

This left the people of the seceded states "deprived of all civil government," at least of the sort that Congress could recognize.

[41] For Bingham's views, see John Syrett, "John Armour Bingham and Reconstruction," unpublished M.A. thesis, University of Wisconsin, 1967, ch. 4. An interesting compromise solution is described in Robert Dale Owen, "Political Results from the Varioloid," *Atlantic Monthly,* XXXV (1875), 660–670. Owen's plan, which he claims had the support of a majority of the Joint

But the presidentially appointed provisional governments were no better. The only authority for the President to act in the matter of southern state government was derived from his capacity as commander in chief of the Union forces. This placed the stigma of military government on all the extant southern governments except Tennessee's. The power to pass on the forms of government to be adopted by the reconstructed states was exclusively a function of Congress.

The first step to be taken toward normalizing relations between these states and the Union, the report continued, was the inauguration of republican forms of government by the people of the ten unrestored states. In any event, whatever new constitutions were drawn up would have to be ratified by the people. Next, the attitude of the southern people must improve: "They should exhibit in their acts something more than an unwilling submission to an unavoidable necessity—a feeling, if not cheerful, certainly not offensive and defiant." Finally, the results of the war would somehow have to be guaranteed: the rebel debt must be repudiated, civil rights must be accorded to freedmen, and the worst rebels disfranchised, temporarily at least. The report ducked altogether the question of Negro suffrage.[42]

Committee at one point, would have struck down all racial restrictions in voting, but not until 1876. This may have represented a fourth position, not as advanced as Sumner's but beyond Lawrence's quantitative view.

[42] H.R. Report 30, 39 Cong., 1 sess., doc. 1273 (1866). The minority report simply reiterated the Democratic viewpoint first announced in 1862: the states are all equal; none are out of the Union; none forfeited their rights; they all have republican forms of government; therefore, they are all entitled to immediate

Because Fessenden's report was designed to reconcile divergent views in the Republican party, it avoided firm ideological or theoretical commitments. The only point made with unmistakable clarity was that Reconstruction was a matter for Congress, not the President. Despite its vague contours, the report was the high-water mark of Republican development of the guarantee clause in the first session. The second session of the Thirty-ninth Congress would concern itself with implementing the theoretical consensus embodied in the report.

The guarantee clause was cited and debated on many occasions in the second session, but its most thorough expostulation came in connection with two measures: the bill admitting Nebraska to the Union and H.R.543, the predecessor of the Military Reconstruction Act of 2 March 1867. Until March 1867 the majority of Republicans in both houses became progressively more radical in the face of Democratic opposition. But passage of the 2 March 1867 Act seemed to exhaust the possibilities of the clause in the minds of the Republican majority. It was never explicitly abandoned, but it was increasingly ignored. Beginning with the Fortieth Congress, Republicans seemed to seek ways to evade the clause, as if its command embarrassed them.

The first order of business for the second session of the Thirty-ninth Congress was the Nebraska admission bill, which had been lost in the welter of more important business in the first session. Republicans had gone so far toward Sumner's views of the guarantee clause that they were prepared to attach a condition precedent to the admission bill forbidding the new state to discriminate on the basis of

readmission. The power to prescribe forms of government belongs exclusively to the people of the states, not to Congress.

race in the matter of political rights. To justify this action, they had to accept something quite close to Sumner's theories. Of course, admitting a new state with conditions precedent was different from readmitting the seceded states, but the principles enunciated could serve as precedent or as analogy for readmission of the southern states.

Nebraska's territorial enabling act (1864) had not imposed any requirement of Negro suffrage on the territory, and the constitution that the state presented in 1867 limited the franchise to whites. Sumner objected and, surprisingly, found his Republican colleagues willing to go along with his views. As J. A. J. Creswell of Maryland explained, it was clear that the Tenth Amendment could not override the powers confided to Congress by the guarantee clause. His colleague James F. Wilson of Iowa began to develop the argument that the clause empowered Congress to supervise all amendments to all state constitutions, even after their admission, but the hammer fell in the middle of his speech, and the point was dropped.[43]

For once Democrats presented a creditable rebuttal to the Republican arguments. Senator Elijah Hise of Kentucky pointed out two weaknesses in the Republican interpretation. First, whatever else republican government might mean, it certainly required self-government. Usually this argument, which had appeared often before, was a dodge or a euphemistic way of insisting that the southern state governments must remain in the hands of white men; "self-government" always had the implicit qualification "white." But Hise argued that now Republicans claimed the power to impose so many conditions on a state's ad-

[43] *Globe*, 39 Cong., 2 sess., App. 57 (8 Jan. 1867); 476 (15 Jan. 1867); 479 (15 Jan. 1867).

mission that the constitution would not be the work of the people it was to govern. Second, Hise pointed out:

You now assume the right and claim the authority, whenever a majority of Congress of the United States may decide that there is some law or some provision of the constitution of a State, or some line of domestic policy which may be adopted by a state, in opposition to your party views, to say that the form of government of that state is not republican.

Whatever Hise's motives or assumptions, the point he raised has some validity. The guarantee clause, after all, can be enforced by statute, which is to say that it is whatever a majority of Congress wants to make of it. But the Republicans had the votes, and the Nebraska bill passed. Johnson vetoed it, and it was promptly repassed over his veto.[44]

Congress then turned to a pending bill, H.R.543, "to reorganize the governments in the seceded states," the forerunner of the Military Reconstruction Act. This bill embodied all the premises of the majority report of the Joint Committee. Section 2 of the bill provided that the state governments created under the auspices of Johnson's proclamations were *de facto* governments whose acts were valid only for municipal purposes. It went on to declare that these governments were not republican in form because of their military origin.

---

[44] *Ibid.*, 189–190 (19 Dec. 1867); 475 (15 Jan. 1867). Charles O. Lerche, "The Guarantee of a Republican Form of Government and the Admission of New States," *J. of Politics*, XI (1949), 578–604 at 591, argues that the Nebraska bill was the zenith of the guarantee clause in Reconstruction. See the same author's "Congressional Interpretations of the Guarantee of a Republican Form of Government during Reconstruction," *J. Southern Hist.*, XV (1949), 192–211.

Republicans took up the bill in a mood of shock brought on by the Memphis and New Orleans racial massacres in the spring of 1866, determined to undo Johnson's governments and provide greater security to ex-slaves. In debates on the bill, both parties rehashed guarantee clause arguments that by then had become stale. Democrats like Michael Kerr of Indiana argued that the guarantee clause was designed by the framers to prevent precisely what the Republicans were about to do: using force to impose a constitution on the people of a state without their consent. They also taunted Republicans with inconsistency. If republican government requires universal suffrage, why did Republicans not support woman suffrage? The Republicans took the question seriously and tried to evade the challenge by definitions of "the people" that were as disingenuous as those of their opponents.[45]

H.R.543 was unsatisfactory to its Republican sponsors, who feared that the machinery for its enforcement might prove ineffectual, and it was referred to the Joint Committee on Reconstruction, which had the effect of killing it. In its place emerged H.R.1143, the first military Reconstruction bill. This bill, originally drafted by George Julian, adopted the premises of H.R.543, but went beyond it in its provisions for military reconstruction. Although eclipsed in the elaborate political maneuvers that were required to get the bill passed, the guarantee clause's importance for the bill's forerunner, H.R.543, was so considerable that the Military Reconstruction Act may properly be considered the fruition of it.[46]

[45] *Globe*, 39 Cong., 2 sess., 350–351 (8 Jan. 1867), 624 (21 Jan. 1867).

[46] The legislative history of H.R. 1143 is well summarized in McKitrick, *Andrew Johnson and Reconstruction*, 473–485. Presi-

The first Military Reconstruction Act divided the ten ex-Confederate states (Tennessee being the exception) into five military districts, each under the command of a brigadier general of the army. The commanding generals were empowered to enforce the laws through regular civil officials or military commissions. They were charged with ultimate responsibility for all peacekeeping activities in their districts, and their authority was nearly absolute.

The Military Reconstruction Acts did not, however, immediately replace the extant civilian governments of the states—a point worth emphasizing since folk belief has it that Congress swept away civilian governments in favor of military commissions and armies of occupation. Rather, the generals were ordered to call for the election of delegates to constitutional conventions. Blacks were allowed to vote at these elections, but certain high Confederate officials were not. A new state constitution had to enfranchise the same classes of persons who voted in the constitutional convention; that is, it had to accord the ballot to Negroes. After the constitution was ratified by a majority of qualified voters, elections were to be held for a regular state government. Not until this civilian government took office would the presidential governments be replaced. The new legislature had to ratify the Fourteenth Amendment. At that point the state's senators- and representatives-elect could present themselves to Congress and request their seats.[47]

The rise and fall of the guarantee clause between 1861 and 1877 paralleled that of Reconstruction itself. Both the clause and Reconstruction generally were in their crescent

---

dent Johnson vetoed the bill and Republicans passed it over his veto the same day.

[47] Act of 2 March 1867, ch. 153, 14 Stat. 428.

phases until March 1867; both began their decade of decline thereafter. There was an interplay of causality. A vigorous policy of Reconstruction would require an expansion of all available constitutional bases to support it, once it was decided not to add radical amendments to the original Constitution (aside from the Thirteenth Amendment). Conversely, when the policy of Reconstruction was contracted and abandoned the guarantee clause would shrink. Its radical potential in an antiradical age would be an unwanted, inconvenient, discomfiting presence. The clause could be ignored only by an astonishing disavowal of principle, but this was exactly what happened after March 1867.

Because Congress soon receded from the positions it took concerning the guarantee power in 1867, we need not conclude that it reversed itself. The clause emerged, stood forward for a time in nearly all its inherent power, and then sunk back to a state of disuse as congressmen, for reasons unrelated to the clause's meaning, abandoned their early determination to hold the people of the southern states to a strict account as the price of readmission to full rights in the Union.

Reconstruction represented the confluence of two earlier streams of interpretation of the guarantee clause. One was the old antislavery argument that slavery and republican government were incompatible. This argument was carried a step forward by Republicans in the late 1860s when they argued that republicanism and the white man's government demanded by the South were equally incompatible. This stream of interpretation was commingled with the second, which insisted that the essence of republican government was popular control of the machinery of government.

But the history of the guarantee clause in Reconstruction is not one of unmitigated failure. If the one great ideal of interracial polities in the southern states was not realized, another was—the United States was now clearly a nation, not a confederation. Thus the nationalizing impetus of the guarantee clause was at last fully realized.

7

Reconstruction:
Diminuendo, 1867–1877

The effective impact of the guarantee clause began to dissipate once the Military Reconstruction Act of 2 March 1867 had been passed. This was not immediately apparent, at least not to the more radical congressional Republicans. Rhetorically, the momentum of the clause's development continued well into the Fortieth Congress (1867–1869). Charles Sumner and others outlined far-reaching applications of it as late as 1868. But by then its force was spent as an element in congressional policy-making, principally because the temporary and forced Republican consensus that produced the March 2nd Act dissolved speedily.

The loss of consensus became increasingly apparent between 1868 and 1874 in three different conflicts that clamored for congressional solution. The expulsion of Negro members from the Georgia legislature in 1868, the political anarchy and near-civil war in Arkansas from 1872 to 1874, and similar conditions in Louisiana in 1872 might all have been handled through application of the guarantee by the Congress. In the latter two the President begged Congress to do something, and the Supreme Court had already given wide berth to Congress to do pretty much as it pleased. Yet Congress refused to act under the guarantee clause. The Republicans seemed thoroughly disenchanted with their experiment in reconstructing southern society and politics. They pursued their own version of a policy of "masterly inactivity," as Republican Senator Oliver Morton called it, and left the Arkansas and Louisiana crises to be resolved by the President.

In the same period the Supreme Court ratified Republican policy in several cases which, if nothing else, allowed for future expansion of the guarantee clause. The net immediate effect of these cases was to leave the clause what it had been since *Luther* v. *Borden*, an open-ended authorization to Congress to work out its own conception of what was required in a republican form of government and to implement this conception as it saw fit. But the northern public seemed as wearied of the southern problem as Congress, and the clause was quietly ignored.

Charles Sumner's penchant for offering declaratory resolutions was undaunted by his persistent failure and by his colleagues' vexation with him. Although his February 1866 resolutions failed, he offered a new and more advanced set at the opening of the second session of the Thirty-ninth Congress (5 December 1866). The December resolutions differed from their February predecessors in that Sumner was now trying to read the principles of the Declaration of Independence into the Constitution via the guarantee clause and to apply these principles to northern as well as southern states as an open-ended assurance of responsive and egalitarian state government. The fourth resolution provided:

That, in determining what is a republican form of government, Congress must follow implicitly the definition supplied by the Declaration of Independence, and in the practical application of this definition, it must, after excluding all disloyal persons, take care that new governments are founded on the fundamental truths therein contained; first, that all men are equal in rights; and secondly, that just government stands only on the consent of the governed.

These resolutions were not denounced as the earlier ones were; they were simply ignored.[1]

Sumner's determination to expand the guarantee clause continued despite two important shifts in the climate of congressional opinion that occurred in the spring of 1867. The first of these was that Congress under its Republican leadership had determined to make the concepts of due process, equal protection of the laws, and equal privileges and immunities embodied in Section 1 of the Fourteenth Amendment the bases of its constitutional renovation in the South. Perhaps Congress could as well have drawn on the concepts of republican government as a basis for drafting the amendment, but it did not. This fundamental decision did not satisfy Sumner, and he determined to offer the guarantee clause as an alternative or a supplement to the majority policy.

Equally important was a change in the mood of Congress, a mood of growing lassitude and withdrawal from pursuing the goals of Reconstruction after passage of the first two Military Reconstruction Acts. Whether Sumner was fully aware of this change in mood is unimportant. What he did perceive was that Congress had at last set up some formidable machinery to accomplish southern Reconstruction. He also saw, correctly, that the policy of

[1] *Globe*, 39 Cong., 2 sess., 15 (5 Dec. 1866).

military Reconstruction was directed primarily toward restoring self-government to the southern states. A few Republican goals, either short-term, like disfranchisement of high-ranking Confederate officials, or permanent and elemental, like repudiation of the Confederate war debt, would be achieved; but Sumner saw no sufficient long-term guaranties for the great humanitarian objectives he advocated. He set about at once to remedy this defect, feeling that such powerful statutory machinery ought to be used to a good purpose. Accordingly he offered a new set of resolutions on March 11th, setting forth his goals for the reconstructed South. These included impartial suffrage, abolition of the Johnson governments, rebel disfranchisement, school desegregation, and homesteads for freedmen.[2]

These resolutions were immediately and thoroughly denounced by two of Sumner's fellow Republicans, John Sherman and Jacob Howard. But James Dixon, the "Johnsonized" Republican from Connecticut (as George Julian called him), glumly reminded Sherman that Sumner had proved to be an accurate prophet: Congress had come around to adopting a position that was startlingly radical when first proposed by Sumner during the war. This was close to the truth, and it did not sweeten the mood of moderate Republicans as the summer of 1867 wore on. The increasingly surly behavior of Sumner's colleagues toward him cannot be wholly accounted for by his lack of tact or common sense. Sumner had become the conscience of his party, but to men like Fessenden he was simply an officious nuisance.

This antipathy came to a head in July 1867, when Sum-

[2] *Globe*, 40 Cong., 1 sess., 50 (11 March 1867).

ner, still pushing his conception of the guarantee clause, tried to introduce S.124, a bill designed to enforce the guarantee and the Thirteenth Amendment. Its principal objective was Negro suffrage, to be mandatory throughout the Union, not just in the South. This was too much for other Republicans, and Sumner was not even allowed to offer his bill due to a rule recently adopted that limited the nature of bills to be considered for the remainder of the session. But before he was shut off, Democratic Senator Thomas A. Hendricks of Indiana needled the Republicans by observing, with much truth, that Sumner "is simply in advance logically of the other gentlemen of his party when he demands the same legislation for one state that they demand in another." [3]

Undeterred, Sumner carried on his one-man crusade to bring the guarantee clause to its full culmination by bringing up a bill (S.115) that he had introduced earlier and that was almost a duplicate of S.124. Then Sumner made his rhetorical leap that provides the central theme of the guarantee clause's history. It

is a clause which is like a sleeping giant in the Constitution, never until this recent war awakened, but now it comes forward with a giant's power. There is no clause in the Constitution like it. There is no clause which gives to Congress such supreme power over the states as that clause.

He thereby concurred with John C. Calhoun's views of the clause in 1843, though this irony was lost on his Senate colleagues. Unimpressed, they voted by a two-to-one margin against Sumner's motion to take up the bill.[4]

Sumner was not alone in failing to perceive that the

[3] *Ibid.*, 466, 498 (5 July 1867).   [4] *Ibid.*, 614 (12 July 1867).

guarantee clause had become irrelevant. Throughout the Fortieth Congress the clause was summoned by Radical Republicans to support various policy proposals, and it seemed as potent as ever. But this was an illusion.[5]

During intermittent debates on H.R.439, a supplementary Reconstruction bill never enacted, Congress went over the entire guarantee clause again. These debates served as a convenient recapitulation, a sort of valedictory, to the guarantee clause by a Reconstruction Congress. It was by then clear that in any clash of will between Congress and the President, Congress had the final say on the meaning and application of the guarantee. The Democratic construction of the clause, which would have restricted it to ensuring the continuation of pre-existing governments and would have defined "republican" by the standards of 1789, was unequivocally rejected. The states were subordinated to the power of the federal government by the clause: its *raison d'être* was to protect the people, not the administration in power or the old state constitution. Senator Oliver P. Morton of Indiana summed up the expansion of the clause to that point:

That provision [§4] contains a vast undefined power that has never yet been ascertained—a great supervisory power given to the United States to enable them to keep the states in their orbits, to preserve them from anarchy, revolution and rebellion. The measure of power thus conferred upon the government of the United States can only be determined by that which is requisite to guarantee or maintain in each state a legal and republican form of government. Whatever power, therefore, may be necessary to enable the Government

[5] See e.g., *ibid.*, 193 (18 March 1867); 512 (8 July 1867); 656 (15 July 1867).

of the United States thus to maintain in each state a republican form of government is conveyed by this power.[6]

Morton accurately summarized a few characteristics of the clause at the climacteric of its historical development: its ultimate contours remained undefined; it assured the paramountcy of national power over the states; it was plenary in the sense that it granted whatever means were necessary to achieve the goal of republican government in the states. But he slurred over the main issue that Sumner had doggedly pressed forward, namely, what were the requisite characteristics of a republican form of government? Did they include universal manhood suffrage, racial nondiscrimination, and absolute equality before the law?

Morton's reference to the need for putting down "anarchy" and "revolution" in the states would come back to haunt him and his colleagues in the next seven years. The enervation and demise of the guarantee clause after 1867 can be best traced in Congress' inaction in the face of political chaos in Georgia, Arkansas, and Louisiana between 1868 and 1874. By 1872 Republican determination to assure political equality to the Negro had so far shriveled that they could not summon enough support to end virtual civil war in Arkansas and Louisiana.

Under the first Military Reconstruction Act Georgia was placed under the supervision of Generals John Pope and, later, George G. Meade. A constitutional convention then framed a new state constitution. General Meade recognized the state government elected under the new constitution and relinquished all military control to the state's officials.

[6] See remarks of William Loughridge, *ibid.*, 573–574 (16 Jan. 1867); Charles A. Eldredge, 586 (16 Jan. 1867); Oliver P. Morton, 723 (24 Jan. 1868); George H. Williams, 958 (4 Feb. 1868).

Georgia was "readmitted" to the Union under the Omnibus Bill of June 1868. The United States House of Representatives at the same time admitted all seven of Georgia's members to their seats, but no action was taken by the Senate. Military Reconstruction was fully terminated in Georgia by the late summer of 1868.[7]

Although the Georgia constitution forbade racial discrimination at the polls, it said nothing about racial qualifications for office-holding. Taking advantage of this omission, both houses of the Georgia legislature refused to seat the three senators and twenty-nine representatives who were Negroes. To further cloud the legitimacy of the legislature, many of its white members—perhaps fifty-five in all—were ex-Confederates who had not taken the test oath required by the Military Reconstruction Acts. In the fall the Ku Klux Klan reared its hooded head and began intimidating Negroes and Georgia Unionists. After the November presidential elections resulted in the victory of Democratic electors, the regular Republican governor, Rufus Bullock, immediately declared that the entire state government was still "provisional."

The Georgia problem was quickly presented to the third session of the Fortieth Congress (autumn 1868) with two questions. Was Georgia's vote to be counted in the electoral

[7] For details of Reconstruction in Georgia, see three modern studies: Elizabeth S. Nathans, *Losing the Peace: Georgia Republicans and Reconstruction, 1865–1871* (Baton Rouge, 1968); Alan Conway, *The Reconstruction of Georgia* (Minneapolis, 1966); and Olive H. Shadgett, *The Republican Party in Georgia: From Reconstruction through 1900* (Athens, Ga., 1964), as well as two older works: C. Mildred Thompson, *Reconstruction in Georgia* (New York, 1915, Columbia Studies vol. LXIV), and Edwin C. Woolley, *The Reconstruction of Georgia* (New York, 1901, Columbia Studies vol. XIII).

college? Were Georgia's senators to be allowed to take their seats (the House members already having been seated)? Although Congress could temporize on the latter question, it could not on the first. Accordingly, the House Judiciary Committee held hearings on conditions in Georgia and came up with a compromise whereby the results of the electoral college vote were announced with and without Georgia's votes being counted. The Republican ticket of Grant and Colfax had a wide enough margin that it made no difference whether or not Georgia's Democratic votes were counted.

The electoral college compromise did not settle the question of the Georgia senators-elect. The House Judiciary Committee hearings revealed that more was involved in the swamp of Georgia politics than the unseating of the Negro legislators. Governor Bullock had made himself widely unpopular because of his radical stance and his vetoes of railroad-aid legislation, which, at that time, was a chief staple of internal politics in Georgia, as elsewhere in the South. Also at issue were the two Senate seats, the seats of the unsworn state legislators, and the rise of the Klan.

The problem was first dealt with in the Senate, which on 25 January 1869 refused to seat Senator-elect Joshua Hill. This embarrassed the House, which had already seated the Georgia members in the last session of the Fortieth Congress. The first session of the Forty-first avoided that precedent and referred the Georgians' credentials to its Committee on Elections, which recommended that they should not be seated on the basis of insignificant technical defects in the credentials.

So far the guarantee clause had not been important since the electoral college and seating problems were handled under other clauses of the Constitution. But the most important problem remained: what was to be done with the supposedly reconstructed state itself? A rigorous application of the guarantee clause such as that urged by Sumner in 1868 would have left Congress free to remake the Georgia government as it pleased. But Congress was not in a mood for drastic action; it simply did nothing throughout 1869 until President Grant, in his first annual message (6 December 1869), prodded it into action by reminding it that this state of affairs could not continue indefinitely. He suggested that Congress pass legislation to enable the Georgia legislature to reconvene and exclude the nonjuring ex-Confederates; he did not mention the unseated Negro legislators.[8]

Grant's proposal might not have produced any response except that Congress had by then sent out the Fifteenth Amendment for ratification. After its experience with the Fourteenth, it realized that every state's vote counted, and the Georgia impasse presented a chance to pick up Georgia's one necessary vote. Congress therefore opportunistically passed a bill for the re-Reconstruction of Georgia that required its ratification of the Fifteenth Amendment as the price of readmission. Georgia quickly complied by seating the blacks, unseating the unsworn Confederates, and ratifying the Amendment. It was immediately readmitted.

At no point in 1868 or 1869 did Congress try to solve the Georgia matter under the guarantee clause, although this would have been the most appropriate and convenient means. It would have taken only a slight elaboration of the March 1867 congressional consensus on the scope of the guarantee to establish the point that a state is deprived of a republican form of government when thirty-two duly elected legislators are refused their seats because of a caste

[8] Richardson, *Messages,* IX, 3981 ff.

qualification not recognized in the state constitution. Similarly, the seating of unqualified ex-Confederates might have the same effect. In any event, Congress had to resolve the problem posed by the anomalous status of the state, and no other clause in the Constitution seemed so appropriate. Yet in Congress' 1869 detumescent mood, the guarantee clause seemed irrelevant. The attitude of Congress was most clearly stated by Senator Jacob Howard during debates on the 1870 Georgia readmission bill:

> In a general sense, a republican government is a government in which the laws of the community are made by their representatives, freely chosen by the people; it is impossible, in my judgment, to give to the word "republic" any more exact or precise meaning than that. There is no particular standard that I am aware of that can be set up as the test by which the government of a state of the Union can be tried or ascertain whether it is republican or not. It is popular government; it is the voice of the people expressed through their representatives.

In this weary, half-apologetic retreat from radicalism, Howard spoke for his party and for the postwar spirit of reform. With only a slight change of mood, Howard's tired statement might have been spoken by the Democrats a few years earlier.[9]

If the Republican performance was feeble in 1869, it was still better than nothing. By 1872, when Arkansas and Louisiana both degenerated into chaos, even the flickering embers of the old radical fire had smoldered out. The guarantee clause was forgotten just when it was most needed. If ever reason existed for the national government mediat-

[9] *Globe*, 41 Cong., 2 sess., 2022 (17 March 1870).

ing the affairs of the states, it was in Arkansas and Louisiana in 1872, but the reform impulse had so far evaporated that Congress let those states drift in anarchy for two and four years respectively.

Arkansas' government had been declared "provisional" by the 2 March 1867 Act, and a new constitution had been drawn up. By 1868 the Republican party in Arkansas, under the pressures of the anomalous and artificial political circumstances of Reconstruction, demonstrated a fatal fissile tendency by splitting into regular and reform factions, each anathematizing the other. The approach of the 1872 elections, which would elect a whole slate of state officers as well as presidential electors and congressmen, destroyed the balance of forces and shattered all political alliances in Arkansas.[10]

In 1872 there were four factions—they cannot be called parties—in the field: regular Republicans, who supported President Ulysses S. Grant; two reform sects, "Brindletails" and "Liberals," differing only in that the former supported a reform candidate named Joseph Brooks for governor and the latter did not, though both supported Liberal Republican candidate Horace Greeley rather than Grant for Presi-

[10] The summary of Arkansas politics is based on Thomas S. Staples, *Reconstruction in Arkansas, 1862–1874* (New York, 1923, Columbia Studies, vol. CIX). David Y. Thomas, *Arkansas in War and Reconstruction, 1861–1874* (Little Rock, 1926), although written by a professional historian, is a shallow and biased survey. John M. Harrell, *The Brooks and Baxter War* (St. Louis, 1893), succeeds in making the disorder and confusion of the past even more disorderly and confusing in the retelling. Both the latter books, however, reprint some useful documents. A good recapitulation of the violence in both Arkansas and Louisiana is contained in S. Doc. 263, 67 Cong., 2 sess., ser. 7985 (1922), "Federal Aid in Domestic Disturbances, 1903–1922."

dent; and the Democrats, who adopted an avowedly racist platform but supported Greeley and Brooks, apparently reasoning that the enemy of my enemy is my friend. The regulars shrewdly chose a native Georgian, Elisha Baxter, as their candidate for governor. By thus removing the carpetbagger stigma, they disorganized the reform groups.

The election of 1872 was marred by extensive fraud, intimidation, and bribery. It is difficult, even now, to determine which candidate won on the basis of bona fide ballots. But the regulars controlled the state's election-return machinery and declared that their candidate (Baxter) had been elected governor. The Brooks faction in the legislature determined to organize separately and declare Brooks elected. To forestall this, Baxter courted the Democrats with promises of a constitutional convention for 1873 that would remove all political disabilities on whites. With Democratic help, Baxter organized a state government. The mobs that had begun to collect in Little Rock dispersed, and Arkansas seemed to have narrowly averted a crisis.

Unfortunately for themselves and the people of the state, the Arkansas Republicans could not restrain their tendency to fission. The persistent postwar problem of railroad-aid bonds precipitated a new split. To sustain his vetoes on some bond issues Baxter had to woo the Democrats more ardently than ever. This cost him the support of most Republicans, who charged him with corruption, revived Brooks's cause, and began *quo warranto* proceedings to oust Baxter. An Arkansas circuit court judge was prevailed upon to uphold Brooks's claim. He was sworn in by his faction in the legislature and seized the offices of the state government. Both Baxter and Brooks then organized militia forces, and Arkansas teetered at the brink of civil war by the spring of 1874.

The events of this period have ever since been known in Arkansas as "the Brooks-Baxter War."

It was at this point that Grant and Congress were called upon to mediate Arkansas affairs in a way reminiscent of the events of 1842 in Rhode Island. Baxter asked Grant for aid in maintaining his administration under section 4's domestic violence clause, but Grant moved with extreme caution. His attorney general, the one-time Radical Senator George Williams, advised Grant to keep hands off and to use federal troops only to prevent bloodshed. He suggested that the whole problem be left to the Arkansas courts to unravel. A proposed compromise fell apart, however, and skirmishing between rival militia forces grew so ominous that no time was left for bargaining, persuasion, or procrastination.

Williams abandoned his earlier position and submitted a memorandum to the President that stated, without expressly citing Taney's *Luther* opinion, that Grant was obliged to act under section 4 and that Grant must decide for himself which governor was rightfully elected and which government was "republican." Williams concluded that, under the terms of the Arkansas constitution, Baxter was the legitimate governor. Grant immediately issued a proclamation ordering the mobs and armed groups opposed to Baxter to disperse. Thus was the Tyler-Taney precedent of a generation earlier reaffirmed.[11]

This, however, was not the end of the Arkansas matter. Republicans disgruntled at the election of Democrat Augustus H. Garland as governor in 1874 issued an "Address,"

[11] Williams' opinion is in Harrell, *Brooks and Baxter War,* 249–252. Grant's proclamation is in Richardson, *Messages,* IX, 4226–4227.

insisting that Congress, under the guarantee clause, must determine whether a state government existed and must provide a new government for the state if it did not, thus echoing the Dorrites of a generation before. They urged Congress to oust Garland because of irregularities in the election of 1872. This petition produced the appointment of the House Select Committee on Arkansas Affairs, called the "Poland Committee" after its chairman, Representative Luke Poland, a Vermont Republican. The Poland Committee held hearings in Washington and made an investigation in Arkansas. Both Brooks's and Baxter's supporters appeared before the committee and both found authority for their positions in the guarantee clause. Brooks's supporters insisted that Baxter did not receive a majority of the ballots in the 1872 election. Hence, they concluded, Congress must intervene to set aside this "executive usurpation." Baxter's men, cooperating with the Democrats to support the Garland administration, insisted that the clause obliged the federal government to support the regularly inaugurated administration.[12]

Both sides insisted that Congress had power under the guarantee clause to set aside Grant's decision. The President, they urged, must act on the basis of prima facie evidence, but Congress may investigate in a more leisurely way, and if it is satisfied that the President's spur-of-the-moment decision was erroneous, may reverse it and replace the extant government. Neither group, however, under-

[12] The "Address" of the Arkansas State Republican Convention is reprinted in S. Ex. Doc. 25, 43 Cong., 2 sess., ser. 1629 (1875). This document also contains the majority report of the committee. The arguments of Brooks's and Baxter's attorneys are reprinted in S. Misc. Doc. 65, 43 Cong., 2 sess., ser. 1630 (1875).

stood the temper of the congressional Republicans. Poland and his party had no stomach for further involvement in southern state affairs, the guarantee clause notwithstanding. Despite uncontroverted evidence to the contrary, the Poland Committee's majority report concluded that Arkansans had a government that was republican in form, "manned by officers of their choice, and going forward with reasonable quiet and peace." Any "irregularities" in the 1872 election had been cured by the acquiescence of the people. Hence Congress should not interfere in any way with the state government. The House readily acceded to the majority's recommendation by a vote of 150–81, thus leaving the Grant-backed regime in control.

Congress' refusal to settle the 1872 election on the merits was defensible. The "irregularities," as Poland euphemistically called them, probably could not be corrected in 1874, but that did not justify complete congressional noninvolvement. If the guarantee of republican government is to have any meaning, it must surely imply at least that the nation can intervene in state affairs to prevent a civil war from breaking out between partisan factions. This minimal intervention was undertaken reluctantly and after long delay by the President, with no help from Congress. In addition, republican government should also require the purity of the electoral process, if self-government and majority rule are to be anything more than pious slogans. Yet Congress swept under the rug the admissions of Baxter's supporters that the state returning board had acted corruptly in certifying his election. The guarantee clause at the end of the Reconstruction period had become a dead letter; Congress abdicated all responsibility under it.

Conditions in Louisiana between 1872 and 1876 were

worse than in neighboring Arkansas. Election frauds were more blatant; whites resorted to the rope and the faggot more often; newspapers explicitly advocated the lynching of federal officials, army generals, and the President of the United States. Louisiana, at the end of Reconstruction, seemed the antithesis of free republican government.

In 1868 three factions dominated Louisiana politics: the white-supremacist Democrats, a "Conservative Union" group that soon fused with the Democrats, and the regular Republicans. The most prominent of the Republicans was young Henry Clay Warmoth, twenty-six years old when elected governor in 1868. Warmoth was the first governor chosen under the Reconstruction constitution of 1868.[13]

The Louisiana Republican party was just as fissile as Arkansas' under the stresses of local and national politics. Warmoth alienated many white Louisiana voters by his vetoes of railroad-aid bills and most black voters by his veto of a state civil rights bill, losses that he tried to recoup by appeals to moderate Democrats in the state. His increasing hostility to Grant after 1871 stimulated the development of a "customs-house" clique led by James F. Casey, collector of customs for New Orleans and a brother-in-law of Grant's wife. This clique combined forces with another Republican faction led by P. B. S. Pinchback, Negro lieutenant governor, to back William P. Kellogg for governor.

[13] No satisfactory published study of Reconstruction in Louisiana exists. Ella Lonn, *Reconstruction in Louisiana after 1868* (New York, 1918), is the most thorough account, but it is weakened by its Negrophobia and sympathy for the Democrats. It is a sequel to John R. Ficklen, *History of Reconstruction in Louisiana through 1868* (Baltimore, 1910), which is incomplete and superficial. Warmoth tells his own story in Henry C. Warmoth, *War, Politics and Reconstruction* (New York, 1930), a naturally partisan account that is spoiled by omissions.

This left Warmoth's Liberal Republicans a faction without a party, and they in turn shifted their allegiance to the Democrats' candidate for governor, the racist John McEnery.

The 1872 state and national elections in Louisiana, like those in Arkansas, were marked by extensive corruption, intimidation, fraud, and other forms of chicane. The real trouble, however, arose after the election when the returning board met to certify the results. The five-man board was riven by faction; two members resigned, others were appointed, and the board finally split into two groups, one of which certified the election of Kellogg and the other, McEnery. Suits and countersuits were brought in the state courts to void the canvass of both bodies, but the most important legal action took place before United States Circuit Court Judge E. H. Durrell. Durrell, by a series of restraining orders, upheld the returns of the pro-Kellogg group. United States Attorney General Williams ordered federal marshals to enforce all the judge's orders, which effectively threw the weight of the federal government behind the anti-Warmoth ticket.

If the pro-Kellogg returns were accepted, Pinchback would be elected to the United States House of Representatives, and Louisiana's electoral votes counted for Grant. As soon as the Kellogg-Pinchback faction of the legislature met, it impeached Warmoth, which, under the terms of the Louisiana constitution, suspended him from office. Pinchback now became governor. But McEnery claimed that he was elected governor, and that part of the legislature sympathetic to him and Warmoth organized separately. Louisiana was plunged into anarchy under two governments, each of which organized its militia.

This time Congress could not avoid stepping in. The

electoral returns had to be sorted out to determine whether Louisiana's votes should go to Grant or Greeley; both houses of Congress would be faced with rival claimants to seats; everyone outside Louisiana and most persons in the state believed that Judge Durrell's action was improper; and Grant steadfastly refused to do anything beyond what would be minimally necessary to prevent a shooting war from breaking out between the militias. The Senate Committee on Privileges and Elections was ordered to determine whether there was any "legal state government in Louisiana." [14]

The problem of the electoral college vote was speedily solved. Both houses agreed that Louisiana's vote should not be counted. The majority of the Senate Elections Committee concluded that there was no government at all in Louisiana, though they felt that McEnery probably got a majority of the legally cast votes. Referring to the guarantee clause, they insisted that the clause empowered Congress to determine whether a state government existed and whether it was republican:

When the frauds committed are so glaring and widespread as to create public discontent in the state, and the organization of two rival governments threatening civil war, and it is manifest that neither government has been fairly elected, this power of the National Government [the guarantee clause] must be regarded as wise and salutary.

The majority recommended passage of a bill they reported out, S.1621.[15]

[14] *Globe*, 42 Cong., 3 sess., 641 (16 Jan. 1873).

[15] S. Rept. 457, 42 Cong., 3 sess., ser. 1549 (1873) contains the majority report, all three minority reports, and a mass of testimony and affidavits.

The committee chairman, Oliver P. Morton, dissenting, favored recognition of the Kellogg regime, President Grant's position. Morton was the only member of the committee who could be considered a Radical Republican several years earlier, but he ironically insisted that the guarantee clause should not be used to settle the Louisiana question since federal power under the clause was "too great." This marked the full and final abandonment by the once-Radical Republicans of the guarantee clause.

S.1621 was an attempt to cut the Gordian knot of the Louisiana returns by ordering a new election under federal supervision. Whether this would have been successful without more army supervision than Grant was willing to authorize is doubtful since harassment of federal inspectors was widespread in Louisiana. But S.1621 was at least an effort to do something. Wisconsin Senator Matt Carpenter of the committee supported the bill and insisted that Congress had power to impose such a solution on Louisiana under the guarantee clause; but Senator Henry B. Anthony of Rhode Island, one of Grant's men in the Senate, cut the ground out from under him and the rest of the committee majority by insisting that invoking the guarantee clause to undo the 1872 election was too extreme a remedy. Voicing the sentiments of most of his Senate colleagues, Anthony argued that Judge Durrell's action was a nullity because a political question was involved. On this, at least, there was complete agreement in the Senate.

Most of the senators also seemed to feel that if Congress took any action at all, state governments would exist only "at the sufferance of Congress." Missouri Senator Carl Schurz, another one-time Radical who had by then exchanged his earlier concern about Negro rights for other reform activities, killed what little Republican enthusiasm was left either for the bill or for the guarantee clause by providing a disingenuous and self-contradictory rationale for congressional inaction. Schurz argued that, although McEnery was properly elected, a republican government did exist in Louisiana under Kellogg and that it was functioning successfully. This was patently untrue—neither regime could collect taxes—but Kellogg's was satisfactorily republican for the idealists-turned-opportunists who now composed the Republican party.[16]

S.1621 was rejected and Congress soon adjourned. This threw the whole problem back into the lap of the President, who would have gladly avoided all responsibility for it. But Grant had earlier warned Congress that if they did nothing, he would uphold whatever regime was recognized by the Louisiana courts. Since this happened to be the Kellogg group, Grant issued a dispersal proclamation, ordering Kellogg's opponents to disband. Despite savage objections by Louisiana Democrats, Grant's action was successful, and Kellogg was maintained in power by occupation-army bayonets long enough to produce a similar electoral impasse in 1876 that had far more serious consequences for the nation than the 1872 elections.

Reaction to the decisions of Congress and the President was ambivalent. The *Central Law Journal* strongly condemned Grant's support of the Kellogg regime in Louisiana based on judicial decisions because any court action on a political question was void. This organ of the midwestern bar insisted that the President must not quash an insurrec-

[16] *Globe*, 42 Cong., 3 sess., 1520–1521, 1854–1874 (20 Feb., 27 Feb. 1873).

tion aimed at overthrowing a usurper, that is, Kellogg.[17]

An even more prestigious assertion of this view was a widely read article by the eminent treatise-writer, judge, and law professor, Thomas M. Cooley, in the *International Review* of 1875. The failure of Reconstruction in its attempt to reorder southern society produced a reaction against federal power under the guarantee clause, and Cooley became an exponent of this reaction. He argued that the federal and state governments were dual sovereignties that could not cross the invisible boundary between their domains. Cooley insisted that because of this dual sovereignty, federal interference in state affairs should occur only on the most extraordinary occasions, which he rigidly defined as a change to monarchical governments.

The federal government, Cooley continued, had no power to pass on the validity of election returns; it had to support whatever regime was in power. Nor could it intervene because the state excluded some of its citizens from the franchise; representative government did not require that all male adults should vote. Racial discrimination at the ballot box was perfectly compatible with republican government. Cooley's reaction against the progressive interpretation of the guarantee clause was so violent that he adopted the most conservative Whig views of the 1840s and Democratic views of the 1860s: those excluded from the ballot could seek a remedy only from those enfranchised, and if they resorted to insurrection the federal government must use all its force to repress them.[18]

[17] Anon., "The Louisiana Question," *Central L.J.*, I (1874), 475–476.

[18] [Thomas M. Cooley], "The Guarantee of Order and Re-

Cooley agreed that republicanism was not a question for the courts; *Luther* v. *Borden* had settled that. But it was not properly a matter for Congress or the President either, unless a state government had indisputably become a monarchy. Mere "wrongs and abuses" in the operation of state government could not call the guarantee into operation. The state agencies (courts, returning boards, or whatever else the state constitution specified) could pass on the legitimacy of a state regime, and the federal government's protective power extended only to the properly accredited regime. This conservative conclusion was further qualified by Cooley's insistence that a regime established by usurpation or violence could become legitimate if the people tolerated it for any length of time. Thus was a constitutional rationalization provided for the "redemption" of the South. In the words of an approving commentary on Cooley's views, the federal government must enforce the guarantee even if that made it "the constant and permanent agent of repression." Reaction against the progressive promise of the guarantee clause could not go further.[19]

The United States Supreme Court's involvement with

---

publican Government in the States," *International Rev.*, II (1875), 57–87. Although the article was published anonymously, it was an open secret that Cooley was the author, as indicated by comment on it in other journals.

[19] Anon., "The Guarantee of Order and Republican Governments in the States," *Central L.J.*, II (1875), 18–20. See also Cooley's *Treatise on Constitutional Limitations which Rest upon the Legislative Power of the States of the American Union* (4th ed., Boston, 1878), 23, and his *The General Principles of Constitutional Law* (Boston, 1880), 194–197. See also Herman von Holst, *The Constitutional Law of the United States of America* (Chicago, 1887), 239–242; William A. Dunning, "Are the States Equal under the Constitution," *Pol. Sci. Q.*, III (1888), 425–453.

the guarantee clause was peripheral throughout the Reconstruction period. After its decision in the *Prize Cases* (1863) recognizing presidential and congressional discretion in the conduct of the war, the court did not deliver a prominent opinion on the nature of the Union and the relation of the states to the nation until it handed down its opinion in *Mississippi* v. *Johnson* on 15 April 1867. Hence for all the crescendo period of the guarantee clause's development, the Supreme Court silently acquiesced in congressional policy. It did not speak until the clause's development had peaked and had begun its decline.

The Court was suddenly drawn into the disputes over the nature of the Union by Mississippi's petition in April of 1867 for an injunction against President Johnson to restrain him from enforcing the Military Reconstruction Act. Chief Justice Salmon P. Chase, who wrote the Court's opinion, was so eager to avoid passing on the legality of the act that he treated the injunction action as if it were a petition for a mandamus and applied the legal doctrine governing mandamus—relief lies only for ministerial, not discretionary, acts—in a suit where it was inapplicable. This difficulty Chase dismissed by saying that the same general principles covered both types of proceedings.[20]

Mississippi v. *Johnson* had not raised guarantee clause

---

[20] *Mississippi* v. *Johnson*, 4 Wall. 475 (U.S. 1867). In private correspondence, Chase had made it clear that he believed Congress and the President should have a free hand in restoring the states under any theory they wished to adopt. See Chase to John R. Young, 29 June 1867, in Robert B. Warden, *The Private Life and Public Services of Salmon Portland Chase* (Cincinnati, 1874), 667. See also Chase to William P. Mellen, 26 March 1862, in Jacob W. Schuckers, *The Life and Public Services of Salmon Portland Chase* (New York, 1874), 364.

issues, but its companion case, *Georgia* v. *Stanton*, did. At-torneys for Georgia sought to enjoin Secretary of War Edwin M. Stanton and two generals from enforcing the Military Reconstruction Act. United States Attorney General Henry Stanbery replied that the petition in effect asked the Court to pass on a political question, something that it had refused to do in *Luther* v. *Borden.* Justice Samuel Nelson, writing for the majority (the Chief Justice con-curred; no dissents), accepted Stanbery's argument. Holding that the Court had no jurisdiction over the subject matter because it involved a political, not a judicial, question, Nelson dismissed the petition.[21]

No one denied that military supervision of Georgia's government was incompatible with any definition of a "re-publican form of government." The only real question presented to the Court on the merits was whether the ex-traordinary conditions of the Civil War and the postwar South made it necessary to suspend the guarantee briefly until self-government by Georgians could be resumed under conditions that insured the permanence of a state govern-ment under the Constitution. This dilemma—can the Con-stitution be abrogated briefly for its own preservation—had been easy enough to confront when Confederate armies marched from the Potomac to the Mississippi, but it was ex-cruciatingly difficult after Appomattox. The Court was therefore not altogether wrong in deciding *Georgia* v. *Stanton* as it did; it presented a metajudicial question for which the courts could not very well provide enforceable solutions. Yet the issue was not entirely the simple matter of deciding which arm of the federal government was to be responsible for Reconstruction, which was the effect of the

[21] *Georgia* v. *Stanton*, 6 Wall. 50 (U.S. 1868).

Court's disposition of the Georgia case on the jurisdictional point. The guarantee clause was more than a grant of power to the nation over the states; it was as well an assurance of republican government to the people of the states, and this raised the subsidiary questions of who constituted "the people," what is a "state," and who has the power to answer these first two questions.

Georgia v. *Stanton* had the effect of leaving these questions to Congress to resolve. Congress had become disenchanted with its solutions and tried to withdraw from the field, though it did so with extremely bad grace. With the executive branch at loose ends under Grant, it was likely that the Supreme Court should be called upon again to resolve the problem. This eventually came about in another action, *Texas* v. *White*. This time the justices decided to tackle the questions head-on.

Texas v. *White*, like the earlier Georgia and Mississippi cases, was an original action before the Supreme Court in which the Court could properly take jurisdiction only if Texas was a "state" within the meaning of Article III, conferring such jurisdiction. One of the defendants in the action (a suit brought to recover certain federal securities disposed of by the secessionist government of Texas during the war to pay for military medical supplies) challenged Texas' right to bring an original action in the Supreme Court, claiming that Texas was not a state in the Union at the time suit was brought (15 February 1867). This raised issues that the Court had avoided in *Georgia* v. *Stanton*. Chief Justice Chase for the majority (Robert C. Grier, Noah H. Swayne, and Samuel F. Miller dissenting) held that there are three possible definitions of "state," and the Constitution uses the word in all three senses. It can refer to the people of the polity, the political unit itself, or the geographic area within the jurisdiction of the polity. The guarantee clause has particular reference to a state in the first sense, the people, and was inserted to benefit the people.[22]

But Chase perceived what many others had not: the problem of Reconstruction was one of bringing both institutions and individuals back into their proper relation to the Union. Individuals might retain their relation and allegiance to the Union, but the relation of the states had been disordered by secession. In terms strongly reminiscent of Representative Shellabarger's forfeited-rights theory, Chase held that the rights of the state-as-institution were "suspended" by secession. The proper relation of the states to the Union had to be restored, and the guarantee clause was the peacetime means of doing so, just as the militia clause of Article I conferred wartime authority. The nature of the guarantee was pre-eminently a political question for Congress rather than the executive; the President's governments instituted under his powers as commander in chief were "provisional."

This raised the vital question: what restraint existed on Congress when it enforced the guarantee? "Discretion in choice of means is necessarily allowed," Chase answered. If the means chosen are "necessary and proper" to carry out the guarantee and are not "unsanctioned" by the Constitution, Congress has complete latitude. Chase found nothing in the Constitution inconsistent with the governments set up under military Reconstruction.

[22] *Texas* v. *White*, 7 Wall. 700 (U.S., 1869). The conclusions of this case on the nature of the Union and secession were re-affirmed in *White* v. *Hart*, 13 Wall. 646 (U.S., 1871).

The net impact of the Mississippi, Georgia, and Texas cases was to leave primary responsibility for enforcing the guarantee clause with Congress. The Court did not exclude judicial enforcement of the clause and acknowledged that the President had a provisional power under it. To this extent the Supreme Court confirmed Reconstruction policies and recognized the guarantee clause as an open-ended grant of power to the nation over the states.

The Supreme Court is a creature of its age, more or less responsive to the predominant mood of the time. Hence it is no surprise that when Congress and northern public opinion grew weary of the Negro and Reconstruction, the Court reflected this weariness. At a time when the postwar constitutional amendments might have established new substantive standards of republicanism for the Union, in their backhanded guarantee of civil and political equality, the Court as well as the nation was overcome by a spirit of lassitude, and the promise of the amendments was put in abeyance for a half-century.

The Supreme Court's retreat from the palmy days of the guarantee clause began with *Minor* v. *Happersett* in 1875. In a dictum incidental to his holding that the Fourteenth and Fifteenth Amendments did not confer the right of suffrage on women, the new Chief Justice Morrison R. Waite stated that the power of a state over the qualifications of its voters is "supreme" until Congress acts on the question. Waite did not hint at how far Congress might cut into this supremacy, but another of his dicta on the nature of republican government must have had an ominous ring to friends of Negro suffrage.

The guarantee is of a republican form of government. No particular government is designated as republican, neither is the exact form to be guaranteed, in any manner especially designated. . . . The guarantee necessarily implies a duty on the part of the states themselves to provide such a government. All the states had governments when the Constitution was adopted. . . . These governments the Constitution did not change. They were accepted precisely as they were, and it is, therefore, to be presumed that they were such as it was the duty of the States to provide. Thus we have unmistakable evidence of what was republican in form, within the meaning of that term as employed in the Constitution.

Waite concluded that it was too late to argue that female disfranchisement was inconsistent with republican government since all the original states disfranchised women. Waite came perilously close to endorsing some of the principal Democratic conceptions of the guarantee clause as they were advanced to impede national power during Reconstruction.[23]

The Supreme Court did not finally dispose of some of the most sharply contested issues of the Reconstruction era until long after their original political significance had disappeared. In doing so, it adopted all that was valid in the Democratic position after the war. It did not thereby invalidate the Republican arguments; rather, its holdings were conditioned by the dual-sovereignty views of Judge Cooley and others. In re *Duncan* (1891) illustrates this. It raised the question whether a certain Texas statute regulating criminal appeals and procedure was valid. Chief Justice Melville W. Fuller stated that such a question was for the

[23] *Minor v. Happersett,* 21 Wall. 175 (U.S., 1875). Waite was personally sympathetic to the cause of woman suffrage, but he was a conservative Republican who disliked reformers. See C. Peter Magrath, *Morrison R. Waite: The Triumph of Character* (New York, 1963), 119, 153.

state alone to resolve and presented no issue that could be properly decided by a federal court. To buttress his point, he cited the guarantee clause and stated, "the distinguishing feature of that form is the right of the people to choose their own officers for governmental administration, and pass their own laws in virtue of the legislative power reposed in representative bodies, whose legitimate acts may be said to be those of the people themselves." Such a dictum would have been explosive in 1867, but the reaction from radical Reconstruction was so complete by 1891 that it passed unnoticed.[24]

One of the most important Democratic challenges to Republican Reconstruction policy was the assertion that Congress could not impose conditions on the admission of states without destroying the equality of the states in the Union. This challenge was taken up by the Supreme Court in 1910 in the case of *Coyle* v. *Smith*. The enabling act for the admission of Oklahoma, New Mexico, and Arizona stipulated that the Oklahoma state capital must remain at the town of Guthrie until 1913. This was challenged on the grounds that it placed Oklahoma in an inferior status as compared with the older states since Congress could not force any state within the Union to locate its capital at a designated place and since the location of the state capital was none of Congress' business. A majority of the Court eagerly agreed. Brushing aside objections that this presented a political question under the guarantee clause, Justice Horace H. Lurton held that

when a new state is admitted into the Union, it is so admitted with all the powers of sovereignty and jurisdiction which

24 In re *Duncan*, 139 U.S. 449 (1891).

pertain to the original States, and that such powers may not be constitutionally diminished, impaired or shorn away by any conditions, compacts or stipulations embraced in the act under which the new State came into the Union, which would not be valid and effectual if the subject of congressional legislation after admission.

The Court thereby cast serious doubt on one of the most important means of enforcing Reconstruction more than a generation after Reconstruction was abandoned.[25]

The Court had earlier suggested, in *Collector* v. *Day* (1871), that the existence of the states was necessary for the vitality of the federal government. It came back to this point in *South Carolina* v. *United States* (1905), a case wherein the state of South Carolina challenged the validity of the federal internal revenue license taxes on state-owned "dispensers," that is, liquor stores. Justice David J. Brewer, writing for the majority, reiterated a mild version of the doctrine of dual sovereignty and reaffirmed the holding of *Collector* v. *Day*, permitting the federal government to tax income of a state official. He admitted that the states are "supreme" in internal police matters and stated that the guarantee clause marked the uttermost limit of the federal government's power to intervene in state affairs. But he denied that the dispensers were instrumentalities of the state and thus upheld the validity of the federal tax.[26]

The most suggestive part of Brewer's opinion in the *South Carolina* case, however, was a dictum that took him far afield from the issues before the Court. To strengthen

[25] *Coyle* v. *Smith*, 221 U.S. 559 (1910) (McKenna and Holmes, J.J. dissenting without opinion).

[26] *Collector* v. *Day*, 11 Wall. 113 (U.S., 1871); *South Carolina* v. *United States*, 199 U.S. 437 (1905) (White, Peckham, and McKenna, J.J. dissenting).

his holding, Brewer pointed out that the states could not deprive the federal government of its tax base by taking over various economic activities. He went on:

There is a large and growing movement in this country in favor of the acquisition and management by the public of what are termed public utilities, including not merely the supply of gas and water, but also the entire railroad system. Would the state by taking into possession these public utilities lose its republican form of government?

In context, the implied answer seemed to be something like "obviously not," an unlikely position for the highly conservative Brewer. But whether Brewer expressed his own feelings accurately or not, he had touched on the problems that provoked the next major reappearance of the guarantee clause, the proliferation of experiments in state government during the Progressive Era. *South Carolina* v. *United States* bridged two eras characterized by vastly different conceptions of state power. In both periods the guarantee clause played a role in controlling this power.

Despite the Supreme Court's later doubts, Republican policies in Congress during the early years of Reconstruction established precedents of lasting validity. Although the particular problem of restoring states to their proper relations with the nation is not likely to arise again, the assumptions which underlay Republican policy-making may prove useful for dealing with other problems.

During congressional Reconstruction, the guarantee clause underwent a subtle but important shift in meaning. The clause reads, "the United States shall guarantee to every State in this Union a Republican Form of Government," but as applied by Congress in 1867 the clause seemed to become "the United States shall guarantee a republican government to the people in every state." The beneficiaries of the guarantee, as the Supreme Court emphasized in *Texas v. White*, were the people, not the abstraction called the "state." The concept of a state as an entity that could have rights, be injured or punished, and be the beneficiary of a guarantee, was moribund (but not dead) by 1877.

The clearest precedents of all from the Reconstruction period were negative. It was plain by 1870 that the guarantee was not merely of the forms of government, individual rights and liberties, structures and powers of state government that existed in 1789. "Republican form of government" was seen to be a fluid phrase, a reminder by those who lived at the end of the eighteenth century that every generation must formulate for itself the fundamental aspirations in America's revolutionary promise. The phrase was certainly not meant to freeze these hopes in an eighteenth-century mold in which they would impede improvement and evolution.

The guarantee was likewise not to be for the exclusive benefit of existing regimes in the states. Congress did not sweep away extant state governments or expel the men it found occupying state office, though there is no doubt that it would have done so had white southerners continued their recalcitrance after March 1867. But Congress did demonstrate that it would not automatically impose the guarantee to perpetuate a regime. Congress did not go to the opposite extreme either; it recognized that under proper conditions the reasoning that guided President Tyler's action in 1842 would be valid. Sometimes the guarantee could be best effected by federal support of the existing form of government or officers, at least temporarily. But Reconstruction established that this was not an absolute and binding rule and that at other times the enforcement of the guarantee would have in view the eventual disestablishment or restructuring of the state government.

If the guarantee did not sanctify the forms of government or the extant officeholders, neither did it perpetuate state constitutions or vital social arrangements, like slavery, that they protected. Quite the reverse; the guarantee might require the destruction of state-protected institutions inimical to republicanism. The victory of the abolitionist view that slavery was incompatible with republican government stands as an assurance that whatever is antithetical with the republican ideal will be swept away, no matter how much violence it may do the state constitutions.

Most of the rejected limitations on the guarantee clause were urged by Democrats, usually with a callous opportunism. Yet one point in the Democratic argument was valid: republican government means self-government. This right of self-government could be temporarily impaired but only for the purpose of assuring its eventual and permanent triumph. This paradoxical conclusion was inescapable if there was to be any realistic restoration of the Union. A second point was implicit in the first; self-government means government by all the people. Caste had no place in a republic. Eventually this was to mean that political power could not be the exclusive privilege of the property owner or the taxpayer or the white man or the males.

PART III

DESUETUDE

8

The Progressive Era

Since 1867 the guarantee clause has lingered in a state of desuetude. It has emerged only twice: in the years 1900–1920 it was the focus of debates over some of the new forms and functions undertaken by the state governments, and in 1962 the 113-year-old connection between the clause and the doctrine of political questions was severed.

Two salient features of the clause's history converged during the Progressive era. First, attorneys revived and read into the guarantee clause an early "natural-law" interpretation of the principles of republican government. This use of the clause was decisively repudiated by the courts. Second, the doctrine of judicial abstention in political question cases was restated forcefully by the Supreme Court, thereby removing the courts further than ever from an active role in developing the substantive standards of republicanism. Both developments culminated in the 1912 decision of *Pacific States Telephone and Telegraph Co.* v. *Oregon,* a case that ranks with *Luther* v. *Borden* and *Baker* v. *Carr* as one of the three most important in the history of the guarantee clause.

A natural-law conception of the guarantee clause originated before the Civil War. Antislavery theorists believed that slavery was incompatible either with the specific guarantee of republican government in the text of the Constitution or with the vaguer ideal of republican liberty. Opponents of slavery were not alone in measuring society's institutions against their concept of republican government. Contemporary judges were just as vigorously working out a natural-law rationale of metaconstitutional limitations on legislative power and came close to finding textual support in the guarantee clause. Like the antislavery theorists, they first postulated characteristics of republican government as a test of the constitutional legitimacy of some governmental innovation in a case before them. Unlike slavery's opponents, though, they did not quite succeed in reading these characteristics into the guarantee clause. That possibility was averted because judges linked higher-law doctrines to the due process clauses of the federal and state constitutions in the 1850s, which resulted in the appearance of so-called substantive due process after 1890. Ironically, it was in the heyday of substantive due process that a natural-law interpretation of the guarantee clause reappeared.

The fountainhead of higher-law judicial theory in America is the seriatim opinion of Justice Samuel Chase of the United States Supreme Court in the 1798 case of *Calder* v. *Bull*.[1] Lawyers today remember this case, if at all, only for its holding that the ex post facto clause of the United States Constitution applies only to criminal, not civil, cases. Yet the dicta of Justice Chase concerning higher-law restraints on legislative power were the source of what Edward Corwin called "the basic doctrine of American constitutional law."[2] Chase stated:

[1] 3 Dall. 386 (U.S. 1798).
[2] Edward Corwin, "The Basic Doctrine of American Constitutional Law," *Mich. L. Rev.*, XII (1914), 247–276.

I cannot subscribe to the omnipotence of a state legislature, or that it is absolute and without control, although its authority should not be expressly restrained by the constitution or fundamental law of the state. . . . The purposes for which men enter into society will determine the nature and terms of the social compact; and as they are the foundation of the legislative power, they will decide the proper objects of it. The nature and ends of legislative power will limit the exercise of it. . . . There are acts which the federal or state legislatures cannot do without exceeding their authority. There are certain vital principles in our free republican governments which will determine and overrule an apparent and flagrant abuse of legislative power. . . . An Act of the legislature (for I cannot call it a law) contrary to the great principles of the social compact cannot be considered a rightful exercise of legislative authority. . . . The genius, the nature, and the spirit of our state governments amount to a prohibition of such acts of legislation: and the general principles of law and reason forbid them.

Chase here insisted that, even apart from explicit restraints on legislative power in the American constitutions, other restraints were derived from "certain vital principles in our free republican governments." These principles protected both "personal liberty" and "private property." Nowhere in his digression did Chase cite a specific clause of the Constitution as authority for his position; if the limitations he outlined existed at all, they were the creatures of judges' opinions. This prospect dismayed Chase's associate, Justice James Iredell, who in another seriatim opinion in the same case condemned the idea that judges could bind legislatures by their notions of justice.

The judge-made principles of higher law that Chase found in the social compact or in the spirit of republican governments were developed more extensively in the state than in the federal courts. This occurred because Chief Justice John Marshall in 1819 aborted the line of development begun by Chase. It had at first seemed that Supreme Court justices would expand Chase's principles. Justice William Paterson, on circuit in 1795, had anticipated them when in a jury charge he condemned a hypothetical law taking the property of "A" and giving it to "B" because "it is inconsistent with the principles of reason, justice and moral rectitude; it is incompatible with the comfort, peace and happiness of mankind; it is contrary to the principles of social alliance in every free government; and lastly, it is contrary both to the letter and spirit of the constitution." [3]

For a time this tandem reliance on general principles and the letter of the Constitution characterized the thinking of the Marshall court. Thus in *Fletcher* v. *Peck* (1810) Marshall voided a statute by which Georgia sought to undo the Yazoo land frauds because the repealer violated both "general principles which are common to our free institutions" and "the particular provisions of the Constitution of the United States," including the obligation of contracts, bill of attainder, and ex post facto clauses. As if to emphasize this alternative approach of Marshall's, resting both on meta-constitutional principles and on specific clauses, Justice William Johnson, concurring in a separate opinion, argued that the contracts clause was inapposite and that the Georgia law was voided only by "a general principle, on the reason and nature of things: a principle which will impose laws even on the Deity." [4]

Justice Joseph Story was even more enthusiastic for such

[3] *Van Horne's Lessee* v. *Dorrance*, 2 Dall. 304 (C.C.D.Pa., 1795).
[4] 6 Cranch 87 (U.S., 1810).

reasoning in an 1815 case, *Terrett* v. *Taylor,* in which he came close to reading higher-law principles into the guarantee clause. Holding unconstitutional a Virginia religious disestablishment statute that divested the Episcopal church of some glebe lands, Story insisted that the notion that a legislative grant of land was revocable "is utterly inconsistent with a great and fundamental principle of a republican government, the right of the citizens to the free enjoyment of their property legally acquired." Elsewhere in the opinion, echoing Justice Paterson, Story based his reasoning on "the principles of natural justice, upon the fundamental laws of every free government, upon the spirit and the letter of the constitution of the United States." [5]

Four years later, in *Dartmouth College* v. *Woodward* (1819),[6] Marshall was forced to abandon this conveniently bifurcated approach to limitations on legislative power. Marshall's narrowly focused reasoning there was based exclusively on the obligation-of-contracts clause; he did not mention "general principles common to free republican institutions" or any comparable formulae of Chase's *Calder* opinion. After the *Dartmouth College* case, natural-law reasoning appeared occasionally in the opinions of Supreme Court judges,[7] but it was no longer used as the basis for invalidating a state statute in a major case like *Fletcher* v. *Peck.*

By contrast, the state courts were more hospitable to higher-law principles.[8] Connecticut judges cited the "social

[5] 9 Cranch 43 (U.S., 1815).   [6] 4 Wheat. 517 (U.S., 1819).

[7] See *Corfield* v. *Coryell,* 6 Fed. Cas. 546 (No. 3,230) (C.C.E.D.Pa., 1823); *Johnson and Graham's Lessee* v. *M'Intosh,* 8 Wheat. 543, 572 (U.S., 1823); and *Wilkinson* v. *Leland,* 2 Pet. 627 (U.S., 1829).

[8] On this subject see generally Benjamin F. Wright, *American Interpretations of Natural Law* (Cambridge, Mass., 1931), ch. 9; and

compact" as a restraint on the power of the state legislature
to meddle with vested rights because it implied principles
that "underlie all legislation, irrespective of constitutional
restraints." Alabama courts referred to "the very principles
upon which our government is founded" as possibly void-
ing laws "which violate the principles of civil liberty"—a
potentially awkward position for the supreme court of a
slaveholding state. New York decisions found safeguards
for property rights in "the great principles of Eternal Justice" that condemned arbitrary legislation even in the absence of specific constitutional provisions.[9]

The Maryland Supreme Court comprehensively enumerated the sources of higher-law restrictions on legislative
power as "the nature and spirit of the social compact, (in
this country at least) the character and genius of our government, the causes from which they sprang, and the purposes for which they were established." Justice Story, in his
Commentaries on the Constitution, summed up "the general
opinion, fortified by a strong current of judicial opinion,"
that "the fundamental maxims of a free government seem
to require, that the rights of personal liberty and private
property should be held sacred." [10]

It was left to a Delaware court to connect the "funda-

Charles G. Haines, *The Revival of Natural Law Concepts* (Cambridge, Mass., 1930), ch. 1.

[9] *Goshen* v. *Stonington,* 4 Conn. 209, 225 (1822); *Welch* v.
Wadsworth, 30 Conn. 149, 155 (1861); In re *Dorsey,* 7 Porter
293, 377 (Alabama Supreme Court, 1838); *White* v. *White,* 5
Barb. 474 (New York Supreme Court, 1849); *Benson* v. *The
Mayor,* 10 Barb. 223, 244 (New York Supreme Court, 1850).

[10] *Regents of the University of Maryland* v. *Williams,* 9 Gill
& J. 365, 408 (Maryland Supreme Court, 1838); Joseph Story,
Commentaries on the Constitution of the United States . . . (3rd
ed., Boston, 1858), section 1399.

mental maxims of a free government" and the specific command of the guarantee clause. In *Rice* v. *Foster* (1847) [11] the Delaware judges invalidated a state local-option prohibition law because the legislature had exceeded the "limitations on legislative power necessarily involved in a representative republican form of government." A statute is unconstitutional if it is contrary to the "nature and spirit of our republican form of government." The court concluded with a warning to the legislature: any law that "palpably violates the principles and spirit of the constitution, or tends to subvert our republican form of government" is void.

Related to these flourishing ante-bellum concepts of higher law was another development of conservative constitutional thought, also rooted in eighteenth-century ideas. Americans of the 1780s saw the representative character of the state and federal legislatures to be a substitute for direct or simple democracy. Representation preserved the popular element in the composition of government, while at the same time limiting the deliberative body to a reasonable size.[12] Thus Madison could claim in *Federalist* 10 and 14 that representation preserved popular government.

In the hands of Jacksonian-era conservatives, however, the concept of representation became a limitation on popular government, not an assurance of it. Such views were widely aired at the time of the Dorr Rebellion and were stated explicitly by Daniel Webster in his arguments in *Luther* v. *Borden,* where he interpreted legislative representation as a restraint on the power of the people, inhibiting

---

[11] 4 Harr. 479 (Delaware Court of Errors and Appeals, 1847).
[12] In this connection the discussion of democracy and republicanism in Elisha Douglass, *Rebels and Democrats* (Chapel Hill, 1955), viii–ix, is enlightening.

them from acting as they might in some hypothetical simple democracy. As Webster saw it, the regular functioning of a representative legislature precluded the people from taking power into their own hands.[13]

In the turmoil of the Civil War and Reconstruction these parallel ante-bellum gropings toward a conservative interpretation of republican government were eclipsed. The force and sweep of Radical Republican interpretations of the guarantee clause forced Democratic conservatives to fight a rear-guard action based on ideas worked out in the slavery debates rather than on judicial elaborations of higher-law ideas. By the end of the nineteenth century, however, as the federal courts began emphatically to stake out claims for power to invalidate federal and state legislation, the earlier conservative interpretations were revived. They furnished rationales that judges could use to strike down state legislation they found offensive to their sense of right and justice. The natural-law tradition supplemented the vague generality of the guarantee clause in a period when judges were favorably disposed toward judicial activism.

This commitment to judicial activism as a means of protecting the people from their official servants was suggested by the United States Supreme Court in the 1891 case of In re *Duncan*. The Court there construed the guarantee clause as assuring representative government, but warned that "while the people are thus the source of political power, their governments, National and state, have been limited by written constitutions, and they have thereby set

---

[13] See the recapitulation of Webster's arguments in Samuel P. Lyman, *The Public and Private Life of Daniel Webster* (Philadelphia, 1852), I, 290 ff.

bounds to their own power, as against the sudden impulses of mere majorities." In an earlier case, before the concept of "freedom of contract" had been subsumed in the due-process clause, the Court warned the states that the right "to follow any lawful calling, business, or profession . . . may in many respects be considered as a distinguishing feature of our republican institutions" and therefore above state interference.[14]

Taking their cue from the United States Supreme Court, state supreme courts periodically warned legislators that the guarantee clause implies, in the words of the Supreme Court of Errors of Connecticut, "fundamental principles of morality and justice which no Legislature is at liberty to disregard." State courts later construed the clause so as to prohibit legislatures from taxing for a private purpose and from creating bureaus in the state government that could "supervise and control" any of the three branches of government. A federal court, the Fifth Circuit Court of Appeals, warned the Alabama legislature that the guarantee clause not only forbade it from inhibiting freedom of speech and press, but also authorized Congress to secure freedom of communication in the state if restricted by the legislature.[15]

Encouraged by this tentative resuscitation of natural law as embodied in the concept of a republican form of government, attorneys representing litigants who opposed some innovation in the structure of state or local government

[14] In re *Duncan*, 139 U.S. 449 (1891); *Dent* v. *West Virginia*, 129 U.S. 114 (1889).

[15] Appeal of Allyn, 81 Conn. 534 (1909); *Beach* v. *Bradstreet*, 85 Conn. 344 (1912); *State* ex rel. *Licking Township* v. *Clamme*, 134 N.E. 676 (Indiana, 1922); *Heimerl* v. *Ozaukee County*, 256 Wis. 151 (1949); *Powe* v. *U.S.*, 109 F. 2d 147 (5th Cir., 1940).

argued that the innovation was forbidden by the guarantee clause. Such arguments took a variety of forms. Sometimes it was claimed that the principle of the separation of powers was violated by a merger of functions in a new agency, thus denying to the people an essential element of republican government. At other times counsel insisted that the legislature had improperly delegated its powers, as where it empowered an independent commission to set railroad rates.

These attempted applications of the clause were regularly rejected by the state courts, usually on the grounds that the challenged innovation did not so far blur the lines between the departments of government as to negate the republican character of the state. Thus in the two generations between 1871 and 1937 state courts permitted legislatures to pardon an indicted individual before trial, consolidate city and county government, authorize home rule in the cities, establish regulatory commissions with rate-setting powers, create new forms of city government, set up old-age pension funds, and devise new modes of valuing property for tax purposes. The courts similarly accepted gubernatorial appointments to police juries and university regents boards. None of these changes in the structure and organization of state government ran afoul of the guarantee clause.[16]

[16] *State* v. *Nichols,* 26 Ark. 75 (1871); *People* ex rel. *Elder* v. *Sours,* 31 Colo. 369 (1903); *Kies* v. *Lowrey,* 199 U.S. 233 (1905); *Village of Satatoga Springs* v. *Saratoga Gas, Electric Light and Power Co.,* 191 N.Y. 123 (1908); *Eckerson* v. *City of Des Moines,* 137 Iowa 452 (1908); *Siler* v. *Louisville & N.R.R. Co.,* 213 U.S. 175 (1909); *Louisville & N.R.R. Co.* v. *Greenbrier Distillery Co.,* 170 Ky. 775 (1916); *Santee Mills* v. *Query,* 122 S.C. 158 (1922); *State* ex rel. *Porterie* v. *Smith,* 184 La. 263 (1935); *State* ex rel. *Peterson* v. *Quinlivan,* 198 Minn. 65 (1936); In re *Interrogatories by the Governor,* 99 Colo. 591 (1937); *Michigan Cent. R.R. Co.* v. *Powers,* 201 U.S. 245 (1906).

Another form of challenge to expanded governmental functions in the Progressive era was more direct. Attorneys insisted that certain statutes, in themselves and apart from their effect on the structure of state government, violated the republican government guarantee. This approach was no more successful than the others. The courts let legislatures revise voting procedures, enlarge municipal boundaries, control water use, impose gross-receipts taxes, permit local governmental units like boards of education to tax, authorize state sales of liquor, and create regulatory commissions.[17]

Disputes about the new forms and scope of metropolitan government provided another occasion for guarantee clause challenges. Late in the nineteenth century American cities were well launched on the spectacular growth that has resulted in the modern megalopolis. This growth created territorial expansion, demands for city home rule, greater scope for local initiative and referenda, and changes in the form of city government. Pressures for institutional changes in city government were intensified by muckraking publicists who exposed the corruption and inefficiency that they felt were a natural product of rule by the bosses and the machines.

These pressures were resisted in different ways by persons with widely varying interests. Owners of land on the city outskirts sought to stem the expansion of municipal

---

[17] *Cook* v. *State*, 90 Tenn. 407 (1891); *Forsyth* v. *Hammond*, 166 U.S. 506 (1897); *Osborne* v. *San Diego Land and Town Co.*, 178 U.S. 22 (1900); *State* v. *Pacific States Tel. & Tel. Co.*, 53 Ore. 162 (1909); *Susman* v. *Board of Public Education*, 228 Fed. 217 (D.C.W.D. Pa. 1915); *Weaver* v. *Cuff*, 52 S.D. 51 (1927); *Riggins* v. *District Court*, 89 Utah 183 (1935); *Highland Farms Dairy* v. *Agnew*, 300 U.S. 608 (1937).

boundaries since incorporation would bring higher taxes and land-use restrictions. Rural and small town representatives in the legislatures, with a visceral fear of the cities as sinks of vice and refuges of alien ethnic groups, opposed all forms of urban expansion. Conservatives in town and country alike looked with jaundiced eyes on the radical political innovations which the cities seemed to breed. All these and others who felt their interests affected by the shift of political gravity to urban centers looked to the courts as bulwarks against change. They hoped the guarantee clause could be a vehicle for presenting their antiurban protests in justiciable form.

The courts, national and state, chose to meet this challenge head-on, rather than avoiding it by the political question rationale. The first city-related question that presented guarantee clause issues to reach the United States Supreme Court was the aggrandizement of adjacent territory by cities. In *Forsyth* v. *Hammond* (1897) a landowner whose land was about to be incorporated within city limits objected to a peculiar provision in the Indiana statutes that permitted this to be done by a court order. Justice David J. Brewer, writing for a unanimous court, held that a change in municipal boundaries was primarily a question for the states, not the national government. Nothing in the Constitution, particularly not the guarantee clause, prohibited such an issue from being decided by the state courts. The preservation of legislative control in such matters, Brewer held, was not one of the "essential elements" of a republican form of government.[18]

The Court's seeming willingness to decide what did and did not constitute an essential element of republican gov-

[18] 166 U.S. 506 (1897).

ernment encouraged other litigants in city government cases to urge the guarantee clause as a brake on change. When the Colorado legislature consolidated the government of Denver with that of the surrounding county and bestowed expanded powers of self-government on the new body, county residents unsuccessfully challenged the consolidation in the state courts. The Colorado Supreme Court held that neither consolidation nor home rule destroyed the republican form of government in the state.[19]

Two principal innovations in the form of city government, the city commission and the manager-council, were also tested in the courts. The United States Supreme Court did not rule explicitly on the matter, so the state courts had the issue to themselves. While they upheld the new forms without exception, they also evolved a new doctrine restricting the applicability of the guarantee clause to statewide government. The state courts pointed to the wide variations in local government at the time the Constitution was adopted and concluded that the clause neither restricts the form of local government nor limits the degree of popular direct participation in city or county government.[20]

Three related reforms of the Progressive era, the initiative, the referendum, and the recall, ran a gauntlet of guarantee clause challenges. Although the initiative and recall are recent innovations in the structure of American state government, the referendum is at least as old as the nation. Referenda were held on the Revolutionary constitutions of

[19] *People* ex rel. *Elder* v. *Sours*, 31 Colo. 369 (1903).

[20] *Eckerson* v. *City of Des Moines*, 137 Iowa 452 (1908); *People* ex rel. *Springfield* v. *Edmands*, 252 Ill. 108 (1911); *Walker* v. *Spokane*, 62 Wash. 312 (1911); *Mayor of Jackson* v. *State*, 102 Miss. 663 (1913); *Hile* v. *City of Cleveland*, 107 Ohio St. 144 (1923); *Sarlls* v. *State*, 201 Ind. 88 (1929).

Pennsylvania, New Hampshire, and Massachusetts in the 1770s. Revisions in the constitutions of Connecticut, Maine, Rhode Island, New York, Virginia, Georgia, Tennessee, and North Carolina were approved by referenda in the first half of the nineteenth century. Referenda were also used extensively throughout the nineteenth century on various legislative issues, the most common being local-option liquor laws, the location of state capitals, and bonded indebtedness. State supreme courts overwhelmingly upheld the constitutionality of such referendum provisions, though they seldom adverted to problems arising under the guarantee clause.[21]

The Grange and Populist movements, the muckrakers, and the whole coalition of late nineteenth- and early twentieth-century reform movements provided the impetus for an expanded use of the referendum, particularly on a statewide basis, and introduced two innovations, the initiative and the recall. These three devices for "restoring government to the people" provoked vehement debate. Their supporters saw them as panaceas that would sweep away many imperfections in state government. Their opponents believed the reforms would destroy the historic forms of American government and replace them with anarchy or communism.[22]

These polemics were soon translated into constitutional terms, and the guarantee clause assumed a prominent place

[21] The best single study of the referendum, initiative, and recall in the United States is still Ellis P. Oberholtzer's *The Referendum in America* (New York, 1912).

[22] A bibliography of the literature of support and opposition, with some annotations, covering the period to 1912, was compiled by the Library of Congress, *Select List of References on the Initiative, Referendum, and Recall* (Washington, 1912).

in the debates among lawyers. To supporters of the reforms, it seemed obvious that if republican government must be responsive to the people, the reforms merely improved on the original republican system. They also used an old conservative argument—that the forms of state government extant in 1789 were presumptively republican—to defend the local-option type of referenda, citing the New England town meetings. Backers of the reforms also insisted that since Congress had seated the representatives from those states that authorized some form of initiative or referendum procedure, the constitutionality of those devices had been authoritatively passed on by the only body competent to do so. By analogies to the law of agency, they argued that the people were the principals, the legislators the agents, and there was nothing novel in the principal binding the agent by instructions or superseding his authority.[23]

Opponents of the three devices had the better of the argument in the law journals because of their ingenious construction of such scant favorable authority as existed in state and federal cases. *Rice* v. *Foster*, though it had since been expressly repudiated by conventions and legislatures, remained the foremost relevant precedent. For the *Rice* judges, as well as for later opponents of the initiative and

[23] "The Constitutionality of the Initiative and the Referendum," *Yale L.J.*, XIII (1903), 248–250; O. H. Myrick, "The Initiative and the Referendum," *Cent. L.J.*, LXVIII (1909), 383–390; W. A. Coutts, "Is a Provision for the Initiative and Referendum Inconsistent with the Constitution of the United States?" *Mich. L. Rev.*, VI (1907), 304–317; Willis L. Hand, "Is the Initiative and Referendum Repugnant to the Constitution of the United States?" *Cent. L.J.*, LVIII (1904), 244–248. Oberholtzer, *Referendum in America*, chs. 13 and 19, believed that neither device ran afoul of the guarantee clause, though he thought both were pernicious in their potential effects and were proposed by socialists and cranks.

referendum, "republican" and "representative" were synonymous. Explicitly citing Edmund Burke's speech to his Bristol constituents, the Delaware court had insisted that representative government implied that the discretion of the people's representatives could not be trammeled by instructions, much less overruled or superseded. Further, they reasoned, the separation of powers forbade a delegation of any legislative power, even to the whole people. "Pure democracy" was as antithetical to a republican form of government as monarchy, with republicanism standing as a sort of mean between extremes. The Delaware court had flatly held that the guarantee clause prohibited local-option referenda.

To supplement this precedent, opponents of the referendum and initiative seized on two important dicta from United States Supreme Court opinions that they believed confirmed their conservative view of representative institutions. The first was an observation of Chief Justice Morrison Waite in *Minor* v. *Happersett* (1875):

The guarantee is of a republican form of government. No particular government is designated as republican; neither is the exact form to be guaranteed in any manner especially designated. Here, as in other parts of the instrument, we are compelled to resort elsewhere to ascertain what was intended. . . . In all [state governments in 1789] the people participated to some extent through their representatives elected in the manner specially provided. These governments the Constitution did not change.[24]

Chief Justice Fuller had suggested in In re *Duncan* (1891):

[24] 21 Wall. 162 (U.S., 1875).

By the Constitution a republican form of government is guaranteed to every state in the Union and the distinguishing feature of the form is the right of the people to choose their own officers for governmental administration and pass their own laws in virtue of the legislative power reposed in representative bodies whose legitimate acts may be said to be those of the people themselves.[25]

The notion of representative government was a two-edged sword. To the liberal thinkers of the late eighteenth century who advocated representative government as opposed to autocracy, it was a means of assuring the people a voice in law-making through control of those whom they chose to represent their interests. But the idea at least partly atrophied in the following century so that it came to mean that the people surrendered their sovereign legislative power to their representatives, who could only be controlled by being voted out at the next election. Variants on this theory, echoing *Rice* v. *Foster*, were that the elected representatives could not delegate their power nor surrender any portion of it and that the separation-of-powers doctrine required that all legislative power be vested in the legislature and no portion of it in the people.

Whatever version of this conservative theory was advocated, its proponents invariably insisted that the republican form guaranteed by section 4 was purely representative government. Anticipating the John Birch Society by half a century, they insisted that America was a republic, not a democracy, that the initiative and referendum led to "pure democracy," and that pure democracy led to communism and expropriation.[26]

[25] 139 U.S. 449 (1891).
[26] D. C. Lewis, "Arizona's Constitution—The Initiative, The

Despite (or perhaps because of) these arguments, opponents of the reforms met only with defeat in the courts where they brought suit to challenge the innovations; state courts invariably upheld the initiative and referendum. The Minnesota Supreme Court rendered the earliest and the leading opinion on the matter, holding that neither the initiative nor the referendum was inconsistent with republican government. This view was reaffirmed by the Oregon Supreme Court as it applied to statewide referenda in three cases that were quickly accepted elsewhere as authoritative. The Oregon court's reasoning was followed by the supreme courts of California, Oklahoma, and Texas.[27] By 1912 the initiative and referendum seemed secure from judicial attack. Undeterred by their failure in the state courts, however, opponents of the initiative and referendum turned to the United States Supreme Court, using as their vehicle one of the Oregon cases.

The decision in this case, *Pacific States Telephone and*

Referendum, The Recall—Is the Constitution Republican in Form?" *Cent. L.J.*, LXXII (1911), 169–177; Glenway Maxon, "Is the Referendum Anti-Republican?" *ibid.*, 378–381; T. A. Sherwood, "The Initiative and Referendum under the United States Constitution," *Cent. L.J.*, LVI (1903), 247–251; E. C. Gottry, "Is Republican and Representative Government Synonymous?" *Cent. L.J.*, LXXIII (1922), 222–228; Charles R. Brock, "Republican Form of Government Imperilled," *Am. Bar Assn. J.*, VII (1921), 133–134; Joseph F. Ingham, "Republican in Form," *Dick. L. Rev.*, XXXIV (1930), 193–217.

[27] *Hopkins* v. *City of Duluth*, 81 Minn. 189 (1900); *Kadderly* v. *Portland* 44 Ore. 118 (1903); *Kiernan* v. *Portland*, 57 Ore. 454 (1910); *State* v. *Pacific States Telephone and Telegraph Co.*, 53 Ore. 162 (1909); In re *Pfahler*, 150 Cal. 71 (1906); Ex parte *Wagner*, 21 Okla. 33 (1908); *Bonner* v. *Belsterling*, 104 Texas 432 (1911).

Telegraph Co. v. *Oregon* (1912), was doubly significant.[28] In the short run, it laid to rest all challenges to the constitutional validity of the referendum and initiative under the guarantee clause. In the long run it extended Taney's *Luther* dicta concerning political questions and exalted them to the status of a holding. *Pacific States* and later decisions (aptly referred to as its "progeny") remained the fundamental law concerning the relationship of the political question doctrine to the guarantee clause until their authority was weakened fifty years later in *Baker* v. *Carr*.

Oregon had amended its constitution in 1902 to permit the use of the initiative in statewide political issues. By initiative Oregon voters enacted a gross-receipts tax. The taxpayer-telephone company mounted a two-pronged attack on this initiated measure in both the Oregon and the United States Supreme Courts. Its attorneys first argued that the tax was invalid because the mode of enacting it, the initiative, was inconsistent with a republican form of government. Reiterating ideas used by Daniel Webster and his Whig contemporaries, they argued that the representative nature of republican government prevented the people from taking legislative functions into their own hands. The Oregon Supreme Court rejected this contention on its merits, and the United States Supreme Court refused to rule on it.

The second prong of the telephone company's attack was on substance of the measure. The company's attorneys claimed that the tax itself violated the guarantee of republican government. The courts reacted similarly, Oregon's ruling against the company, the United States Supreme Court avoiding the substantive issue.

[28] 223 U.S. 118 (1912).

In the high court, Chief Justice Edward D. White, for a unanimous bench, chose to treat the issue as jurisdictional: he asked whether federal courts could take jurisdiction of suits presenting the questions raised by the company's attorneys. White adopted arguments made by counsel for the state that both challenges were nonjusticiable because all guarantee clause questions were for the political branches of the government, not the courts. "The single issue," he said, is "whether the enforcement [of the guarantee clause], because of its political character, is exclusively committed to Congress or is judicial in its character." He concluded that it was exclusively for Congress. White thought that if the Court should consider the guarantee clause question and find that adoption of the initiative did deprive Oregon of republican government, all Oregon statutes passed since 1902 would be thereby held invalid.

Lest there be any misunderstanding about the continuing authority of *Luther* v. *Borden*, Chief Justice White quoted from it at length and held it to be "absolutely controlling." Adopting some of Taney's points as relevant to the case at hand, White insisted that to uphold the company on the jurisdictional point would destroy the state and national governments, would obliterate the distinction between judicial and legislative departments, and would lead to an "inconceivable expansion of judicial power."

The impact of *Pacific States* in its time was considerable. Both state and federal supreme courts after 1912 dismissed many suits simply on its authority without re-examining its assumptions. Thus both the Washington and United States Supreme Courts declined to hear a challenge to the state's workmen's compensation statute solely on the basis of *Pacific States*. State and national tribunals dismissed attempts

to overturn Louisiana's "Free Text Book Act," which provided for lending textbooks to both public and parochial
school children in the state, citing *Pacific States* as controlling authority. The United States Supreme Court similarly
disposed of attacks on eminent domain authority being
given to a drainage district and on price-fixing by a state
milk-control commission.[29]

Pacific States, like *Luther* v. *Borden*, has been read as a
blanket prohibition of suits challenging legislation on the
grounds that it deprives the state of a republican form of
government. Whether the case's authority is that broad,
however, should still be open to question. It was an attack
on a gross-receipts tax only in form; in substance the company hoped to overturn an amendment of the Oregon constitution authorizing the initiative. The company's counsel,
in both state and national courts, sought to foist off on the
justices a theory of republican government that was a
throwback to Whig conceptions of representative government. The courts could not accede to these completely
reactionary doctrines. In addition, if courts struck down the
initiative and referendum they might thereby invalidate all
legislation based on either device in eleven trans-Mississippi
states (South Dakota, Oregon, Nebraska, California, Iowa,

[29] These "progeny" cases include: *State* v. *Mountain Timber
Co.*, 75 Wash. 581 (1913); *Mountain Timber Co.* v. *Washington*,
243 U.S. 219 (1917); *Borden* v. *Louisiana State Board of Education*,
168 La. 1006 (1929); *Cochran* v. *Louisiana State Board of Education*, 281 La. 370 (1930); *O'Neill* v. *Leamer*, 239 U.S. 244 (1915);
Highland Farms Dairy v. *Agnew*, 300 U.S. 608 (1937). See also
Kiernan v. *Portland*, 223 U.S. 151 (1912); *State ex rel. Topping*
v. *Houston*, 94 Neb. 445 (1913); *Marshall* v. *Dye*, 231 U.S. 250
(1913); *State ex rel. Foote* v. *Board of Commissioners*, 93 Kans.
405 (1914); and *Ohio ex rel. Davis* v. *Hildebrant*, 241 U.S. 565
(1916) on the constitutionality of the initiative and referendum.

Utah, Nevada, Montana, Oklahoma, Arkansas, and Colorado) that had adopted some version of these reforms. Although the Court overstated the consequences, its instincts were sound in seeing that the company's position in *Pacific States* implied far-reaching results that would greatly unsettle affairs in the new western states. Another difficulty facing the Court was that Congress had already spoken on the issue by admitting Oklahoma into the Union in 1907 with referendum and initiative provisions in her constitution.[30]

The result in *Pacific States*, if narrowly confined to the factual situation presented there, was defensible. Chief Justice White's loose and extravagant language, however, promoted a constitutional doctrine of judicial abstention that went considerably beyond *Pacific States* and even further beyond any modern rationale upholding that decision.

The powers of the state government, the forms of city government, and the validity of the initiative and referendum were the broad issues that brought the guarantee clause to the attention of the state and federal courts in the Progressive era. Although many of the state supreme courts, and the United States Supreme Court on occasion, spoke on the merits and determined what did or did not constitute a republican form of government, after 1912 the authority of *Pacific States* was so widely accepted that the guarantee clause remained in desuetude, receiving only occasional notice in the courts. Thus the guarantee clause failed to sup-

[30] For a parallel criticism of *Pacific States* directed at the narrower problem of the role of the courts in reapportionment, see Arthur E. Bonfield, "*Baker* v. *Carr*: New Light on the Constitutional Guarantee of Republican Government," *Calif. L. Rev.*, L (1962), 245–263.

plement the due process clause as a vehicle for higher-law doctrines. Fifty years later it similarly failed to supplement the equal protection clause as a guarantee of political equality.

9

Baker v. Carr (1962)

The benchmark reapportionment case, *Baker* v. *Carr* (1962), held that suits attacking the malapportionment of state legislatures are justiciable in federal courts; that is, they present issues that courts are capable of resolving and may therefore be litigated. This holding had both a negative and a positive effect on the development of the guarantee clause. Its negative impact was due to the refusal of Justice William Brennan, writing for the *Baker* majority, to base his opinion on the clause; Brennan relied entirely on the equal protection clause of the Fourteenth Amendment. This refusal to ground *Baker* and subsequent reapportionment cases on the guarantee clause seemingly thrust the clause back into its customary place on the fringes of American constitutional development. It now seems clear that the clause will not play any important role in the reapportionment of state legislatures or congressional districts.

In a more positive way, however, *Baker* v. *Carr* may have given the clause an impetus toward expansion unequaled since Reconstruction. Justice Brennan's opinion sharply restricted the scope of the political question doctrine. *Luther* v. *Borden* and later judicial elaborations of it were not overruled because the Court, as it often does, preferred to circumvent a doctrinal obstacle rather than to meet it head-on, but the political question doctrine has lost vitality as a restraint on judicial implementation of the guarantee clause. Thus the principal barrier to the clause's interpretation by the courts has been removed. Given the willingness of the United States Supreme Court of the last two decades to expand both judicial and federal power, the future of the clause seems bright.

Since the end of the nineteenth century, state and federal courts had been asked to order reapportionment of congressional and state legislative districts. For federal constitutional grounds, petitioners relied on the due process, equal protection, and guarantee clauses. These actions were often successful in state courts.

The political question doctrine did not prevent state supreme courts from holding that republican or representative government required the political equality of one voter vis-à-vis another and that courts had the duty to enforce this equality. They undertook this duty in a variety of ways, sometimes by striking down innovations in the mechanisms of legislative procedure, such as cumulative or weighted voting; sometimes by upholding stringent election laws regulating the counting of ballots; sometimes by affording equitable relief to force election officials to do or refrain from doing certain acts; and sometimes simply by holding reapportionment statutes unconstitutional.[1]

---

[1] *Maynard v. Board of Canvassers*, 84 Mich. 228 (1890); *Cook v. State*, 90 Tenn. 407 (1891); *Attorney General v. Apportionment Commissioners*, 224 Mass. 598 (1916); *State ex rel. Harte v. Moorhead*, 99 Neb. 527 (1916). A minority of state courts refused to review apportionment disparities. See *Fergus v. Kinney*, 33 Ill. 437 (1928); *State ex rel. Smiley v. Holm*, 238 N.W. 494 (Minn., 1931),

Federal courts, on the other hand, refused to countenance malapportionment suits. Since such suits were usually begun in state courts in actions seeking equitable relief (mandamus, injunction, or declaratory judgment), federal courts on review held either that equitable relief is discretionary with the state court and that federal courts will not review the state court's discretion, or that the issues presented were nonjusticiable under *Luther* v. *Borden*.[2]

This line of federal authority was capped in 1946 by *Colegrove* v. *Green,* an action challenging malapportionment of congressional districts rather than state legislative districts. Petitioners sought to restrain the governor of Illinois from holding the 1946 congressional elections because the state's congressional districts varied so widely in population that the congressman from the Seventh District (Cook County) represented nine constituents for every one represented by his downstate colleague from the Fifth District. From a dismissal of the suit by the federal district court, the plaintiffs appealed directly to the United States Supreme Court.

Justice Felix Frankfurter, the pre-eminent modern defender of the political question doctrine, delivered the judgment—not the opinion—of the Court. Only Justices Stanley F. Reed and Harold H. Burton concurred in Frankfurter's opinion. Justice Wiley B. Rutledge concurred in the result but disagreed with Frankfurter's reasoning. Justices Hugo Black, William O. Douglas, and

---

rev'd on other grounds, sub nom. *Smiley* v. *Holm,* 285 U.S. 355 (1932); *Breedlove* v. *Shuttles,* 183 Ga. 189 (1936).

[2] *Green* v. *Mills,* 69 Fed. 852 (4th Cir., 1895); *Taylor and Marshall* v. *Beckham,* 178 U.S. 548 (1900) (dictum); *Keogh* v. *Neely,* 50 F. 2d 685 (7th Cir., 1931).

Frank Murphy dissented. Since Chief Justice Harlan Fiske Stone had recently died and Justice Robert H. Jackson was absent, only seven justices heard argument, and only three of these supported the Frankfurter position. Nevertheless, Frankfurter's opinion held sway for sixteen years as authority for the proposition that courts must abstain from reapportionment disputes. He also authoritatively stated that "violation of the great guaranty of a republican form of government in states cannot be challenged in the courts."[3]

Colegrove enabled Justice Frankfurter to unburden himself of his long-accumulated anxiety that the Court was not applying the political question doctrine in its full rigor. In a terse and donnish opinion, he tried to return the doctrine to its *Pacific States* pre-eminence: "Nothing is clearer than that this controversy concerns matters that bring courts into immediate and active relations with party contests. From the determination of such issues this Court has traditionally held aloof." But his opinion was brief and ambiguous on the central question, which was whether the Court, as a constitutional matter, lacked jurisdiction of reapportionment suits or whether the Court's refusal to take jurisdiction was discretionary. Frankfurter merely said that "due regard for the effective working of our Government revealed this issue to be of a peculiarly political nature and therefore not meet for judicial determination." He concluded with a powerful aphorism, "Courts ought not to enter this political thicket," which became a shibboleth for all those who opposed judicial reapportionment.

The guarantee clause did not affect the outcome of *Colegrove*. Appellants in their briefs hesitantly suggested the ar-

[3] *Colegrove v. Green*, 328 U.S. 549 (1946).

gument that had formerly been successful in state cases: representative government requires equality of weight for all ballots; hence gross malapportionment is forbidden by the guarantee clause. Frankfurter brusquely dismissed this argument on the authority of *Pacific States.*[4]

Frankfurter spoke for a minority of the Court. To make a majority for the result, Justice Rutledge's concurring opinion must be taken into account. He agreed with the dissenters (and disagreed with Frankfurter) that the courts could take jurisdiction of a congressional reapportionment suit. Thus on the crucial issue, constitutional jurisdiction, the real split on the Court was 4–3 in favor of jurisdiction; later citations of *Colegrove* to support a doctrine of absolute nonjusticiability misread the opinions that went to make a majority in favor of dismissal. Rutledge concurred in dismissing because, as a matter of judicial discretion, he felt the issue so sensitive that courts should intervene only if it was "compelling" to do so.

The dissenters, speaking through Justice Black, anticipated *Baker* by insisting that the issue was justiciable, that appellants made a showing that they were denied equal protection because their vote was diluted, that no political questions were presented, and that appropriate equitable relief could be fashioned.

Despite *Colegrove's* seemingly definitive disposal of the guarantee clause and reaffirmation of *Pacific States,* chinks began to appear in the armor of the political question doc-

[4] Brief for appellant, *ibid.* For criticisms of the Frankfurter opinion, see Robert B. McKay, *Reapportionment: The Law and Politics of Equal Representation* (New York, 1965), 66–70; Note, "Challenges to Congressional Districting: After *Baker* v. *Carr,* Does *Colegrove* v. *Green* Endure," *Colum. L. Rev.,* LXIII (1963), 98–116.

trine and in the *Colegrove* rationale. In an article in the 1958 *Harvard Law Review*, Anthony Lewis, Supreme Court reporter for the *New York Times*, attacked *Colegrove* directly. He argued that the political question doctrine received too mechanistic an application at the hands of Justice Frankfurter. Lewis thereby belled the cat: *Colegrove* was no longer to be unquestioningly obeyed. Frankfurter's opinion now had to withstand intensive and critical scholarly analysis.[5]

With the authority of *Colegrove* called into question and with population shifts exacerbating the malapportionment of most legislative and congressional districts, it was only a question of time before the United States Supreme Court would again be faced with the legal and political issues of reapportionment litigation. When a federal district court in Tennessee dismissed a suit seeking a declaratory judgment and an injunction to compel reapportionment of the Tennessee legislature, the stage was set for *Baker* v. *Carr*.

As the *Baker* case came up from the district court, two issues were presented. First, did the district court have jurisdiction of the subject matter of the action? Second, was the case justiciable; that is, did the petitioners present a claim for which a federal court could grant relief? Both issues were in reality the two sides of the same coin. A third question, the standing of the petitioners, apparently was debated sufficiently in conference to merit separate attention in the principal *Baker* opinions. This latter question was whether the petitioners had any interest for which they could seek judicial protection.[6]

[5] Anthony Lewis, "Legislative Apportionment and the Courts," *Harv. L. Rev.*, LXXI (1958), 1057–1098.
[6] *Baker* v. *Carr*, 369 U.S. 186 (1962).

The petitioners offered to prove that the constitution of Tennessee required decennial reapportionment by the state legislature; that the Tennessee General Assembly had not reapportioned since 1901, thereby disobeying the plain command of the constitution; and that population shifts within the state, with the malapportionment already existing in 1901, resulted in a gross malapportionment of the state legislature. They requested that the federal court either reapportion the legislature on the basis of the Tennessee constitution's formula or order elections to be held at large until the legislature did the reapportioning.

The majority in *Baker*, as Justices Brennan and Potter Stewart were at pains to point out, held only that: (1) the district court had jurisdiction of the subject matter of the action; (2) the plaintiff stated a justiciable cause of action, which, if established, would entitle him to relief of some sort; and (3) the plaintiff had standing to bring the action. In other words, the Supreme Court technically did nothing more than tell the district court that it was wrong to throw the plaintiffs out of court at the outset. Yet Justice Brennan's discussion of the three issues greatly altered the Court's attitude toward reapportionment, political questions, and the guarantee clause.

Justice Brennan, speaking for himself and four of the majority (Justice Douglas disagreed), explicitly rejected the guarantee clause as authority for deciding each of these points. He relied instead on the equal protection clause, which was perhaps more familiar to the Court. Just two years before, in *Gomillion* v. *Lightfoot* (1960), the Court had struck down the Alabama legislature's attempt to redraw the city of Tuskegee's boundaries so as to place nearly all the city's Negro voters outside its political limits. In

Gomillion the Court had relied on the Fifteenth Amendment, not the Fourteenth, but it took no great insight to see that the force of the equal protection or due process clauses might be great enough to breach the defenses of nonjusticiability that went back through *Colegrove* and *Pacific States* to *Luther* v. *Borden.*[7]

It would have seemed, as it did to Justice Frankfurter and other critics of the *Baker* opinion, that *Colegrove* must either preclude the *Baker* result or be overruled. Justice Brennan, however, pointed out that this assumption was based on a misreading of the three *Colegrove* opinions. A majority (Justice Rutledge and the three dissenters) had

[7] The Court's reliance on an equal protection rationale for its decision has been the subject of much scholarly criticism. See especially Robert G. Dixon, *Democratic Representation: Reapportionment in Law and Politics* (New York, 1968), 135–137, 265; Phil C. Neal, *"Baker* v. *Carr:* Politics in Search of Law," *Sup. Ct. Rev.* (1962), 252–327; Mark DeWolfe Howe, *The Garden and the Wilderness: Religion and Government in American Constitutional History* (Chicago, 1965), 145–146; Robert G. Dixon, "Reapportionment in the Supreme Court and Congress: Constitutional Struggle for Fair Representation," *Mich. L. Rev.*, LXIII (1964), 209–278; James B. Atleson, "The Aftermath of *Baker* v. *Carr*—An Adventure in Judicial Experimentation," *Calif. L. Rev.*, LI (1965), 535–572; Jerold Israel, "The Future of *Baker* v. *Carr,*" *Mich. L. Rev.*, LXI (1962), 107–146; Paul A. Freund, "New Vistas in Constitutional Law," *U. Pa. L. Rev.*, CXII (1964), 631–646; Paul G. Kauper, "Some Comments on the Reapportionment Cases," *Mich. L. Rev.*, LXIII (1964), 243–254; Robert G. McCloskey, "Foreword: The Reapportionment Case," *Harv. L. Rev.*, LXXVI (1962), 54–74; Alexander Bickel, "The Durability of Colgrove v. Green," *Yale L.J.*, LXXII (1962), 39–45; Robert G. Dixon, "Legislative Apportionment and the Federal Constitution," *Law & Contemp. Probs.*, XXVII (1962), 329–389; Philip B. Kurland, "Foreword: 'Equal in Origin and Equal in Title to the Legislative and Executive Branches of the Government,'" *Harv. L. Rev.*, LXXVIII (1964), 143–176.

held that federal courts did have jurisdiction of the subject matter because the suit presented a substantial federal question, was a "case" or "controversy" within Article III, and came under the appropriate jurisdictional statute (28 U.S.C. §1343).

Brennan held that the *Baker* suit was an Article III case or controversy within the jurisdiction of the federal courts because he found that it was a bona fide action seeking redress of an individual's federally protected rights under the equal protection clause. For Justice Frankfurter, by contrast, the suit was just an officious individual's attempt to have a federal court declare an entire state government unconstitutional.

A similar dispute between the majority and the minority arose over the question of standing, and again equal protection was the nub. To the majority Baker plainly had standing in a federal court to seek redress of the state's denial of the equal protection of its laws to him as an individual. To Justice Frankfurter, Baker was merely a citizen having no individual interest greater than any other resident of Tennessee seeking to have a court force Tennessee to administer its government according to law.

Finally, on the justiciability point, Brennan held that any equal protection suit was justiciable unless it was merely a vehicle for bringing into the Court a political question with no real Fourteenth Amendment claim present. Then Brennan found that none of the elements that made political questions nonjusticiable in the past were present in *Baker.* Justice Frankfurter, on the other hand, argued that the equal protection claim was a sham, a guarantee clause case in disguise. He believed all the reasons that the Court had formerly found for holding guarantee clause actions nonjusticiable were applicable to *Baker.*

Justice Frankfurter's insistence that *Baker* was really a guarantee clause case forced Brennan to explain at length why no guarantee clause questions were involved. By somewhat involuted reasoning, he concluded that guarantee clause claims are nonjusticiable only because they present elements of a political question and not because they touch on matters of state governmental organization. *Luther* v. *Borden* was distinguishable because it was a "pure" guarantee clause case with no other constitutional rights asserted. By a review of the major guarantee clause cases decided after *Luther* v. *Borden*, Brennan concluded that "reliance on the Guaranty Clause could not have succeeded" in *Baker* because the clause presents no "judicially manageable standards."

This conclusion did not command unanimity among the majority justices, though it did receive Frankfurter's approval. Justice Douglas, concurring separately, argued that many of the political question precedents were erroneous. Taney's dicta in *Luther* that the guarantee clause was enforceable only by Congress or the President were "not maintainable." Douglas stated:

The abdication of all judicial functions respecting voting rights . . . states no general principle. It is indeed contrary to the cases discussed in the body of this opinion [*Nixon* v. *Herndon, Smith* v. *Allwright, United States* v. *Classic*]—the modern decisions of the Court that give the full panoply of judicial protection to voting rights. Today we would not say with Chief Justice Taney that it is no part of the judicial function to protect the right to vote of those to whom it is denied by the written and established constitution and laws of the state.

For Douglas, "the right to vote is inherent in the republican form of government" guaranteed by section 4.

Justice Frankfurter's dissent explored at great length the reasons for judicial abstention in apportionment cases. Unlike Justice Harlan, who saw nothing in the Fourteenth Amendment that required equally weighted ballots, Frankfurter dissented principally because it was beyond the competence of courts to enforce whatever substantive standards did exist. "There is not under our Constitution a judicial remedy for every political mischief, for every undesirable exercise of legislative power," he warned.

The heart of Frankfurter's criticism of the majority position appears in a paragraph attacking the basic assumptions of the majority justices who viewed reapportionment as a matter of equal protection:

What, then, is this question of legislative apportionment? Appellants invoke the right to vote and to have their votes counted. But they are permitted to vote and their votes are counted. They go to the polls, they cast their ballots, they send their representatives to the state councils. Their complaint is simply that the representatives are not sufficiently numerous or powerful—in short, that Tennessee has adopted a basis of representation with which they are dissatisfied. Talk of "debasement" or "dilution" is circular talk. One cannot speak of "debasement" or "dilution" of the value of a vote until there is first defined a standard of reference as to what a vote should be worth. What is actually asked of the Court in this case is to choose among competing bases of representation—ultimately, really, among competing theories of political philosophy—in order to establish an appropriate frame of government for the state of Tennessee and thereby for all the States of the Union.

This is what he meant when he characterized *Baker* as "in effect, a Guarantee Clause claim masquerading under a different label."

Two fundamental points of *Baker* v. *Carr* were reaffirmed emphatically in *Reynolds* v. *Sims* (1964),[8] the decision which held that apportionment of state legislatures must approximate as closely as possible the standard of one man–one vote. These were, first, malapportionment of state legislatures runs afoul of the equal protection clause. Thus the issues of the reapportionment cases are fundamentally questions of equal protection, not due process or republican government. Second, the guarantee clause is irrelevant to the problems of reapportionment. As Justice Brennan said in *Baker*, "any reliance on that clause would be futile."

Thus it would seem that the clause's possible expansion has been aborted again. Yet Justice Brennan, in the same opinion wherein he shoved the clause back into disuse, also imposed narrow restrictions on the political question doctrine. Perhaps the real significance of *Baker* lies outside reapportionment. It may be that, in the long run, Justice Brennan's digression on the political question doctrine will have a greater and more lasting effect on the Court's business than its exploitation of the equal protection clause.

In the Progressive era cases, Chief Justice Taney's generalizations in *Luther* v. *Borden* about the need for courts to abstain from cases presenting political questions took on a life of their own. Some federal and state judges seized on the political question doctrine so eagerly that responsible commentators as early as the 1920s accused them of contriving a *deus ex machina* out of the doctrine that permitted them to avoid deciding a case whenever they felt it would be inconvenient, embarrassing, or impolitic to decide.[9]

As the twentieth century wore on, the fabric of the doc-

---

[8] 377 U.S. 533 (1964).
[9] See Maurice Finkelstein, "Judicial Self-Limitation," *Harv. L. Rev.*, XXXVII (1924), 338–364, and a rebuttal by Melville Weston,

trine began to fray. State courts, especially the elective benches of the western states, ignored the doctrine and passed on the merits of questions that other courts had held "political." The lower federal courts occasionally evaded *Luther* by holding that a case did not present a political question merely because it would have political repercussions or because political rights were involved.

Finally in the 1950s scholars and judges subjected the doctrine to scrutiny on its merits and found it wanting in many ways. Professor John P. Frank summed up their conclusions in 1954: "The doctrine of political questions is currently undergoing a most undesirable expansion." It is a "magical formula which has the practical result of relieving a court of the necessity of thinking further about a particular problem." It encouraged other branches of government to dodge questions, especially those related to personal liberty. Frank thus concluded that the doctrine was "contrary to the spirit of our institutions" and should be "sharply confined to cases where the functional reasons justify it." [10]

A useful result of this criticism was a thorough review of the doctrine in the law reviews. By the 1950s the doctrine had proliferated to such an extent, and the relevant precedents had been so rarely collected or analyzed, that this was a more difficult task than it might at first appear. As Frank had said, the doctrine is "more amenable to description by infinite itemization than by generalization."

"Political Questions," *Harv. L. Rev.*, XXXVIII (1925), 296–333. These were followed by a doctoral dissertation published in 1936, Charles G. Post, *The Supreme Court and Political Questions* (Baltimore, 1936, Johns Hopkins Univ. Studies in Hist. and Pol. Sci., ser. 54).

[10] John P. Frank, "Political Questions," in Edmund Cahn, ed., *Supreme Court and Supreme Law* (Bloomington, Ind., 1954), 43.

Nevertheless, legal scholars took on the problem and tried to categorize the precedents in two ways: by making explicit the rationale underlying political question cases, or by enumerating the standards usually cited by a court for holding a question nonjusticiable because political.

Those who sought a rationale to explain why a court invoked the doctrine concluded that it was based on the concept of separation of powers. Either because the Constitution sorted out the duties of the three branches of government or because the three branches tried to work out such an allocation in practice, it seemed convenient to explain abstention by the attractively simple conclusion that courts do judicial business, leaving political business to the political branches.[11]

Another explanation of the doctrine, one that rejected the quest for rationale, was put forward by Alexander Bickel shortly before the *Baker* decision. Bickel's explanation was perhaps intended to be prophetic and admonitory. The sources of the doctrine, he argued, are

the court's sense of a lack of capacity, compounded in unequal parts of the strangeness of the issue and the suspicion that it will have to yield more often and more substantially to expediency than to principle; the sheer momentousness of it, which unbalances judgement and prevents one from subsuming the normal calculations of probabilities; the anxiety not so much that the judicial judgment will be ignored, as that perhaps it

[11] David Fellman, "The Essential Nature of American Constitutional Law," in Morris O. Forkosch, ed., *Essays in Legal History in Honor of Felix Frankfurter* (Indianapolis, 1966); Weston, "Political Questions"; Willard Hurst, "Review and Distribution of National Powers," in Cahn, ed., *Supreme Court*; Note, "Judicial Attitude Toward Political Question Doctrine: The Gerrymander and Civil Rights," *Wash. U. L. Q.*, III (1960), 292–301.

should be, but won't; and finally . . . the inner vulnerability of an institution which is electorally irresponsible.[12]

The search for all-encompassing rationales was usually found unsatisfactory, either because they did not cover many cases or because they explained nothing and merely rephrased the question. Because of these difficulties, other scholars took a different tack, that of categorizing standards for political question cases. They discovered fourteen. By the 1960s the doctrine was thus found to be protean. Although each of the enumerated standards was defensible when applied to the proper factual circumstances, taken together they suggested an unwieldy doctrinal proliferation.[13]

The United States Supreme Court found its first chance to prune the doctrine's growth in the *Baker* case. Justice Brennan for the majority eagerly seized the opportunity. He apparently realized that any attempt to find a rationale for the doctrine that would fit all cases and that would be more than tautological was likely to fail. A recapitulation of the standards would not do for his purposes, since several of them might preclude the result that he desired to

[12] Alexander Bickel, "Foreword: The Passive Virtues," *Harv. L. Rev.*, LXXV (1961), 40–79.

[13] See Weston, "Political Questions"; Frank, "Political Questions"; McCloskey, "Reapportionment Case"; Herbert Wechsler, "Toward Neutral Principles of Constitutional Law," *Harv. L. Rev.*, LXXIII (1959), 1–35; William L. Taylor, "Legal Action to Enjoin Legislative Malapportionment: The Political Question Doctrine," *So. Cal. L. Rev.*, XXXIV (1961), 179–189; Louis L. Jaffe, "Standing to Secure Judicial Review: Public Actions," *Harv. L. Rev.*, LXXIV (1961), 1265–1314; Bickel, "Passive Virtues"; Note, "Injunctive Protection of Political Rights in the Federal Courts," *Harv. L. Rev.*, LXII (1949), 659–669; Walter F. Dodd, "Judicially Non-Enforcible [*sic*] Provisions of Constitutions," *U. Pa. L. Rev.*, LXXX (1931), 54–93.

reach in *Baker*. Yet the doctrine's challenge had to be met lest the Court lay itself open to the charge that, by ignoring precedents embodying the doctrine, it considered its fiat unrestrained. Brennan hit on a third course that proved convenient for his purposes: he composed a legal taxonomy, listing five principal categories of cases to which the political question doctrine might apply. Four of these need not concern us here: the executive's conduct of foreign affairs, the dates of the duration and the end of hostilities, the validity of statutory enactments, and the status of Indian tribes.

The fifth category of cases affected by the political question doctrine, however, guarantee clause cases, is of the utmost importance. Brennan began by striking at one of the principal trunks of the doctrine: he stated that the political question doctrine applied only to the federal judiciary's relations with the President and Congress, not its relationship to the state governments. With this one blow he hacked away the foremost impediment to the Court's use of the guarantee clause. *Luther* v. *Borden* now stood naked to the winds.

Then, by an analysis of the five categories of cases, Justice Brennan confined the political question doctrine to a drastically reduced scope of operation:

Prominent on the surface of any case held to involve a political question is found [1] a textually demonstrable constitutional commitment of the issue to a coordinate political department; [2] or a lack of judicially discoverable and manageable standards for resolving it; [3] or the impossibility of deciding without an initial policy determination of a kind clearly for non-judicial discretion; [4] or the impossibility of a court's undertaking independent resolution without expressing lack of the respect due coordinate branches of government; [5] or an unusual need for unquestioning adherence to a political decision already made; [6] or the potentiality of embarrassment from multifarious pronouncements by various departments on one question.

Any one of these elements would be fatal to justiciability, but if none is present, the case should not be dismissed merely because it presents a political question. "The courts cannot reject as 'no law suit' a bona fide controversy as to whether some action denominated 'political' exceeds constitutional authority," Brennan stated. Rather, the courts must look to "the precise facts and posture of the particular case" to determine whether one of the fatal elements is involved. The question can no longer be decided, if it ever could, by "semantic cataloguing."

The political question doctrine had at last been made manageable. It now remained only to apply its new standards to the guarantee clause. Justice Brennan insisted that the guarantee clause cases remained nonjusticiable only because they "involve those elements which define a 'political question.'" This nonjusticiability "has nothing to do with their touching upon matters of state governmental organization." In a lengthy review of Taney's *Luther* v. *Borden* opinion, Brennan suggested that the judiciary could determine what a republican form of government meant or required so that the second of his six criteria, the lack of standards or criteria to guide the Court's decision, "might fall away," as he put it. He later emphasized that only the restricted political question elements make a guarantee clause case nonjusticiable.[14]

The Court's new political question standards are vaguely

[14] 369 U.S. at 217–227.

worded, but the *Baker* opinion gives some clues as to what the Court feels would be held justiciable under the new dispensation. Brennan held that none of his standards precluded the *Baker* result under the equal protection clause. From this and from dicta scattered throughout the opinion, we may discern the outlines of the Court's future approach to the political question hurdle in guarantee clause cases.

The first controlling standard, "a textually demonstrable constitutional commitment of the issue to a coordinate political department," obviously does not make a guarantee clause case nonjusticiable. The wording of the clause does not limit its enforcement to the political branches. From the domestic violence and invasion clauses that make up the remainder of section 4, we might conclude that the decision of Congress or the President to authorize or to use troops to suppress violence or invasion would not be reviewable, although even that is doubtful.[15] But no such impediment affects the guarantee clause.

Justice Brennan disposed of the second standard in a footnote when he said that a court could determine the characteristics of a republican form of government. Even if he had not, the Court's willingness and ability to find standards under the equal protection clause suggests that the Court would not be embarrassed by "a lack of judicially discoverable and manageable standards" in guarantee clause cases.[16]

[15] Clarence C. Ferguson, "The Inherent Justiciability of the Constitutional Guaranty against Domestic Violence," *Rutgers L. Rev.*, XIII (1959), 407–425, concludes that the domestic violence clause is justiciable.

[16] Cf. Arthur E. Bonfield, "*Baker* v. *Carr*: New Light on the Constitutional Guarantee of Republican Government," *Calif. L. Rev.*, L (1962), 245–263, who argues that only the first two Bren-

It would seem that the third criterion, "the impossibility of deciding without an initial policy determination of a kind clearly for nonjudicial discretion," should preclude judicial enforcement of the guarantee clause, except for three countervailing considerations. First, as *Baker* implied and as *Reynolds* held, such a policy determination ("equally-weighted votes" in reapportionment cases) can easily be made by courts under the equal protection clause. Second, this "policy determination" criterion is perhaps controlled by the same considerations that control the second ("manageable standards"). In other words, if the Court can find standards, it will probably not consider itself making a policy determination that is for nonjudicial discretion. Last, the Court has not been modest under former Chief Justice Earl Warren in making policy determinations which, if they are not plainly for nonjudicial discretion, at least involve the Court in breathtaking policy innovations.

The fourth consideration, potential conflict with Congress or the President, was gratuitously brushed aside in *Reynolds*. There the Court was faced with the argument that Congress had admitted states whose constitutions contained provisions assuring malapportionment. Therefore, it was argued, either Congress' finding that the state's government was republican was binding on the Court or that it was at least evidence that the provisions were not invidious or unreasonable. Chief Justice Warren, for the majority, noted that Congress had probably not considered the malapportionment problem and that, even if it had, it could not thereby deprive individual voters of their constitutionally guaranteed right to an equally weighted ballot. Apparently,

---

nan standards are applicable in guarantee clause cases and that the remainder will be irrelevant in most factual situations.

with Congress and the President in an acquiescent humor, the Court will not fret about conflicts with them.

The last two criteria, not upsetting political decisions already made and speaking with one voice, are chiefly applicable to foreign policy issues. Except for something like the Dorr Rebellion, it is unlikely that they will ever be relevant in cases coming up under the guarantee clause.

Hence none of the Court's new political question considerations will necessarily preclude it from hearing guarantee clause cases. Each case, as Justice Brennan stated, must be considered on its merits, in the light of its own specific factual complications. Judges had assumed for more than a century that *Luther* v. *Borden* absolutely denied justiciability to guarantee clause cases because they invariably presented political questions, and later cases did nothing to correct this assumption.

Now that is all changed. Under the innocuous *Baker* standards, many guarantee clause cases will have an entrée into the courts. Those that do not fall under the ban of the *Baker* criteria will present the Court with new opportunities to evolve substantive standards of republican government and to enforce these on the state governments.

Epilogue

Charles Sumner's simile of 1867 remains pertinent. The guarantee clause, he claimed, "is like a sleeping giant in the Constitution, never until this recent war awakened, but now it comes forward with a giant's power." In the short run Sumner was wrong; as he spoke the giant was already lapsing back into his customary somnolence, to stir only fitfully in the Progressive era and in the early 1960s. In the long view, however, Sumner may yet be proved correct: "There is no clause which gives to Congress such supreme power over the states as that clause."

After almost two hundred years of development, the clause is still in some ways the enigmatic challenge that it was in 1787. We do not have—and never will have—an authoritative definition of republican government. We continue to enjoy the opportunity of working out for ourselves the answers to this problem. In doing so, we are helped by a knowledge of the clause's history, which provides no ready-made answers to our present problems, but which can suggest lines of development that could be projected from the past.

In leaving us the guarantee clause, the framers provided few specific guides to its application. They did make it clear that the clause established federal supremacy over the states, which was to be preserved by the use of force to put down insurrectionary challenges, if necessary. The framers meant to preclude certain characteristics of government, such as orders of nobility. They wished to establish others permanently—popular representation, limited government, the paramountcy of a written constitution and the subordination of ordinary legislation to it, the separation of powers, and functional safeguards against the concentration of power. Some of the framers' views have been purposely discarded, as for example, their belief that republicanism and slavery were compatible; others, like their fear of kings and aristocracies in America, are irrelevant today. In the guarantee clause they left us a command—ambiguous and hence protean—that could realize the ideals and aspirations they had embodied in the Declaration of Independence, the preamble to the federal Constitution, and the libertarian elements of the state constitutions.

The guarantee clause developed unevenly before the Civil War. State and federal courts tentatively and unsuccessfully tried to graft onto it the vigorous growth of higher-law limitations on legislative power. President Tyler in the Dorr Rebellion construed the guarantee as obliging him to support extant state governments against extralegal political challenges; he wisely limited presidential power under the clause by insisting that he could not overturn a state government merely because it did not conform to his personal standards of republicanism. The United States Supreme Court subsequently declined to undertake enforcement of the clause in *Luther* v. *Borden* when doing so would force it to resolve political questions.

While judges were tentatively linking the guarantee clause to higher-law theories of limited government, anti-

sion." Though such a reactionary approach has occasionally represented the beliefs of a respectably large minority, there seems to be little chance that it will ever again be influential.

Closely allied to this repressive position, but less extreme, is a view of the federal relationship under the guarantee clause that emphasizes the independence of the states and the right of their people to untrammeled self-government. The clause would prohibit most federal intervention in the states' affairs, except for unimaginable occasions when a state's government might somehow become tyrannical. This state-sovereignty position was first advocated in the writings of John Taylor of Caroline, who insisted that the clause was only a mutual guarantee among the states and not a grant of power to the federal government.[1] This theme was modified in the writings and speeches of pro-slavery thinkers to allow the federal government to suppress slave uprisings. It persisted in the arguments of Reconstruction-era Democrats, who sought to resist national interference in the readjustment of race relations in the South after slavery was abolished. It was faintly and innocuously echoed in several United States Supreme Court decisions at the end of the nineteenth century that emphasized the equality of status enjoyed by all states and their rights to internal self-government.

This state-sovereignty approach was best articulated by moderate Democratic opponents of Republican Reconstruction, who insisted that a fundamental characteristic of republican government was the right of the people of a state to govern themselves, free of any supervening power that could impose basic policy decisions on them. Seen from

[1] See John Taylor, *Construction Construed and Constitutions Vindicated* (Richmond, 1820), 308–313.

tion of our society's democratic goals." More specifically, Bonfield suggests that the clause is as enforceable by the federal courts as by Congress, that it incorporates fluid higher-law concepts (his term is "natural justice"), and that the characteristics of republicanism must be "dictated by contemporary values. Those values will not only include the present spirit of the national government, but also the current expectations of the American people," such as access to the ballot and "equal access for all to housing, employment, education, transportation and numerous other things, when sufficiently touched with a public interest." They also include many of the libertarian guarantees of the Bill of Rights.[5] Much of Bonfield's interpretation is supported by the history of the clause, but it has not yet gained widespread acceptance among federal judges or congressmen.

There are two variants of the activist approach, one emphasizing the role of federal courts, the other the role of Congress and the states. The judicial-activist view, antithetical to *Pacific States* and its progeny, would construe the clause as a warrant for federal courts to overturn legislative or executive actions because of their inconsistency with higher-law imperatives. Though eclipsed since *Luther v. Borden* and the failure of the state courts to work out an explicit higher-law rationale for the guarantee clause, this judicial-activist position may yet develop vigorously since the political question hurdle has been lowered or removed in *Baker* v. *Carr*.

Bonfield and other advocates of judicial activism inter-

[5] Arthur E. Bonfield, "The Guarantee Clause of Article IV Section 4: A Study in Constitutional Desuetude," *Minn. L. Rev.*, XLVI (1962), 513–572.

pret the guarantee clause as a bulwark of individual rights. This position has received the sanction of the Fifth Circuit Court of Appeals, which in 1956 affirmed a federal district court's use of the clause to protect individual liberty. In *Hoxie School District* v. *Brewer* (1956), the District Court for the Eastern District of Arkansas enjoined a number of individuals and organizations, including the Arkansas White Citizens Council and something that called itself "White America, Inc.," from harassing school district officials who were trying to implement a school desegregation program in the wake of *Brown* v. *Board of Education.* The District Court's action, according to the Court of Appeals, was immediately and entirely effective. Citing the guarantee clause, the District Court held that the school district officials had a right to ask the court to protect "their sacred right to function their offices [*sic*] and to live as citizens under a government of laws and not of men." If the anti-integrationist actions of the respondent individuals and organizations were not restrained, the petitioners would be deprived of representative government in violation of the guarantee clause.[6]

The *Hoxie* case is unusually significant because the respondents were private parties, not connected with the state. Hence their actions could not be reached under federal statutes of the time because the due process and equal protection guarantees of the Fourteenth Amendment were available only to restrain "state action." To whatever extent the state-action limitation on the Fourteenth Amendment remains potent today, the due process clause must be supplemented by federal judicial power derived

[6] *Hoxie School District* v. *Brewer,* 137 F. Supp. 367 (D.C.E.D. Ark., 1956); aff'd. *Brewer* v. *Hoxie School District,* 238 F.2d 91 (5 Cir., 1956).

from some other source to reach private, unofficial acts. In *Hoxie* that source was the guarantee clause.

The judicial-activist approach presents two difficulties. First, *Baker* v. *Carr* notwithstanding, judges might find it difficult to work out judicially enforceable standards of republicanism, and even more difficult to enforce these standards on the states, particularly when the President and Congress are unenthusiastic. Second, from a libertarian viewpoint, judicially devised standards of republicanism might not always be desirable. Judicial activism under the guarantee clause was first espoused by judges hostile to reform, innovation, and popular political power that might threaten property relationships.

A more promising interpretation of federal power under the guarantee clause, the legislative-activist, places primary responsibility on the state and federal legislative branches of government for implementing the guarantee. Constitutional scholars have recently expressed concern that constitutional issues are thought by legislators, lawyers, and the man in the street to be esoteric technical questions best left to the specialists of the bar and bench.[7] This undesirable but widespread attitude places excessive responsibility on the courts to resolve constitutional problems that are fundamentally not esoteric and that require political rather than judicial resolution. Those concerned with an excessive "judicialization" of constitutional development therefore call for the legislative and executive branches to play a greater role than they do currently in resolving constitutional issues.

In this view, the primary responsibility, in point of

[7] Donald G. Morgan, *Congress and the Constitution* (Cambridge, Mass., 1966); Alexander M. Bickel, *The Supreme Court and the Idea of Progress* (New York, 1970).

both time and logic, for assuring republican government to the people lies with the states since the guarantee clause assumes that the states have a republican form of government. Should the states default, Congress rather than the courts must step in. The legislative-activist position was grounded in *Luther* v. *Borden* and fully expounded by Reconstruction-era Republicans. Though its emphasis on the political question doctrine has been rejected by the United States Supreme Court, Taney's *Luther* opinion still places on Congress primary responsibility for carrying out the clause's command. A modern proponent of the legislative-activist view, William W. Crosskey, concurs and sees the clause as the "chief source" of congressional authority over the states, especially in implementing the right to vote.[8]

The two activist positions are mutually compatible. The courts should act to enforce the guarantee in appropriate cases, yet leave to Congress the role—more congenial to a deliberative body—of working out broad standards of republicanism. Responsibility for enforcing the guarantee should be seen as complementary between the judicial and the political branches of government.

An activist view of the guarantee clause is dominant among scholars and commentators today and is reinforced by the clause's history. Whether this view will prevail indefinitely is problematical, but its present ascendancy augurs a greatly expanded role for the guarantee clause in the American federal system. The history of the clause provides few firm precedents to answer future problems of federalism. We shall never undergo another period of

[8] William W. Crosskey, *Politics and the Constitution in the History of the United States* (Chicago, 1953), I, 522–524.

Reconstruction, nor are the circumstances of the Dorr Rebellion likely to be repeated. Nevertheless, the past provides general answers to the enigmas of the clause that substantiate the activist position.

The first of these enigmas is the meaning of "the United States." It now seems clear that this phrase was used in a nonexclusionary sense, so as to comprehend all three traditional branches of the federal government. The Supreme Court in *Luther* v. *Borden* established beyond question that the guarantee power was invested primarily in Congress and was delegable in some ways to the President. Later the principal barrier to judicial participation in the guarantee function, the political question doctrine, was substantially lowered so the courts can now play a more activist role than in the past. Thus "the United States" today means "Congress, the President, and the federal courts."

The beneficiaries of the guarantee are, textually, "every State in this Union." Since Reconstruction this has meant "the people of the various states" or "the people of the United States as a whole." Most Americans no longer consider the states to be anthropomorphic entities capable of having rights or enjoying the benefits of the guarantee. The idea that the people of the whole nation are the proper beneficiaries of the guarantee is a recrudescence of Montesquieu's dictum that in a federation all constituent polities must be republican. In the United States today the loss of republican characteristics in one state has an impact on all other states. All are equally concerned with the preservation of republicanism throughout the Union.

The Supreme Court has implied that the guarantee obligation presumes that the states must preserve their republican character. The nation must step in when the states default or threaten to default, but the states are continuously obligated to preserve their republicanism.

The verb "guarantee" is also broadly defined by the clause's past. The Reconstruction experience suggests that there are virtually no effective limits on the power of the federal government when it enforces the guarantee, not even specific clauses of the Constitution. For example, Article I, section 3, and Article V both expressly mandate that a state shall at all times have its quota of two senators in the United States Senate and that nothing shall ever be done without the consent of the state to reduce that representation; yet the process of Reconstruction, based in part on guarantee clause assumptions, swept aside those two provisions. This does not make the guarantee clause a supraconstitutional joker in the deck, but it does give point and substance to the warnings of Reconstruction-era Democrats and conservative Republicans that the guarantee powers must be used sparingly, with sensitivity, and only after mature deliberation.

The power to "guarantee" is prophylactic as well as reactive. The national government need not sit by an idle spectator to the loss of republicanism, even where that loss was sanctioned by time, custom, mores, written and unwritten law, judicial precedent, or the constitutions of the state. Under extraordinary circumstances, even so deeply entrenched an institution as slavery can be rooted out by the guarantee power. The federal government may take the same sweeping actions to prevent a loss of republican government as to restore it. Hence it can remove conditions in the structure of the state governments, in their functioning, or in the social institutions of the people that threaten republican government.

The most open-ended element of the guarantee clause is the phrase "a Republican Form of Government." It will almost certainly be the focus of future debates over the clause; compared with the other three elements, it remains the least defined and the least definable. "A republican form of government" has an ever-increasing minimal content: at first it prohibited kings and nobility; later it was construed to outlaw slavery; today its activist proponents see it as inimical to racial segregation and discrimination and to state inaction when an individual is deprived of rights retained under the Ninth Amendment. There seems to be no practical restriction on the development of the substantive characteristics of republican government.

Whatever interpretation of the clause may come to triumph—whether the clause languishes in disuse or becomes a plenary assurance of individual liberty—its guarantee of republican government will retain the protean potential it has had since 1787: a command that the people of the American states continue in their unending progress toward an American republic. What this republic can become, only we and those who follow us can determine. It is up to us to realize the promise of the guarantee.

Suggested Secondary Readings

The guarantee clause has developed through interplay between two central characteristics of the American experience: republicanism and constitutionalism. The secondary literature on both is too extensive to be summarized here, but certain works are particularly suggestive.

The writings of Bernard Bailyn and Gordon Wood are indispensable for understanding the origins of America's republican experience. In addition to their studies cited in the first chapter, *The Ideological Origins of the American Revolution* and *The Creation of the American Republic*, respectively, see Bailyn's "Political Experience and Enlightenment Ideals in Eighteenth Century America," *Am. Hist. Rev.*, LXVII (1962), 339–351; *The Origins of American Politics* (New York, 1968); and his edition of *Pamphlets of the American Revolution* (Cambridge, Mass., 1966–), the introduction to which has been reprinted in expanded form as *Ideological Origins*. Wood's valuable brief essay, "Rhetoric and Reality in the American Revolution," *Wm. & M. Q.*, XXIII (1966), 3–32, and *Representation in the American Revolution* (Charlottesville, 1969), should be consulted.

Historians during the Progressive era and their intellectual heirs vigorously contended that the adoption of the federal Constitution and state constitutions like those of Massachusetts (1780) and Pennsylvania (1790) represented a regression from—if not a reaction against—the radical, popular, democratizing tendencies of the earliest years of the Revolution. This theme is stated extravagantly in J. Allen Smith, *The Spirit of American Government* (New York, 1907); in Vernon Louis Parrington's *Main Currents in American Thought: The Colonial Mind* (New York, 1927); and in Charles Beard's *An Economic Interpretation of the Constitution of the United States* (New York, 1913). It was reformulated more temperately by Merrill Jensen in *The Articles of Confederation* (Madison, 1948). The finest brief summaries of Jensen's insistence on the democratizing character of the American Revolution are "Democracy and the American Revolution," *Huntington Lib. Q.*, XX (1957), 321–341, and "The American People and the American Revolution," *J. Am. Hist.*, LVII (1970), 5–35. See also his *The Founding of a Nation* (New York, 1968).

The views of the Progressive historians should be compared with the following reconsiderations of the meaning of republicanism and democracy in the eighteenth century: J. R. Pole, *Political Representation in England and the Origins of the American Republic* (London, 1966); Cecilia M. Kenyon, "Republicanism and Radicalism in the American Revolution: An Old-Fashioned Interpretation," *Wm. & M. Q.*, XIX (1962), 153–182; J. R. Pole, "Historians and the Problem of Early American Democracy," *Am. Hist. Rev.*, LXVII (1962), 626–646; Martin Diamond, "Democracy and the Federalist: A Reconsideration of the Framers' Intent," *Am. Pol. Sci. Rev.*, LIII (1959), 52–68; Richard Buel, Jr., "Democracy and the American Revolution: A Frame of Reference," *Wm. & M. Q.* XXI (1964), 165–190; and Douglass Adair's several writings on the *Federalist* papers, principally "Experience Must Be Our Only Guide: History, Democratic Theory, and the United States Constitution," reprinted in Jack P. Greene, ed., *The Reinterpretation of the American Revolution, 1763–1789* (New York, 1968).

On the related development of constitutionalism in the early period, see Edward S. Corwin's writings, especially "The Basic Doctrine of American Constitutional Law," *Mich. L. Rev.*, XII (1914), 247–276, "The 'Higher Law' Background of American Constitutional Law," *Harv. L. Rev.*, XLII (1928), 149–185, 365–409 and "The Progress of Constitutional Theory between the Declaration of Independence and the Philadelphia Convention," *Am. Hist. Rev.*, XXX (1925), 511–536; Arthur Sutherland, Jr., *Constitutionalism in America* (New York, 1965); Andrew C. McLaughlin, *The Foundations of American Constitutionalism* (New York, 1932); Allan Nevins, *The American States During and After the Revolution* (New York, 1924); Oscar Handlin and Mary Handlin, eds., *The Popular Sources of Political Authority: Documents on the Massachusetts Convention of 1780* (Cambridge, Mass., 1966); Conyers Read, ed., *The Constitution Reconsidered* (New York, 1938).

The character of early American constitutionalism can perhaps be most agreeably approached through several excellent biographies. Madison is the subject of Irving Brant's six-volume *James Madison* (Indianapolis, 1941–1961). Madison's political thought badly needs a satisfactory and comprehensive investigation; Douglass Adair's articles, especially "The Tenth Federalist Revisited," *Wm. & M. Q.*, VIII (1951), 48–67, provide a good starting point. See also Neal Riemer, "The Republicanism of James Madison," *Pol. Sci. Q.*, LXIX (1954), 45–64. Dumas Malone's biography of Jefferson, *Jefferson and His Time* (Boston, 1948–), of which four volumes have appeared, approaches definitiveness, but suffers from the author's adulatory attitude to his subject. James Wilson's thought is ably analyzed in Robert McCloskey's introduction to the reprint of *The Works of James Wilson* (Cambridge, Mass., 1967), and in Charles P. Smith, *James Wilson: Founding Father* (Chapel Hill, 1956). Two studies of Hamilton's impact on constitutional development are helpful, particularly for correcting the biases of Jefferson's admirers, but are not definitive: Gerald Stourzh, *Alexander Hamilton and the Idea of Republican Government* (Stanford, 1970), and Clinton Rossiter, *Alexander Hamilton and the Constitution* (New York, 1964).

The problem of mob violence in America is only beginning to get the scholarly attention it deserves. Pauline Maier's "Popular Uprisings and Civil Authority in Eighteenth-Century America," *Wm. & M. Q.*, XXVII (1970), 3–35, is the most significant recent study. Her conclusions corroborate the interpretations of George Rude, *The Crowd in History* (New York, 1964), which, though it does not deal with America, is highly suggestive for students of American history, especially for Shays's Rebellion and the Whiskey Rebellion. See too Gordon S. Wood, "A Note on Mobs in the American Revolution," *Wm. & M. Q.*, XXIII (1966), 635–643. Two good surveys of federal reaction to local disturbances are U.S. Senate, "Federal Aid in Domestic Disturbances," 67 Cong., 2 sess., ser. 7985, doc. 263 (1922), and Bennett M. Rich, *The Presidents and Civil Disorder* (Washington, 1941). The closely related topic of vigilantism in American history cries for investigation.

The Dorr Rebellion's leaders and theorists, most notably Dorr himself, insisted that their struggle had a conservative object: to return to Revolutionary-era standards of republicanism. Though their understanding of the framers' thought was often superficial or selective, Dorr and his associates participated in the unending process of redefining the character of republican government. Aside from Arthur Mowry's dated *The Dorr War* (Providence, 1901), there are no extended published studies of the Rebellion and *Luther* v. *Borden*, though Peter Coleman's *The Transformation of Rhode Island* (Providence, 1963) briefly reconsiders the Rebellion and gives much useful information about Rhode Island in the Jacksonian period. The Rebellion is the subject of research by several younger scholars today, among them Marvin Gettleman of Brooklyn Polytechnic Institute, George Dennison of Colorado State University, Patrick Conley of Providence College, and Robert L. Ciaburri of the University of Pittsburgh; we may hope that the next few years will see the publication of significant studies by them and others on this too-long-overlooked topic.

Luther v. *Borden* has suffered even more from scholarly oversight. Legal scholars were led to reconsider it in the early 1960s because of its pertinence to the reapportionment controversy, and it had received some attention earlier by students of the political question doctrine, but had not been investigated in its own right until the appearance of Michael Conron's "Law, Politics, and Chief Justice Taney: A Reconsideration of the *Luther* v. *Borden* Decision," *Am. J. Legal Hist.*, XI (1967), 377–388. Although I disagree with Conron's interpretation of the case, his article is a significant re-evaluation of it. More recently, C. Peter Magrath has re-examined *Luther* v. *Borden* from the vantage point of Dorr himself in "Optimistic Democrat: Thomas W. Dorr and the Case of Luther vs. Borden," *R.I. Hist.*, XXIX (1970), 94–112. Regrettably, Magrath's excellent article came to hand too late for me to make more than an incidental use of its interpretations. Charles Warren, *The Supreme Court in United States History* (Boston, 1923), provides much useful incidental information about the case. Biographers of Taney and students of the Supreme Court in this period tend to give the case only slight attention. Carl B. Swisher, Taney's foremost biographer, accords it only footnotes in *Roger B. Taney* (New York, 1935). Charles Grove Haines and Foster Sherwood, *The Role of the Supreme Court in American Government and Politics, 1835–1864* (Berkeley, 1957), is disappointingly noninterpretive. Kent Newmyer's brief survey, *The Supreme Court under Marshall and Taney* (New York, 1968) devotes a paragraph to the case. Maurice G. Baxter, *Daniel Webster and the Supreme Court* (Amherst, 1966), is good on Webster's influence on the Court's decisions.

Many of the questions touched on in *Luther v. Borden* reappeared in different form during Reconstruction, particularly majoritarianism, self-government, and national supervision of state electoral processes. One of the striking characteristics of historians' renewed interest in Reconstruction during the past decade has been an emphasis on these and other constitutional issues. See W. R. Brock, *An American Crisis: Congress and Reconstruction, 1865–1867* (New York, 1963); Rembert W. Patrick, *The Reconstruction of the Nation* (New York, 1967); and Eric L. McKitrick, *Andrew Johnson and Reconstruction* (Chicago, 1960). More important, this awareness has produced constitutionally oriented studies of Reconstruction, among the finest of which are Herman Belz, *Reconstructing the Union: Theory and Policy during the Civil War* (Ithaca, 1969), and Stanley I. Kutler, *Judicial Power and Reconstruction Politics* (Chicago, 1968). The appearance of Howard Jay Graham's essays in his collection *Everyman's Constitution: Historical Essays on the Fourteenth Amendment, the "Conspiracy Theory," and American Constitutionalism* (Madison, 1968) is especially welcome. Arthur Bestor's wise observations in "The American Civil War as a Constitutional Crisis," *Am. Hist. Rev.*, LXIX (1964), 327–352, are equally pertinent to Reconstruction. Jack B. Scroggs, "Carpetbagger Constitutional Reform in the South Atlantic States, 1867–1868," *J. Southern Hist.*, XXVII (1961), 475–493, is a valuable contribution to state-oriented studies.

Despite the high quality of these recent constitutional studies, some of the finest work in this area is now between thirty and seventy years old. See William A. Dunning, *Essays on the Civil War and Reconstruction* (New York, 1904), and his less valuable *Reconstruction, Political and Economic, 1865–*

1877 (New York, 1907). John William Burgess, another Columbia University scholar and contemporary of Dunning's, produced the perceptive *Reconstruction and the Constitution* (New York, 1902). In Dunning's work racism is moderate, in Burgess' virulent; but despite this defect and the astigmatism that it produced, the studies remain valuable for their insights into post-bellum constitutional development. Francis B. Simkins and Robert H. Woody coauthored the finest early study of Reconstruction at the state level, *South Carolina during Reconstruction* (Chapel Hill, 1932), surpassing in quality all the earlier work by Dunning's graduate students, informally known as "Dunning studies."

For specific discussions of the impact of the guarantee clause on Reconstruction, in addition to Belz, *Reconstructing the Union,* see Charles O. Lerche's three related articles: "The Dorr Rebellion and the Federal Constitution," *R.I. Hist.,* IX (1950), 1–10; "The Guarantee of a Republican Form of Government and the Admission of New States," *J. of Politics,* XI (1949), 578–604; and "Congressional Interpretations of the Guarantee of a Republican Form of Government during Reconstruction," *J. Southern Hist.,* XV (1949), 192–211. David Donald's excellent two-volume biography of Sumner, *Charles Sumner and the Coming of the Civil War* (New York, 1960), and *Charles Sumner and the Rights of Man* (New York, 1970) is disappointingly thin on analysis of his political thought.

The recrudescence of the guarantee clause in the reapportionment controversies of the twentieth century can best be understood by reference to a remark of Mark DeWolfe Howe. In *The Garden and the Wilderness* (Chicago, 1965), p. 145, speaking of the reapportionment cases' reliance on an equal protection rationale, Howe said: "Judicial honesty and intellectual morality might be advanced if the [United States Supreme] Court would acknowledge that it is enforcing some other principle than one embodied in either the equal protection clause of the Fourteenth Amendment or in the provision for popular election of congressmen in Article I. Is it time, perhaps, for the Court to announce quite frankly that it means henceforth to exercise the power to guarantee to the nation and the states republican forms of government?" Such a course, Howe thought, would be better than the "disingenuous pretensions" spawned by an attempt to read egalitarian standards into clauses having no such content.

Howe was repeating a commonplace sentiment; see the articles cited in footnote 7 of Chapter 9. Critics of the equal protection rationale, whatever their view as to the justiciability of the reapportionment issues, agreed with Justice Frankfurter's conclusion that *Baker* v. *Carr* was a guarantee clause case parading under the disguise of equal protection. Valid as the point may be, by 1971 it seems likely that Justice Brennan's refusal to see the issue in this light is definitive. Hence the future growth of the guarantee clause lies in different directions. Some idea of its possibilities may be had from a perusal of the several articles of Mitchell Franklin, cited in footnotes 3 and 4 of the Epilogue. Though Franklin perversely insists on reading things into the history of the clause that are simply not there (e.g., the influence of Abbé de Mably and the embodiment of egalitarian ideals before the Civil War), his sweeping proposals for using the clause to strike down all forms of inequality in American society, whether created by governmental action or not, suggest at least one direction in which the clause might develop.

A far more satisfactory statement of this general position was made by Arthur Bonfield in two 1962 articles: "The Guarantee Clause of Article IV Section 4: A Study in Constitutional Desuetude," *Minn. L. Rev.*, XLVI (1962), 513–572, and "Baker v. Carr: New Light on the Constitutional Guarantee of Republican Government," *Calif. L. Rev.* (1962),

245–263. Though written with an eye on the contemporary reapportionment controversy, Bonfield's work suggests a broader scope for the clause, seeing it as a supplement to the Fourteenth Amendment for remedying the deficiencies of the Amendment's protection of individual liberties. This view is especially suitable for judicial implementation.

The most impressive statements of the possibilities of the clause, however, remain Chief Justice Taney's opinion in *Luther* v. *Borden* and Justice Frankfurter's dissent in *Baker* v. *Carr*. These two opinions should not be read as entirely negative—as nothing more than calls for judicial abnegation. In their positive aspects they are a demand for legislative and executive responsibility in enforcing the clause. A merger of the judicial activism demanded by Bonfield and the popular, legislative, and executive responsibility mandated by Taney and Frankfurter will strengthen effective and responsive government at both the state and the national levels.

Index